Where Have All the Democrats Gone?

Where Have
All the
Democrats
Gone?

The Soul
of the Party
in the Age
of Extremes

John B. Judis
Ruy Teixeira

Henry Holt and Company
New York

Henry Holt and Company
Publishers since 1866
120 Broadway
New York, New York 10271
www.henryholt.com

Henry Holt® and ⊞® are registered trademarks of Macmillan
Publishing Group, LLC.

Library of Congress Cataloging-in-Publication Data

Names: Judis, John B., author. | Teixeira, Ruy A., author.
Title: Where have all the Democrats gone? : the soul of the party
    in the age of extremes / John B. Judis and, Ruy Teixeira.
Description: First edition. | New York : Henry Holt and Company,
    2023. | Includes bibliographical references and index.
Identifiers: LCCN 2023017076 (print) | LCCN 2023017077
    (ebook) | ISBN 9781250877499 (hardcover) |
    ISBN 9781250877505 (ebook)
Subjects: LCSH: Democratic Party (U.S.)—Membership. |
    Party affiliation—United States. | Polarization (Social
    sciences)—Political aspects—United States. | United
    States—Politics and government—21st century.
Classification: LCC JK2316 .J84 2023 (print) | LCC JK2316
    (ebook) | DDC 324.2736—dc23/eng/20230530
LC record available at https://lccn.loc.gov/2023017076
LC ebook record available at https://lccn.loc.gov/2023017077

Our books may be purchased in bulk for promotional,
educational, or business use. Please contact your local
bookseller or the Macmillan Corporate and Premium Sales
Department at (800) 221-7945, extension 5442, or by e-mail at
MacmillanSpecialMarkets@macmillan.com.

First Edition 2023

Designed by Meryl Sussman Levavi

Printed in the United States of America

10 9 8 7 6 5 4 3 2 1

For Roberta Lynch
—JOHN B. JUDIS

For Robin Allen, Ian Teixeira,
and Lauren Teixeira
—RUY TEIXEIRA

Contents

Introduction

The Party of the Common Man and Woman

We toured Dundalk, a once prosperous blue-collar town east of Baltimore, where many of its inhabitants worked at the huge Bethlehem Steel plant at Sparrows Point that at its peak employed 30,920 workers or at the General Motors plant in White Marsh that had employed 7,000. Dundalk, which is almost entirely white, was dependably Democratic in presidential and congressional elections until 2004, when its residents narrowly backed George W. Bush against John Kerry. Its local administration was solidly Democratic, but in 2014 it became Republican. In the 2016 election, it backed Trump by 62 percent to 33 percent over Clinton. In 2020, Trump won Dundalk by 57 percent to 40 percent.

We interviewed Robert Price, who is in his fifties and worked at the GM and Bethlehem plants and now works at a shipyard. Price says he took "the last train of industrialism out of the station." Price, who in 2004 went to Iowa to campaign for labor Democrat Dick Gephardt, now supports Trump. As we are driving to Dundalk, we asked him why so many white workers have left the Democratic Party and turned to Trump and the Republicans. "I mean a lot of it is AM radio," he says. "There is a racist element to it. There is no question of that." But he rejects that as too simple an explanation. "To me there are only two groups of people, the globalists and the nationalists, and unfortunately the Democrats have wound up appearing to be the friends of the globalists. And the nationalists, the black people at work, they are veterans, they side with the right, the Republicans. In other words, it's more about class than color, it's more about nationalism than race."

We turn into Dundalk, and he continues, "I think the blue-collar working-class people are the more nationalistic people. I think the Democrats are what we used to call the jet-setter class. They are the ones who go to Europe on vacation. They are the ones who don't care where the stuff is made. I think the working class has caught on to that."

There are now hundreds or even thousands of small towns and midsize cities across America where working-class Americans express opinions about the Democrats that resemble what Robert Price described. While Dundalk is predominately white, you can now find similar sentiments in small towns where many of the inhabitants are Hispanics or Asians or among some working-class blacks. Of course, they know that not all the people who are Democrats are jet-setters or globalists, but that's how they now see the leaders of the Democratic Party and their political outlook. These working-class voters used to be the life-blood of the Democratic Party. This book is about why they are abandoning the party, and why it matters.

The Great Divide

The Democratic Party has had its greatest success when it sought to represent the common man and woman against the rich and powerful, the people against the elite, and the plebians against the patricians. During the height of Jacksonian democracy, which endured two decades, Democrats spoke for the newly emigrated, the working man, and the small farmer against the merchant and banking class of northeastern Protestants. During Franklin Roosevelt's New Deal, Democrats represented the "forgotten American" and "the people" against the "economic royalists" of Wall Street and corporate boardrooms. As Frances Perkins, Roosevelt's secretary of labor, put it, "The 'new deal' meant that the forgotten man, the little man, the man nobody knew much about, was going to be dealt better cards to play with."

Both the Jacksonian and the New Deal Democrats had their failings—and they were egregious in Jackson's case. Jackson waged a brutal war against the Indians and was a slave owner, but Jackson and Martin Van Buren, his political guru and successor, presided over the expansion of American suffrage and the birth of the modern American party system and defended the Union against the first threat of southern secession. Roosevelt compromised with southern segregationists to win needed support to pass Social Security and other pathbreaking measures. These measures vastly expanded the federal government's responsibility for the welfare of its citizens, including the old and disabled. Roosevelt also signed legislation that enabled workers to vote for unions, laying the basis for the modern labor movement and for modern American pluralism, where labor could provide a countervailing force to the power of business. These reforms narrowed the gap between the people and the powerful. They contributed to decades of prosperity and to growing equality. They were as close as America has come to a social democratic politics and polity.

Over the last thirty years, the Democrats have continued to claim to represent the average citizen. In his 1992 campaign, Bill Clinton championed "the forgotten middle class" and promised to put "people before profit." Barack Obama pledged that the "voices of ordinary citizens" would "speak louder" than "multimillion-dollar donations." Hillary Clinton in her 2016 campaign promised to "make the economy work for everyday Americans." And Joe Biden was running in 2020 to represent "the people":

> They're the reason why I'm running. These are people that build our bridges, repair our roads, keep our water safe, who teach our kids, look, who race into burning buildings to protect other people, who grow our food, build our cars, pick up our garbage, our streets, veterans, dreamers, single moms.

Biden's appeal was clearly genuine, but over the last decades, Democrats have steadily lost the allegiance of "everyday Americans"—the working- and middle-class voters that were at the core of the older New Deal coalition. Initially, most of these voters were white, but in the last elections, Democrats have also begun to lose support among Latino and Asian working-class voters as well.

How did this happen? There is an original reason, for which the Democrats were hardly to blame. Democrats were the principal supporters of the Civil Rights Act of 1964 and the Voting Rights Act of 1965—measures that went a long way toward ending racial segregation and Jim Crow, but that angered many southern whites and, to a lesser extent, some whites in the North. "Well, I think we may have lost the South for your lifetime—and mine," Lyndon Johnson told his aide Bill Moyers after he signed the 1964 bill. According to Moyers, it was said "lightly" and was a "throwaway thought," but it proved at least partly true. With the exception of a few far-right groups, however, Americans have reconciled themselves to those bills. Democrats regularly win elections in Virginia, the seat of the southern Confederacy, and many of the northern and southern suburbs formed by white flight now vote for Democratic candidates. And Americans elected an African American president in 2008 and reelected him in 2012.

There is no single factor that has driven working-class voters out of the Democratic Party. They include:

- Democrats' support for trade deals that led to factory closings in many small towns and midsize cities in states that were once Democratic strongholds.
- Democrats' support for spending bills that the working and middle classes paid for but that were primarily of benefit to poor Americans, many of whom were minorities.
- Democrats' enthusiasm for immigration of unskilled workers and the party's opposition to measures that might reduce illegal immigration.
- Democrats' support for abortion rights (and opposition to any restrictions on these rights).
- Democrats' support for strict gun control.
- Democrats' support for and identification with the quest for new identities and lifestyles, particularly among the young, and denigration of all those who were not supportive.
- Democrats' insistence on eliminating fossil fuels.
- Democrats' opposition to open displays of religiosity.
- Democrats' support for the desecration of national symbols, such as the flag or national anthem, to dramatize discontent with injustices.
- Democrats' use of the courts and regulations to enforce their moral and cultural agenda, whether on the sale of wedding cakes or the use of public men's and women's bathrooms.

Not all Democrats are in line with these actions or beliefs. But overall, they came to characterize the party, as Robert Price would tell you. Some of these stances have to do directly with economics; others with culture. The differences over them are often taken to distinguish the college-educated professional from those who do not have college degrees, but they equally, if not more accurately, arise from the differences in economic geography—what we call the "Great Divide" in American politics.

On one side of the divide are the great postindustrial metro centers like the Bay Area, Atlanta, Austin, Los Angeles, Chicago, Boston, New York, and Seattle. These are areas that benefited from the boom in computer technology and high finance—the areas economist Robert Temin dubs "FTE," for finance, technology, and electronics. These areas are heavily populated by college-educated professionals, but also by low-skilled immigrants who clean the buildings, mow the lawns, and take care of the children and the aged. The professionals, who set the political agenda for these areas, welcome legal and illegal immigrants; they want guns off the street; they see trade not as a threat to jobs but as a source of less expensive goods; they worry that climate change will destroy the planet; and, among the young, they are engaged in an anxious quest for new identities and sexual lifestyles. A majority of them are Democrats.

If you want an extreme counterpart to Dundalk, it is Mountain View, a posh town (population 80,000) that is part of Silicon Valley. Alphabet (Google) and Meta (Facebook) are both headquartered there. Its main drag boasts chic boutiques and restaurants. Starter houses go for nearly $2 million, and rents run $3,000 a month for a one-bedroom. Many incomes are in the six-, seven-, or more figure range. The area once leaned Republican. In 1980, Ronald Reagan defeated Jimmy Carter by 13 points in Santa Clara County. It is now overwhelmingly Democratic. Biden won 83 percent of the vote in 2020. Its congressman is Ro Khanna, who was national cochair of Bernie Sanders's 2020 presidential campaign.

But its Democratic politics diverge from the older New Deal liberalism. His constituents, Khanna explained to us in an interview in his Capitol Hill office, are drawn to the Democrats primarily by social issues. They are "vehemently pro-choice, vehemently pro-gay marriage, vehemently for reasonable gun safety legislation. Yeah, vehemently pro-immigration in terms of recognizing that immigrants improve the nation, and care deeply about climate." Former Mountain View mayor Lenny Siegel said about the politics of Mountain View's residents, "They are progressive on national issues, but they don't want to see dense housing built near them." Mountain View has a minimum wage of $18.15, but in 2020 its residents backed an initiative restricting parking by recreational vehicles (the only viable housing for many of the lower-wage service workers) in their small city.

The cost of housing is a big issue for young tech workers, but they are indifferent to labor unions. "The thing about tech people," Siegel told us, "is that they can easily find another job if they are unhappy. If they stay at the same job for too long, it looks bad on their résumé. There is a lot of occupational mobility. People who are unhappy can solve the problem themselves." That could change, of course, with the wave of layoffs that began in early 2023, but Siegel expects the downturn to be temporary.

On the other side of the divide are the small towns and midsize cities that have depended on manufacturing, mining, and farming. Some of these places have prospered from newly discovered oil and gas deposits, but many are towns and cities like Muncie, Indiana; Mansfield, Ohio; and Dundalk that have lost jobs when firms moved abroad or closed up shop in the face of foreign competition. The workers and small businesspeople in these towns and cities want the border closed to illegal immigrants, whom they see as a burden to their taxes and a threat to their jobs; they want to keep their guns as a way to protect their homes and family; they fly the American flag in front of their house; they go to or went to church; they oppose abortion; some may be leery of gay marriage, although that is changing; many of them or members of their family served in the military; they have no idea what most of the initials in LGBTQIA+ stand for. A majority of them are now Republicans and many are former working-class Democrats.

The underlying divisions are economic, but the political battles between the parties now manifest themselves as a continuation of the culture wars that began in the late 1960s. In the 2021 and 2022 election, for instance, Democrats and Republicans fought over abortion rights, crime and the police, voter fraud and suppression, critical race theory, sexual education, and border security. These differences between the parties and their candidates have been reinforced and hardened by what we call the "shadow parties." These are the activist groups, think tanks, foundations, publications and websites, and big donors and prestigious intellectuals who are not part of official party organizations, but who influence and are identified with one or the other of the parties.

The labor movement used to play a dominant role in the Democrats' shadow party and kept it rooted in working-class concerns, but it had to take second or third place during the Clinton and Obama years to Hollywood, Silicon Valley, and Wall Street, together with various environmental, civil rights, and feminist groups. Currently, the shadow party includes organizations like the American Civil Liberties Union, the Sunrise Movement, Planned Parenthood, and Black Lives Matter, publications such as the *New York Times*, MSNBC, and Vox, foundations like Ford and Open Society, and think tanks like the Center for American Progress.

These shadow institutions have articulated the outlook of many young professionals in the large postindustrial metro centers and in college towns. On many of the cultural issues concerning race, gender, and immigration that divide our politics, they have taken the most radical positions. Their counterparts on the right include the Koch Network, Heritage Foundation, the Center for Renewing America, Turning Point USA, Fox News, Breitbart.com, and the Claremont Institute. These groups on the left and right subsist within their own closed universes of discourse, each shadow party using the extremes of the other to deflect criticism of their own radicalism.

With the parties at roughly equal strength—the Democrats' losses in small-town America have been made up by their gains in the metro centers, and particularly in the suburbs—the parties have rarely enjoyed undivided rule. In the last forty-four years, one party has held the White House and both houses of Congress in only fourteen of them. The civics books will say that this rough equality encourages constructive compromise, but in the last three decades, it has more often been a recipe for gridlock and stalemate, epitomized in battles over increasing the debt limit and in repeated government shutdowns. This stalemate has increased voters' distrust of Washington and of government.

In recent years, elections have increasingly been decided by which party can make the other party's radical extremes or the politicians who represent those extremes the main issue. In 2016, Donald Trump succeeded in making the election about "Crooked Hillary." In 2018 and 2020, the Democrats were able to make the election about Trump's excesses. In 2022, Democrats won elections where the issue was Republican opposition to abortion rights and insistence that the 2020 election was stolen, whereas Republicans won when the issue was Democrats' wanting to defund the police or decriminalize illegal immigration.

Democratic Pluralism

There is a danger to democracy lurking in this transformation of the parties into cultural warriors. American democracy was originally based on the Jeffersonian idea that roughly equal property ownership (by white males) would undergird political equality and democracy. That notion was dashed on the rocks of the industrial revolution, which created a society of distinct economic classes. It was then hoped by liberals and progressives in the early twentieth century that the intrinsic economic and political power of the lords of industry and finance would be counterbalanced by the power of labor unions in the workplace and by a party that represents the working and middle classes in the political realm. And that was the democratic pluralism that, with some obvious flaws, New Deal liberalism bequeathed and that dominated American politics from the 1930s up through the 1960s.

But that hope for democracy has also been shattered. During the last half century, the labor movement, under assault from business and Republicans, has precipitously declined, particularly in the critical private sector. And the Democratic Party has ceased to be seen and to function as the party of the people in competition with the party of business. The consequences have been profound. Business and finance, through a plethora of lobbies that began springing up in the 1970s, have gotten their way time and again. The tax code has been dramatically rewritten to favor the wealthy and corporations, including those with subsidiaries overseas, at the expense of working America; trade deals have been signed that have aided multinational corporations, investment banks, and insurance companies but screwed American workers; finance, with its propensity to instability, and its emphasis on short-term returns, has been enhanced at the expense of manufacturing; at the behest of the most retrograde elements, social programs have been sabotaged or rejected that would have provided American workers with the same security in health care, childcare, and employment that European workers simply take for granted; and conservative court decisions have gutted post-Watergate measures designed to limit the inordinate influence of corporations and the wealthy on political campaigns.

In our view, one prerequisite for reviving the promise of American democracy is the reemergence of a political party whose primary commitment is to look after the country's working and middle classes. It could be the Republicans who end up being this party. There are new intellectual currents within the Republicans' shadow party that are skeptical about the reign of big business and free market ideology and endorse a version of industrial policy. These include the think tank American Compass and the journal *American Affairs*. We wish them well. But we worry that they will be ignored because of the Republicans' traditional commitment to business and the strength of business groups and donors within the Republicans' shadow party. That was evident in the new House Republican majority's first act in January 2023, which was to slash funds for the Internal Revenue Service that had been targeted for uncovering tax dodging by the wealthy. The Republicans, too, have a radical side whose propensities for violence and contempt for democracy outweigh the foibles of the Democrats' cultural radicals.

We place our hopes for change in the Democratic Party. We see evidence in the Biden administration's first two years of a reevaluation of the party's economic priorities on trade, taxes, and labor and on national economic growth that tries to bridge the Great Divide. The Democrats seem to have turned a corner from their deference to free markets and free trade during past administrations. The influence of Wall Street and Silicon Valley remains a problem with the Democrats, but the main problem we see with today's Democratic Party is the cultural insularity and arrogance that surfaced clearly during Hillary Clinton's 2016 presidential campaign.

Most of the stands the party and its groups take on issues

like race, crime, immigration, climate, sex, and gender have a rational basis and justification. There has been police brutality; the country's eleven million illegal immigrants constitute an exploitable underclass that needs to be integrated into society; transgender people have suffered discrimination; and climate change is a genuine threat to the planet's future. There are reasonable reforms that address these, but the radical solutions and the censorious outlook advanced by the Democrats' shadow groups and by some Democratic politicians have been wrongheaded and divisive.

Many Democrats simply refuse to recognize this. Instead, they have succumbed to what we call the "Fox News Fallacy"— namely, that if Fox or the *Washington Free Beacon* or some Republican operative denounces Democrats for their stance on criminal justice or illegal immigration or gender affirmation, there can be no basis for those charges. Prior to the 2022 election, for instance, as Republicans were blaming Democratic support for defunding the police for a rising crime wave in big cities, Democratic pundits and politicians derided the very idea of a widely documented crime wave. The *Washington Post*'s Philip Bump wrote a column aptly entitled, "Crime Is Surging (in Fox News coverage)." Democrats' unwillingness to acknowledge the mote in their own eyes has hurt the party's chances to win back working-class voters like Robert Price.

The America of today is vastly different from the America of the 1930s, but what the Democrats need today is a general approach to politics that is similar to that of the New Deal liberals. The New Deal liberals were liberal, progressive, and social democratic in their economic views, dedicated to creating a better balance of power between labor and business and security against poverty, unemployment, disease, and old age, but by today's standards, the New Deal Democrats were moderate and even small-c conservative in their social outlook. They extolled "the American way of life" (a term popularized in the 1930s); they used patriotic symbols like the "Blue Eagle" to promote their programs. In 1940, Roosevelt's official campaign song was Irving Berlin's "God Bless America." Under Roosevelt, Thanksgiving, Veterans Day, and Columbus Day were made into federal holidays. Roosevelt turned the annual Christmas tree lighting into a national event. Roosevelt's politics were those of "the people" (a term summed up in Carl Sandburg's 1936 poem "The People, Yes") and of the "forgotten American." There wasn't a hint of multiculturalism or tribalism. The Democrats need to follow *this* example. They need to press economic reforms that benefit the working and middle classes, but they need to declare a truce and find a middle ground in today's culture war between Democrats and Republicans so that they can once again become the party of the people.

Part I

The
Great
Divide

Chapter One

The Rise and Fall of the Emerging Democratic Majority

In 2002, we wrote a book, *The Emerging Democratic Majority*, which predicted that by the end of the first decade of the twenty-first century, the Democrats would have established a majority. It would not be an overwhelming and long-lasting majority like that which Franklin Roosevelt and the Democrats had enjoyed, with only a few breaks, from 1932 to 1980, but it would amount, on average, to an advantage over several decades. We pointed to new groups within the Democratic coalition, including college-educated professionals and single women, and to the growing numbers of minority voters.

These voters were concentrated in postindustrial metro centers that we termed "ideopolises." These metro centers such as Boston, New York, the Raleigh/Durham Research Triangle, Chicago, Seattle, Austin, Omaha, Los Angeles, and the Bay Area predominately produced ideas rather than material goods. To win elections, Democrats would still need a significant share of working-class votes, and the votes of people who lived in small towns and midsize cities that had relied on manufacturing or mining, but they would not need the solid majorities that had sustained the New Deal party. We expected that Democrats would hold on to enough of these voters, many of whom had voted Democratic for decades, to win national elections and retain an overall edge in congressional elections.

In the wake of the Democrats winning the White House and Congress in 2008, our prediction appeared to have been confirmed. We were hailed as seers. It even seemed to us possible that the new president, Barack Obama, in responding effectively to the financial crash and the Great Recession, could create a Roosevelt-like majority that would consign the Reagan–Bush Republicans to the same sorry fate as the Coolidge–Hoover Republicans. But the Democrats' dominance lasted only two years.

In 2010, Republicans won back the House and netted 6 governorships and would have won back the Senate if not for several wacky Tea Party candidates who proved unelectable. In the remaining elections during the second decade, the parties alternated control of the White House and Congress, and Republicans built an edge in statehouses. In 2022, the Republicans narrowly won back control of the House but Democrats retained narrow control of the Senate. American politics was stuck in a teeter-totter between the parties. The majority we predicted had not emerged. What had happened? Where did we and where did the Democrats go wrong?

Where We Went Wrong

We did get the new groups right. In *The Emerging Democratic Majority*, we argued that professionals, women, and minorities were displacing the old New Deal blue-collar working class as the key ingredients in a new Democratic majority. Professionals were, broadly speaking, college-educated workers whose success at work was measured by the quality of the product or service they produced. They were not private-sector managers who were judged by whether they mobilized workers to bring in the highest return, nor were they salespeople who were judged on their bottom line. They included nurses and teachers, software programmers and engineers and scientists. Once typified by the dentist or doctor who ran his own business and was a loyal Republican, professionals began voting Democratic in the late sixties and by the 1988 election were supporting Democrat Michael Dukakis over Republican George H. W. Bush. In polling, professionals appear in the ranks of voters with a postgraduate education, although their actual ranks include many people with only four-year degrees.

Their increase in numbers reflected the dramatic change in American capitalism that took place after World War II. In the 1950s, professionals made up only about 7 percent of the workforce in the United States. But as the country has moved away from a blue-collar industrial economy to a postindustrial one that produces more ideas and services, they have grown dramatically to 24 percent of the labor force, more than triple their level in the 1950s. They were drawn to the Democrats by the party's support for blacks' and women's rights, consumer and environmental protection, and its identification not so much with the average American but with the public interest, most clearly articulated beginning in the 1960s by consumer and good government advocate Ralph Nader. Some professionals like nurses, teachers, and social workers also joined unions and, like other union members, tended to support Democrats rather than Republicans.

The second group was women and particularly single and working women. They, too, were growing in number. Around half of adult women are now unmarried and their labor force participation in the twenty-first century has been pushing 60 percent, up from under 40 percent in 1960. As a group, women had tilted Republican as late as 1976, but in reaction to the Republican identification with the religious right and opposition to the welfare state, many women began voting Democratic in

1980. A substantial gender gap arose that is now a regular feature of our elections. In 2020, women supported Biden over Trump by 13 points, while men supported Trump by 6 points, producing a 19-point gender gap.

The third group was minorities. Blacks had begun voting Democratic during the New Deal and, after the Republican repudiation in 1964 of the civil rights reforms, became uniformly Democratic. Democrats had historically been the party of immigrant groups and Republicans the party of Anglo-Saxon Protestants. Hispanics, except for Miami's Cubans, had earlier been Democratic, and after the 1965 reform of immigration law, their numbers expanded rapidly. Most Asians had been voting Republican. In the 1990s, however, they started to come around. In California, they were driven by a perception that Republicans were hostile to immigrants.

Our calculation was that as the numbers of college-educated voters, working women, and minorities grew, and as postindustrial metro centers grew, if Democrats were able to hold on to about 40 percent of the white working class, with close to an even split in heavily white working-class Rust Belt states, Democrats would more likely than not win the presidency and Congress and a majority of statehouses. We viewed the working class to be generally workers without a college degree who earned a wage rather than an annual salary and worked in jobs where they had little, if no, authority over the goods or services they produced.

We expected that this new majority would emerge by the end of the first decade of the twenty-first century, and when Obama won in 2008, it seemed to confirm our prediction. Obama, benefiting from Republican candidate John McCain's failure to convince the public that he could handle the Great Recession, won not only the vote of the new Democratic groups from the sixties, but also white working-class voters in states like Michigan, Wisconsin, and Iowa.

Besides carrying all the states Democrat John Kerry won in 2004, Obama carried the southwestern states of Colorado, Nevada, and New Mexico and the southern states of Florida, North Carolina, and Virginia (the first time Democrats had carried that state since 1964). He also swept the industrial Midwest, adding Iowa, Ohio, and even Indiana to Michigan, Minnesota, Pennsylvania, and Wisconsin. Democrats gained 21 seats in the House and 8 seats in the Senate on top of their wins in the 2006 midterms.

Obama took better advantage than any of his predecessors of the emerging Democratic groups and of their rising share of the electorate. According to Catalist, among rising groups, Obama received 79 percent support among nonwhite voters, carrying black voters by 88 points, Hispanic voters by 32 points, and Asian voters by 22 points. He also carried women by 16 points, single women by 35 points, and voters under thirty by 30 points. We hadn't included younger voters in our calculation, but these voters, who as late as the 1980s had favored Republicans, appeared to be still another entry in the new majority, as the millennial generation came of voting age. Among the burgeoning ranks of white college-educated voters, Obama made a historic breakthrough and carried them by a point and white college-educated women by 9 points. And he dominated the postgraduate vote as a whole by 18 points, reflecting the Democrats' growing strength among professionals.

Obama's victory bore out our prediction that, based on the growth of postindustrial metropolitan areas, the Democrats would even begin to do well in southern states they had been losing since 1980. In North Carolina, which had not gone Democratic since Jimmy Carter's run in 1976, Obama won by dominating the state's thriving metro areas. In Mecklenburg County, the fast-growing heart of the Charlotte metro area, Obama bested McCain by 24 points, an amazing 44 points better than Michael Dukakis did when he lost the county in 1988.

Obama cleaned up in North Carolina's Research Triangle, which includes Raleigh and Durham, and three major universities. Obama won Wake County, where the Raleigh metro area is located, by 14 points, a 29-point swing since 1988, when Dukakis lost the county by 15 points. Obama won the Durham metro area by an overwhelming 40 points, a 30-point improvement over Dukakis's modest 10-point advantage in 1988.

Obama combined this strong performance with a dramatic reversal of the prior Democratic decline among white working-class voters. In 2004, according to the exit polls, Kerry lost these voters by 23 points. Obama cut the Democratic white working-class deficit to a comparatively modest 13 points nationally, and he carried the white working-class vote in states like Michigan and Wisconsin. Obama carried Macomb County, the home of Chrysler autoworkers, by 9 points, which Kerry had lost in 2004. In a 1986 study, consultant Stanley Greenberg had immortalized Macomb as the home of the Reagan Democrats.

But Obama's coalition proved to be as fleeting as Reagan's. In the 2010 election, his majority disintegrated. Midterm elections are normally bad for the incumbent party, but the drubbing the Democrats received went far beyond the expected. They lost 63 seats in the House, as the House flipped from 256 to 179 Democratic control to 242 to 193 Republican control. In doing so, Democrats lost the House popular vote by 7 points. The Republicans gained House seats all over the country but were especially successful in the upper Midwest where Obama and the Democrats had seemed to make a breakthrough. House delegations in Indiana, Illinois, Michigan, Ohio, Pennsylvania, and Wisconsin— all states that Obama won—flipped from majority Democratic to majority Republican. The key was the defection of white working-class voters. According to Catalist, Democratic congressional support among white working-class voters in Wisconsin went from

6 points Democratic in 2008 to 20 points Republican in 2010, a dramatic reversal of 26 points.

Democrats also lost 6 Senate seats and 6 governorships, and the main losses were in the industrial Midwest. They lost Senate seats in Illinois, Indiana, Pennsylvania, and Wisconsin, and governorships in Iowa, Wisconsin, Michigan, Ohio, and Pennsylvania. They also lost a net of 680 state legislative seats. Democrats had controlled 61 state legislatures and Republicans 36; now Republicans controlled 60 and Democrats only 36, an almost complete reversal.

While Democrats' support fell across virtually all voting groups, the most consequential shift was among white working-class voters. They abandoned the Democrats in droves. The Democratic deficit among these voters ballooned to 23 points in 2010. And these voters were at the time close to half of all voters—and considerably more than half in the upper Midwest where a good deal of the carnage took place. We had gotten the new voting groups right. Even in 2010, the Democrats continued to have an edge among college-educated professionals, single women, and minorities, but we were dead wrong about the Democrats' ability to hold on to the working-class whites. By losing the white working class so decisively, the Democrats lost their majority.

Losing the Heartland

In underestimating the defection of the white working class, we also underestimated the Democrats' difficulties in bridging a geographical and industrial divide. In the election, a political divide that cut across America, and which dated back at least thirty years, became a chasm. This Great Divide pitted the dynamic postindustrial metro areas of the country, concentrated in coastal America (although not exclusively) and dominated by the outlook of the burgeoning professional class, against the working-class areas in the small towns, rural communities, and midsize cities scattered across the Heartland that still depended upon manufacturing and resource extraction. As the decade of the 2010s progressed, this divide was to became the fulcrum that defined the contest between the political parties.

In Ohio, the Democratic popular vote for the House fell from a 5-point advantage in 2008 to a 12-point deficit in 2010. Five Democratic incumbents were tossed out of office as a red wave swept across the state. Consider Ohio's Sixth Congressional District that runs along the southeast side of the state and borders Kentucky, West Virginia, and Pennsylvania. The district goes from rural Lucasville through Athens and older Ohio River industrial towns and eventually reaches the Youngstown city limits. It was the home to steel and auto plants and to coal-fired power plants. Incumbent Democrat Charlie Wilson, who had carried the district by 30 points in 2008, lost to Republican Bill Johnson by 5 points in 2010, a stunning 35-point reversal.

That same thing happened in Ohio's Sixteenth District, located in the northeast of the state, and including manufacturing towns like Wooster, Akron, and Canton. Incumbent Democrat John Boccieri, who had won the seat by 11 points in 2008, lost decisively to Republican Jim Renacci by 11 points in 2010, a swing of 22 points. And what happened in these Ohio congressional districts happened in other districts that were heavily dependent on manufacturing and mining. These areas were once the center of Democratic Party strength, but now, along with rural, farming areas, they were becoming part of the Republican political base.

In 2012, Obama easily won reelection largely because he was able to portray his opponent, Mitt Romney, as a plutocrat who had opposed the auto bailout and was generally indifferent to the fate of American workers. Romney, like McCain, allowed the Democrats' presidential candidate to run as the candidate of the common man and woman and to revive the image of Republicans as the party of the uncaring rich. But Republicans retained control of the House of Representatives and added another governorship to their total, and in the 2014 elections, the Democrats' weakness among the white working class and on one side of the Great Divide reemerged with a vengeance.

In 2014, the Democrats lost 13 seats in the House and a stunning 9 Senate seats, losing their majority. In the states, Republicans gained 2 gubernatorial seats (for a total of 31) and attained control of another 10 state legislative bodies to total 67. The key to the Democratic losses was once again the defection of white working-class voters. The national deficit among these voters increased to 25 points in 2014. In Wisconsin, where Obama had received 53 percent of the white working-class vote in 2008, and where Democrats and their union allies were in an all-out effort to defeat Governor Scott Walker, they could muster only 42 percent of that vote in a losing effort.

Trump's Telling Victory

Some Democrats dismissed their losses as the result of a low-turnout midterm election, but in 2016, the Democrats' deficit among working-class voters in industrial America became the most important factor in Donald Trump's completely unexpected defeat of Hillary Clinton and for Republican success in retaining control of the House and Senate and adding to their control of statehouses. In these elections, Republicans won almost everywhere outside the big cities, and they won the bulk of white working-class votes.

Clinton lost three states, Florida, Iowa, and Ohio, that Obama had carried twice, and three Rust Belt states, Michigan, Pennsylvania, and Wisconsin, which were part of the "Blue Wall" of states the Democrats had carried in every presidential election since 1992.

That made for a 306–232 Electoral College victory for Trump. Clinton did win the popular vote, and some Democrats would rationalize their defeat by blaming it on the Electoral College, but much of Clinton's margin was the result of her advantage in California where she campaigned and Trump did not, and Trump's relatively narrow margin in Texas, where he also didn't campaign. In the 2016 House vote totals, Republicans edged the Democrats by a percentage point.

Trump's victory was attributable, above all, to the shift of white working-class voters into the Republican column, including many who had voted for Obama. In the country as a whole, the Republican advantage among white working-class voters went up 6 points to a staggering 31 points. Our forecast of Democratic success among professionals, single women, and minorities held. Clinton increased the Democratic margin among white college voters by 6 points from Obama's victory in 2012, but white working-class voters are far more numerous than their college-educated counterparts, particularly in the midwestern states where the election was decided.

In Iowa and Ohio, where Clinton got blown out, white working-class voters moved massively toward the GOP. In Iowa, where Obama had tied Romney among these voters, Clinton lost them by 57 percent to 36 percent, a shift of 23 points from the

Democratic Margins Among the White Working Class

State	Obama 2012 (%)	Clinton 2016 (%)	Margin Shift
Iowa	0.2	-22.8	-23.2
Ohio	-16.4	-31.9	-15.5
Michigan	-10.0	-21.0	-11.0
Pennsylvania	-20.3	-29.4	-9.1
Wisconsin	-5.5	-18.8	-13.3

Source: Rob Griffin, Ruy Teixeira, and William H. Frey, "America's Electoral Future: Demographic Shifts and the Future of the Trump Coalition," Center for American Progress, April 2018.

previous election. In Ohio, Clinton lost white working-class voters by 31 points, a shift toward the GOP of 15 points from 2012. In Michigan, Clinton lost these voters by 21 points, in Pennsylvania by 29 points, and in Wisconsin by 19 points. These massive deficits among white working-class voters explain why she lost these states that Obama had won.

The Great Divide also widened from 2012. Counties that shifted strongly toward Trump tended to be dominated by working-class whites and dependent on blue-collar jobs battered by automation and international trade. In addition, many of these communities had seen declines in civic life and increases in deaths of despair from alcoholism, drug abuse, and suicide. In 2012, Obama had won Iowa's Howard County, which was typical of Iowa's many small rural farming counties, by 21 points. In 2016, Clinton lost it to Trump by over 20 points. In 2008 and 2012, Obama had won Clinton County in eastern Iowa, a manufacturing center, with big employers like Archer Daniels Midland, by 23 points. But in 2016, the county swung by a massive 28 points toward Trump and the GOP, giving him a 5-point advantage over Clinton.

In Ohio, it was the same story. In 2012, Obama carried Ashtabula, the hometown of Trump's U.S. trade representative, Robert Lighthizer, and once a thriving steel and port town, by 13 points in 2012. But Trump crushed Clinton in the county by 19 points in 2016, the first time a Republican presidential candidate had carried the county since the Reagan landslide of 1984. Obama had carried nearby Trumbull County, anchored by the formerly prosperous, and now opiate-plagued, industrial town of Warren along the Mahoning River, by 23 points in 2012. But Trump carried the county by 6 points in 2016, a swing of 29 points from the previous election. It was the first time the county had voted Republican in a presidential election since Richard Nixon had routed George McGovern in 1972.

In 2012, Obama easily won Kenosha County in southeast-
ern Wisconsin, which was once a center of auto manufacturing, by 12 points, but Trump carried it in 2016 by a third of a
point, the first time a Republican had carried the county since
the McGovern election in 1972. The same thing happened in
Racine, another manufacturing town. Bill Clinton and Obama
had carried Luzerne County, centered on the blighted industrial
town of Wilkes-Barre in northeastern Pennsylvania, but in 2016
Trump blew out Hillary Clinton in the county by 19 points.

The Mythic Majority-Minority

While we were rethinking our theory of an emerging Democratic majority, some Democratic theorists like Steve Phillips of
Democracy in Color and the Center for American Progress were
doubling down on the theory. They argued that while working-
class whites were abandoning the Democratic Party, minorities,
who were dependably Democratic, would, as they continued
growing and became the majority of the population by 2045,
ensure ever-easier Democratic, victories. The calculation was
that if minorities (led by blacks, Hispanics, and Asians) were still
voting collectively three-quarters Democratic, by the time 2045
rolled around Democrats would only have to get a little over 30
percent of the white vote to win elections. That vote should be
easy to get from professionals and working women and young
people. Republicans might well retain their overwhelming support among the white working class, but it would mean progres-
sively less as that group declined as a share of the electorate.

There are two problems with this thesis. The first has to do
with who is identified as "white." The Census has relied on a
methodology that is uncomfortably close to the slave-era racist
"one-drop rule," which said that if a person had one drop of black
blood, they were "black." The Census practice has therefore clas-

sified Hispanics and Asians as being minorities on the basis of their ancestry even if they are of mixed race and identity themselves as white. The only citizens identified as white for purposes of projecting the rise of a "majority-minority" nation are those who identified as white and *checked no other boxes*. This is known as "white alone non-Hispanic." But if they had checked the white box *and* other boxes, those other identifications (Hispanic, Asian, etc.) are viewed as overriding their white identification and making them part of the minority population. Furthermore, as sociologists Richard Alba, Morris Levy, and Dowell Myers have shown, as intermarriage rates increase, high percentages of the children of mixed-race or ethnic marriages, one of whose parents is white, identify themselves as white. In other words, if what matters in politics is how voters identify themselves racially or ethnically, the size of the "white vote" more broadly defined may not actually change as much over time as "majority-minority" advocates anticipate.

The second problem is that even by the most generous recounting of who is Hispanic or Asian, Democrats can't count on members of these groups to continue voting for them in high percentages. This was even apparent in 2014. In 2014, two Obama administration veterans, funded by progressive foundations, set up a group, Battleground Texas, that proposed to make Texas Democratic on the strength of its becoming a majority-minority state.

Their first test was the gubernatorial race pitting the Republican attorney general Greg Abbott, a hard-line conservative who had sued the government on abortion, voting rights, environmental regulations, and the enforcement of the Affordable Care Act, against Democratic state senator Wendy Davis, who had acquired a national reputation when she staged a one-woman filibuster against a bill banning abortions after twenty weeks. But in the final tally, Abbott routed Davis by 20 points. He lost the Hispanic vote by only 55 to 44 and carried Hispanic men. But the clearest indication of trouble with the rising American majority and majority-minority thesis would come in the 2020 election and was affirmed in the 2021 and 2022 elections.

In 2020, Democrats assumed that they would easily win the Hispanic vote against a president with a history of vitriolic statements against Mexico and Mexican Americans and hostility toward illegal immigration, but Trump actually improved his vote with Hispanics from 2016. The most notable results came in Texas. Trump got over 40 percent among voters in the predominately Hispanic border counties along the Rio Grande River, and he actually won Zapata County, which had not voted for a Republican presidential candidate since 1920. Republican Tony Gonzales won Texas's Twenty-third Congressional District, which extends west from the outskirts of San Antonio and is 69 percent Hispanic. That district, which Clinton had carried in 2016, went for Trump.

Trump also dramatically improved his vote among Hispanics in Florida, and not just among the traditionally Republican-

Declining Latino Democratic Support

Two-party Latino Democratic margin, 2016 and 2020 presidential elections

	2016	2020	2016–20 Shift
National	41	23	-18
Texas	28	10	-18
Florida	32	0	-32
Wisconsin	34	16	-18
Pennsylvania	46	32	-14
Arizona	38	26	-12
Nevada	38	20	-18

Source: Yair Ghitza and Jonathan Robinson, "What Happened in 2020," Catalist, May 2021; and Yair Ghitza and Haris Aqeel, "What Happened in 2022," Catalist, May 2023.

leaning Cuban vote but among Puerto Ricans and other Hispanics. In Nevada, Trump reduced the Democratic advantage among Latinos by 18 points from 2016. Trump improved his performance among Hispanics by 18 points in Wisconsin, 14 points in Pennsylvania, and 12 points in Arizona and among urban Hispanics in Chicago, New York, and Houston. In Chicago's predominately Hispanic precincts, Trump improved his raw vote by 45 percent over 2016.

Nationally, Latinos in 2020 shifted sharply to Trump and reduced Democrats' overall margin among this group by 18 points. Cubans had the largest shift of 26 points, but Puerto Ricans moved by 18 points to Trump, Dominicans by 16 points, and Mexicans by 12 points. Among Hispanics, the largest shifts were among working-class voters. According to a Pew analysis, Trump got 41 percent nationally of the working-class Hispanic vote.

In the presidential race, Democrats' margin among Asian Americans (an unwieldy category that spans Indian American software moguls and Filipino home health aides) seems to have held up—a result in part of Trump's use of terms like "Kung Flu" to describe the COVID-19 pandemic. But in some congressional races, there were signs of Asian discontent with Democrats. In California's heavily Asian Orange County, two Korean American Republicans defeated Democratic incumbents. Democrats continued to enjoy huge margins among black voters, but even here, those margins declined in 2020 by 5 points relative to 2016. According to the Catalist data, Trump won 13 percent of black men.

Democrats failed to gain back much ground nationally among Hispanic voters in the 2022 election, improving their margin relative to 2020 by just a point. Latino men remained a clear weak spot for the Democrats, with 42 percent casting their House ballots for Republicans. Democrats also continued to do worse among working-class Hispanics than among their college-educated counterparts. Compared to 2018, the Democratic advantage among Hispanic working-class voters fell 13 points, almost triple the decline among Hispanic college voters. Going back even further to the 2012 election, Democrats are down 20 points in their margin among the Latino working class.

In the states, Democratic support among Hispanics generally held steady, though failing to make up ground lost in 2020. But not in Florida. In 2020, Biden had struggled to just a tie among Florida's Hispanic voters. Then, in the 2022 gubernatorial election, Ron DeSantis actually carried the Hispanic vote by 12 points. He won heavily Hispanic Miami-Dade County, historically the Democrats' firewall, by 11 points. He carried Osceola County by almost 7 points—a county where Puerto Ricans, once a dependable Democratic vote, loom large. Statewide, DeSantis split the Puerto Rican vote 50–50 with Democrat Charlie Crist.

In Texas, Republicans got 43 percent of the statewide House vote among Hispanics, losing it by only 10 points to the Democrats. Beto O'Rourke did somewhat better than Biden in the Rio Grande Valley but still carried Hispanics statewide by just 14 points. Democrats' poor showing in House races was the result of working-class Hispanics defecting to the Republicans. Democrats won working-class Hispanics by only 6 points statewide. They won college-educated Hispanics by 24 points, but working-class Hispanics make up three-quarters of the Texas Hispanic vote.

In 2021 and 2022, Democrats also suffered from defections among Asian American voters. In Virginia's 2021 gubernatorial contest, victorious Republican candidate Glenn Youngkin got 44 percent of Asian votes. In that year's New York mayoral contest, Republicans also improved over their 2017 performance by 14 points in heavily Asian precincts. In 2022, Asian voter defection from the Democrats was more broad-based than in 2020.

Nationwide the Democratic advantage among Asian voters declined 13 points relative to 2020. And there were abundant signs that Asian voters in many urban neighborhoods were slipping away from the Democrats. In New York City, the only precinct in Manhattan to vote for Republican gubernatorial candidate Lee Zeldin was in Chinatown. In Brooklyn and Queens, Zeldin outpaced Democrat Kathy Hochul in the heavily Chinese Forty-Seventh and Forty-Ninth Assembly Districts and Seventeenth State Senate District in Brooklyn. Zeldin also won the Fortieth Assembly District based in Flushing, which is dominated by Chinese and Korean immigrants.

In 2022, Democrats lost more ground among black voters, compounding their losses from 2020. Republican House candidates won 12 percent of black voters and 17 percent of black men; the margin for the Democrats among the latter group fell by 8 points compared to 2020. The black decline, together with that among other nonwhites, appears to have been concentrated among working-class voters. From 2020 to 2022, the Democrats' margin among nonwhite working-class voters declined 6 points; from 2018, the decline was 15 points. If you go back even further to 2012, Democrats have lost an amazing 25 points off their advantage among the nonwhite working class.

As was becoming clear in 2014, Democrats no longer can be said to suffer simply from the defection of *white* working-class voters. The term itself had no political meaning until the white backlash that began in the sixties to the civil rights legislation. What began happening in the last decade is a defection, pure and simple, of working-class voters. That's something that we really didn't anticipate when we wrote *The Emerging Democratic Majority*. The loss of working-class voters, who constitute the great majority of the electorate, could undermine Democrats' chances not simply of being the majority party but of being competitive with the Republican Party. It could also make it impossible for Democrats to be the party that represents and seeks to improve the lot of the average American. The question, then, is why the Democrats have lost these voters and what they can do to get them back.

Chapter Two

The Breakup of the
New Deal Coalition

In July 2022, as the midterm elections neared, which many Democrats feared would be disastrous, a group of liberal Democratic politicians and consultants gathered in Washington, the *New York Times* reported, to "discuss ways to counter the narrative . . . that Democrats are now the party of economic elites, while Republicans represent working class Americans." How had things come to this pass? How had Roosevelt's party of the "forgotten American" come to be thought of as the party of "economic elites"?

Our explanation of why this happened requires distinguishing between what happened to the Democratic Party's *electoral* coalition and what happened to its *governing* coalition. A party's electoral coalition is composed of groups that cast their vote at least partly on the basis of their collective identity and similar experience. Working-class whites, many of whom had perceived the Democrats as their party, as the party of the common man and woman, began abandoning the Democrats' electoral coalition in the mid-1960s at about the same time as college-educated professionals began being drawn into it.

A party's governing coalition is composed of its political leaders and of powerful individuals (wealthy donors, celebrities, renowned thinkers) and the representatives of powerful institutions (including businesses, labor unions, foundations, think tanks, universities, the media, religious groups, advocacy groups, and policy groups) that influence the direction that an administration takes in office. After the onset of cable television and the internet, the governing coalition expands into what we will later call the "shadow party."

As C. Wright Mills and G. William Domhoff have argued, there has been a core group of institutions, housed primarily in the upper circles of business and finance, whose leaders, organized in exclusive policy groups, have enjoyed influence within both parties. Prominent representatives from the investment bank Goldman Sachs, for instance, played important roles in the Clinton, George W. Bush, and Trump administrations. Executives from BlackRock, a multinational investment company, served in high positions in the Trump and Biden administrations.

But there are also businesses and labor unions, advocacy and interest group organizations whose leaders have enjoyed influence in one party but not the other. Since World War II, labor unions and their top leaders have primarily exercised influence within the Democratic Party. Many of the advocacy groups that originated in the sixties or earlier—women's, civil rights, environmental, and consumer groups, for instance—have primarily exercised influence within the Democratic Party. Religious right organizations, gun organizations, anti-tax groups, and their leaders enjoy influence primarily in the Republican Party. These kinds of groups are part of a party's governing coalition, although they are usually subordinate to the core elite that Domhoff and Mills described. Unlike the leaders of the core institutions, the degree of their leaders' influence depends on the pressure they can exert on the ground from their followers.

The governing and electoral coalitions of the Democratic Party have been transformed over the last sixty years. The change has occurred in two overlapping phases. In the first phase, the Democratic elites and base divided over support for racial desegregation and civil rights for black Americans. That split led to the Democrats' loss of the white South as a dependable part of its electoral coalition. That change began in the sixties and was not completed until 1994 when white southern voters, including working-class whites, who had enthusiastically backed Ronald Reagan for president, voted en masse for Republicans in congressional races. The departure of the South spelled the end of the New Deal majority.

In the second phase, which began in the 1970s and continues to this day, the decline of the labor movement has given business and financial elites far more sway in the governing coalition over economic policy. As a result, Democratic administrations have taken positions on trade, taxes, and immigration that have worsened the Great Divide and alienated working-class voters. With labor's decline, the party also lost in many areas the principal group that had organized working-class voters to support the Democrats.

At the same time as labor's clout was declining, the influence of pressure and advocacy groups that grew out of the new left, and primarily represented the concerns of the new college-educated professionals, has endured and in some cases grown. A few of these groups have occasionally clashed with financial and corporate interests in the party—over consumer and financial regulation, for instance—but they have often found themselves in happy agreement on issues like gay marriage, a path to citizenship for illegal immigrants, affirmative action, gun control, or limiting fossil fuel use. The party's advocacy of these social issues has rubbed some working-class voters the wrong way and led to their abandoning the Democrats.

In fashionable jargon, the changes in the Democrats' governing coalition over the last fifty years led to the party espousing a combination of neoliberal economics and social liberalism that has alienated working-class voters and led to the changes in the party's electoral coalition. These changes, coming on top of the earlier loss of the white southern working class, have led to a party that looks far different from the New Deal party of the "forgotten American" that Roosevelt wrought in the 1930s. The Democrats could no longer command a consistent majority. With the party's new constituencies, they were locked into a see-saw rivalry with the Republicans.

The Rise and Fall of the New Deal Coalition

The success of the Democrats' New Deal majority depended on their being perceived as the party of "the people" (a term widely used in the thirties) and the Republicans as the party of business and the wealthy. This perception was based on the Republicans' association with the crash and Great Depression and the Democrats with the recovery and subsequent prosperity (regardless of whether, as some economists argue, World War II was the real cure for the Great Depression) and with a set of programs, adopted by the Democrats, that empowered and delivered economic security to the working and middle classes. In his 1932 and 1936 campaigns, Roosevelt framed this perception politically in populist terms—as a defense of the "forgotten American" and the "average citizen" against the "money-changers" and the "economic royalists."

Roosevelt's governing coalition drew on sympathetic corporate lawyers like Adolf Berle, department store magnates like Edward Filene, the founder of the Twentieth Century Fund, big-city mayors and their machines, southern business leaders like Jesse H. Jones, and top aides recommended by Felix Frankfurter at Harvard Law School. The administration was notably lacking in support from Wall Street or big business. Many members of Roosevelt's Business Advisory Council bolted before the

1936 election. Roosevelt's landmark Second New Deal of 1935, which established Social Security, a steeply graduated income tax, and the National Labor Relations Act (dubbed the Wagner Act), which facilitated collective bargaining for labor unions, was driven from below by a rising labor movement and by Huey Long's populist Share Our Wealth clubs.

Through the Wagner Act, the labor movement rapidly grew after 1935. The newly formed Congress of Industrial Organizations (CIO) became an important influence within Roosevelt's electoral coalition. During the 1944 Democratic convention, when Roosevelt, under pressure from southern politicians and business leaders, decided to replace ultraliberal Henry Wallace as vice president with Harry Truman, Roosevelt told his aides to "clear it with Sidney," a reference to Sidney Hillman, the president of the CIO's Amalgamated Clothing Workers of America union. The incident is telling in two ways—in bearing out the influence of southern business on one hand and labor on the other.

The heyday of the New Deal ended with the Fair Labor Standards Act of 1938 that established, among other things, the minimum wage and restriction of hours without overtime. After the 1938 election, and the failure of pro-Roosevelt Democrats to unseat conservative southern Democrats, the coalition between southern conservative Democrats and northern Republicans—the "conservative coalition"—was able to block ambitious initiatives, and after World War II, with the populist surge abated and the labor movement divided internally over the Cold War and Communism, the conservative coalition was able to pass bills making it more difficult for labor unions to organize.

During the 1950s, the labor movement, which merged into the AFL-CIO in 1955, still retained sufficient influence to block efforts to repeal the major New Deal measures and to expand others, including the minimum wage. During the 1950s, about a third of the non-farm labor force belonged to unions. Then in the sixties, the labor movement, augmented by the rise of public employee and service sector unions, helped the Johnson administration win passage of Medicare. In the first Nixon term, with Democrats in control of Congress, the combined force of labor and the new left movements pressured Congress into adopting a spate of new regulatory agencies, including the Environmental Protection Agency (EPA) and the Occupational Safety and Health Administration (OSHA), and into expanding Social Security.

The New Deal Democrats' electoral coalition drew upon the Democrats' older base among southern whites and northern urban ethnics and Catholics, many of whom looked to the Democratic machines for leadership, but it added blue-collar workers, northern blacks, and Jews. The white South, however, remained crucial for Truman in 1948 and Kennedy in 1960 and for Democratic control of Congress. Roosevelt had retained the loyalty of the South by compromising on legislation that southern Democratic politicians and business leaders believed would threaten "Jim Crow" segregation. Southerners had also enthusiastically supported rural electrification and southern agribusiness had appreciated the subsidies from the U.S. Department of Agriculture. But in the aftermath of *Brown v. Board of Education* and the rise of the civil rights movement, the New Deal electoral coalition lost its most dependable base of support.

Democrats opted hesitantly under Kennedy and then energetically under Lyndon Johnson to align the Democrats with the civil rights movement. They were driven by popular support for the movement in the North, which had been fueled by television footage of brutal attempts to suppress civil rights demonstrators and by pressure from sympathetic religious, labor, and educational leaders. The Democrats passed civil rights and voting rights bills and a fair housing bill. They attempted to curb discrimination in hiring, launched a "war on poverty" primarily directed toward urban blacks, and championed "affirmative action" in hiring and government contracts. Democratic judges and politicians also promoted busing as a means to achieve school desegregation. The Democrats knew that these measures would cost them a substantial number of white votes, but they hoped the loss of white votes would eventually be made up by enthusiastic support from blacks in the North and from newly enfranchised blacks in the South. In the 1970s, that would become the strategy and hope of "new South" Democrats like Jimmy Carter and North Carolina governor Jim Hunt.

In the near term, however, Democratic support for desegregation and civil rights, along with the black riots and militant protests in major cities during the mid-sixties, provoked a furious backlash among many white working-class Democrats, especially, but not exclusively, in the South. Alabama governor George Wallace, championing racial segregation—"segregation now, segregation tomorrow, segregation forever," he proclaimed—entered the 1964 Democratic primaries in Wisconsin, Indiana, and Maryland against Lyndon Johnson. Wallace got a third of the vote in Wisconsin and Indiana and 43 percent in Maryland. In 1968, he ran for president and won five southern states. Then in 1972, with Democratic candidate George McGovern championing civil rights, Wallace's vote gravitated to Nixon. Nixon's vote totals in 1972 in forty-five of fifty states closely matched in percentage the total of his and Wallace's vote from 1968.

As will be true in other presidential elections, Nixon's support in 1972 was not entirely attributable to a single cause. Nixon campaigned against school busing to achieve desegregation, but he also campaigned against the new left counterculture—captured in the slogan "Acid, Amnesty, and Abortion"—and campaigned on the promise of recovery from the brief recession in 1970. The opposition to the counterculture and to the demand for abortion rights and equal rights for women would figure later in Republican campaigns and would take voters from the Democrats, but the realignment of the two parties that began in the 1968 and 1972 elections was sparked initially by the backlash against Democratic civil rights and affirmative action measures.

This backlash took two different forms. Some of the support for Wallace, particularly in the Deep South, was predicated on opposition to racial equality. By the 1980s, that kind of appeal would vanish. You could still find it today among marginal groups that advocate white supremacy, but as a popular politics, it disappeared with the end of Wallace's candidacy. Indeed, Wallace himself disavowed his own views when he ran for Alabama governor in 1982. But the backlash also took the form of ethnic resentment that blacks were receiving special favors that were being denied to whites, or that members of the white working class, but not upper class, would have to sacrifice the cohesion of their neighborhoods, their jobs, or their income in the form of taxes to confer what they saw as special favors upon blacks to recompense for past racism.

White working-class grievances often focused on affirmative action. John Kennedy first used the term "affirmative action" on March 6, 1961, in an executive order. He ordered government contractors to "take affirmative action to ensure that applicants are employed, and employees are treated during employment, without regard to their race, creed, color, or national origin." Affirmative action meant "taking action" to end discrimination on the basis of race, creed, color, or national origin. Johnson used the term in the same manner. He issued an executive order on September 24, 1965, requiring federal contractors to take "affirmative action to promote the full realization of equal opportunity for women and minorities." But in the wake of continued rioting and the assassination of Martin Luther King Jr. in 1968, businesses, schools, and the military began to interpret affirmative action as requiring a special effort to employ, admit, or advance blacks.

These grievances about special favors to blacks, which extended to busing and to rising welfare expenditures, were not reducible to simple racism or white supremacy. They were described by Kevin Phillips in his 1969 book *The Emerging Republican Majority*.

> The principal force which broke up the Democratic (New Deal) coalition is the Negro socioeconomic revolution and liberal Democratic ideological inability to cope with it. Democratic "Great Society" programs aligned that party with many Negro demands, but the party was unable to defuse the racial tension sundering the nation. The South, the West, and the Catholic sidewalks of New York were the focus points of conservative opposition to the welfare liberalism of the federal government; however, the general opposition . . . came in large part from prospering Democrats who objected to Washington dissipating their tax dollars on programs which did them no good. The Democratic party fell victim to the ideological impetus of a liberalism which had carried it beyond programs taxing the few for the benefit of the many . . . to programs taxing the many on behalf of the few.

Such racially tinged sentiments would endure as a factor in American politics. They would persist in the opposition to welfare spending and later even to the Affordable Care Act, although in that case, the resentment would not necessarily be directed exclusively at blacks. But unlike in 1968, they would not necessarily be the principal factor driving working-class whites out of the Democratic Party. Economics, relations between business and labor, and social and cultural issues surrounding women's rights and immigration would assume great importance in the critical elections to come.

The Corporate Offensive

After World War II, the United States enjoyed unchallenged industrial superiority. It ran large trade surpluses and acquiesced in Japan and western European countries using tariffs and other barriers to build up their fledgling industries—not only to stave off a Communist challenge but also to create demand for American exports. Many major American corporations, flush with cash, accepted the existence of unions. In 1950, General Motors inked a five-year pact with the United Auto Workers—dubbed "The Treaty of Detroit" by *Fortune*—that became the model for settlements with other auto companies and unionized industries. Wages, profits, and productivity rose in tandem.

But beginning in the late 1960s, business began to feel under threat. With unemployment at less than 4 percent because of Vietnam War spending, and unions demanding new contracts, companies were being forced to grant workers large wage increases. The wages of production workers increased by 6.6 percent a year in nominal terms between 1967 and 1972. At the same time, aided in part by wartime demand, Japan and western Europe not only recovered but became competitive with the United States in basic industries. The global market became sated in textiles, shoes, ships, steel, and other goods, threatening profit margins. In other words, American companies were being squeezed by American workers and rising foreign competition at the same time. In 1971, America ran its first trade deficit in the century.

American business also felt threatened by the new left movements, which, inspired by consumer advocate Ralph Nader, had joined with labor in pressuring Congress to create the new regulatory agencies. The new left movements on campus had also begun to ally with labor. In 1969, General Electric workers went on strike. In February 1970, with the strike still unsettled, 10,000 Boston University students protested the arrival of a GE recruiter. In a special *Business Week* issue on "The Seventies," the magazine warned that "corporations and the middle-and upper-bracket income earners" faced a stiff challenge from "the blacks, the labor unions, and the young. The attacks, retreats, shifting alliances and internal dissension of these groups would make the seventies one of the more tumultuous decades in US history."

Business went on the offensive against unions. In 1965, when unions had filed petitions with the National Labor Relations Board to be recognized as collective bargaining agents, 42 percent of companies immediately complied. By 1973, only 16 percent did. Ignoring the relatively small fines that the NLRB imposed on companies for violating its rules, businesses fired union organizers and began installing replacement workers. Between 1970 and 1980, the number of workers ordered to be reinstated because they were illegally fired increased 216 percent. According to the NLRB, the number of unfair labor practices tripled.

The companies also began moving their plants and outsourcing their production to avoid paying union wages and abiding by government regulations. Auto plants moved from union-dominated cities like Detroit to the rural Midwest or South. Other plants went to Latin America or overseas. By 1974, the largest American companies, including Ford, Kodak, and Procter & Gamble, employed more than a third of their workforce overseas. According to AFL-CIO economist Elizabeth R. Jager, from 1966 to 1970, foreign employment by American firms had grown 26.5 percent, and their sales of goods back to the United States had risen by 130 percent. Companies used the threat of moving south or overseas to suppress union organizing or to hold down wage demands. The corporate offensive had an effect. Unions had represented more than a third of private-sector nonagricultural workers during the 1950s. By 1973, it was down to 24.5 percent; by 1987, 12.7 percent. That diminished labor's ability to win concessions and its influence within the Democratic Party.

Business's second kind of response to the threat to its power and profits consisted in trying to combat the power of labor and of new left groups within Washington and more broadly in the electoral arena. In Washington, businesses built a lobbying presence—later dubbed "K Street" for the street on which many of the law firms and lobbying groups were located. Only 175 businesses had lobbyists in Washington in 1971; by 1982, 2,445 had. The established business organizations, the Chamber of Commerce and the National Association of Manufacturers, grew rapidly during this decade. In addition, CEOs from Fortune 500 corporations came together in 1973 to form the Business Round-table, which became the most powerful business lobby in Washington.

Businesses didn't confine themselves to buttonholing and funding politicians. They also sought to influence public opinion. They poured money into the already established American Enterprise Institute and funded a new policy group, the Heritage Foundation, as well as smaller policy groups like the American Council for Capital Formation. These new business-funded groups claimed to be traditional think tanks like Brookings, but, unlike them, they made only token attempts to be above the partisan fray. Wanting to influence the party in power, businesses and their lobbies had generously funded Democrats as well as Republicans, but once Republicans became competitive in the 1970s, business money began to favor them, especially in closely contested races that could establish congressional majorities. In competitive House races in 1982, corporate PACs (political action committees) gave 84.2 percent of their contributions to Republicans.

The first test of the business lobbies' power came in 1971. The AFL-CIO introduced a bill, sponsored by two Democrats, Massachusetts House member James Burke and Indiana senator Vance Hartke, that would have removed tax incentives for companies to move their production overseas and would have allowed the president to restrict imports and the export of capital when jobs were threatened. But business mounted a furious campaign against the Burke-Hartke bill through the Emergency Committee for American Trade, which had been established in 1967 by Chase Manhattan CEO David Rockefeller and IBM CEO Arthur Watson, to defend the prerogatives of multinationals. The bill never even made it to the floor for a vote. It was a big victory for the business lobbies, and a clear indication of labor's lack of influence over Democratic lawmakers on an issue that was becoming highly salient to working-class voters.

In the early 1970s, the most militant new left movements faded. The anti-war movement barely survived the cessation of the draft, and Nixon's withdrawal in December 1972 ended the movement entirely. The Black Panther Party was the victim of FBI subversion and of the leadership's own criminal inclinations. The student left devolved into irrelevant groupuscules that looked to China's cultural revolution or even North Korea's Juche for inspiration. Of the movements from the sixties, only the women's, environmental, consumer and more moderate civil rights groups still had a following, but they didn't threaten the kind of disruption that the *Business Week* special issue had warned of. With the new left groups relatively quiescent, and labor on the defensive, the business and financial lobbies had carried the day in Washington and, . to some extent, within the Democratic Party's governing coalition. That meant that Democrats would have difficulty serving their working-class constituencies. That would become readily apparent during the Carter administration.

The Carter Debacle

In 1976, in the wake of the Watergate scandal and the 1973–75 recession, Democrats won back the White House and enjoyed Roosevelt-size majorities in Congress—a 62 to 38 advantage in the Senate and 292 to 143 majority in the House. Carter, a successful agribusinessman and Georgia governor, had run as the anti-Watergate candidate. "I'll Never Lie to You" was the title of his campaign book. But he also embraced a version of economic populism. "Too many have had to suffer at the hands of a political economic elite who have shaped decisions and never had to account for mistakes or to suffer from injustice," Carter had declared in accepting the nomination. Carter was not from the party's New Deal wing, but he chose a New Dealer, Minnesota senator Walter Mondale, as his vice president.

Buoyed by their majority, Democrats in Congress advanced an agenda that would have extended and expanded the New Deal. It included the Humphrey–Hawkins Full Employment Act, which would have guaranteed a job to every American—if necessary, through public employment; tax reform that would have increased the tax rates on capital gains and eliminated dodgy business deductions; a new consumer protection agency championed by Nader; and the reform of labor laws to raise the penalties for businesses that blocked union drives by firing organizers or by using the courts to stall implementation of NLRB rulings; a campaign finance reform plan that would extend public financing to House and Senate races and provide for universal voter registration; and a plan to contain hospital costs.

Carter either strongly supported or promised to sign all these measures. Congress had previously passed some of these, but Republican president Gerald Ford had vetoed the measures. Without the threat of a veto, and a cloture-proof majority in the

Senate, the Democrats had reason to believe that they could get their program through.

But Carter and the Democrats proved no match for the newly forged K Street constellation of business groups, think tanks, and policy groups. The business lobbies, with full Republican support, were able to defeat or even reverse Carter and the Democrats' proposals. The Humphrey–Hawkins bill became the Full Employment and Balanced Growth Act. It now paired low unemployment with low inflation and dropped the requirement that government actually guarantee full employment. The main requirement was that the Fed report yearly on its ability to hold down unemployment and inflation. The bill's irrelevance would become clear when the Federal Reserve manufactured a deep recession in 1981.

Businesses formed coalitions to fight these measures, including the Consumer Issues Working Group and the National Action Committee on Labor Law Reform. The business lobbies were able to win over Democrats who never or no longer owed their election to labor union support. If a legislator had relied on union money, business organizations chipped in to replace it. Nader's proposal for a consumer organization never made it to a vote in the House. The Business Roundtable's CEOs jetted to Washington to lobby against labor law reform. Business lobbies outspent the AFL-CIO by $7 million to $2.5 million. The bill failed to get the sixty votes needed to break a filibuster.

In the fall of 1978, after he lost on these other measures, Carter suffered the ultimate indignity: his tax reform proposal that he had championed was turned upside down by the alliance between the business lobbies and the conservative coalition in Congress. Instead of a progressive tax increase on capital gains and corporations, the bill that passed Congress now *reduced* these tax rates. The AFL-CIO and liberal Democrats urged Carter to veto the bill but, beaten by the opposition, Carter jettisoned what remained of his economic populism and signed the bill. Carter's acquiescence bore out the growing influence of business not only within Washington but within the Democratic Party.

Carter's abandonment of New Deal economics and the average American became even clearer in his response to inflation. When the Vietnam War–driven inflation had begun to rise in Nixon's first term, he had responded in August 1971 with wage-price controls, which had cut the inflation rate in half in two years. Inflation would start rising again largely as a result of the Arab oil embargo in 1973 and, when Carter took office, had still not fully abated. The AFL-CIO and liberal economists wanted Carter to seek standby reauthorization from Congress to impose wage-price controls if they were needed. (The unions were against wage controls, but they recognized that the alternative to wage-price controls was to induce a recession.) After his election, Carter met with a group of sixteen businessmen and economists who unanimously recommended that he not seek standby authority, and the next month Carter announced that he would not do so. That took wage-price controls off the table, because after the 1978 election setbacks, it was clear that Carter could not win standby authority for the controls from the new Congress.

When inflation did begin to accelerate in 1978, Carter, echoing Republican critics of New Deal economics, blamed it on budget deficits. "The federal deficit is too high," Carter said in October 1978. "Our people are simply sick and tired of wasteful federal spending and the inflation it brings with it." In response, George Meany, the head of the AFL-CIO, described Carter as "the most conservative president since Calvin Coolidge." The next year, as oil price increases created by the Iranian revolution drove inflation up to 13 percent, Carter appointed banker Paul Volcker to head the Federal Reserve. Carter's choice of Volcker signaled Wall Street's ascendancy within the Democratic governing coalition. Volcker, Carter's domestic policy adviser Stuart

Eizenstat told journalist William Greider, "was the candidate of Wall Street." Wall Street, Eizenstat explained in an oral interview at the Library of Congress, had "concerns in the dollar market."

Inflation was driving down the value of the dollar—gold, once pegged at $35 an ounce, was selling for $850 an ounce in 1979—which was driving down the value of Wall Street's assets. In line with Wall Street's priorities, Volcker began curtailing the dollar supply, which led to a dramatic increase in the dollar's value, skyrocketing interest rate hikes and a recession. Volcker's interventions caused two recessions—a two-quarter one in 1980 that helped defeat Jimmy Carter in the November election and a much sharper one in 1981–82. The 1981–82 recession, in which unemployment reached almost 11 percent, occurred under Reagan's watch but was precipitated by choices that Carter had made in his last two years. Carter's decision to appoint Volcker and adopt his and Wall Street's strategy for fighting inflation had profound political and economic consequences.

Volcker's strategy, aimed as much at jacking up the value of the dollar as reducing inflation, resulted in American goods being priced out of many foreign markets. In the recessions, 90 percent of the jobs lost were in goods production, which made up only 30 percent of the non-farm economy. Manufacturing was particularly hard hit. Jobs were permanently lost in autos, steel, machinery, and textiles. Some midwestern towns and cities would never fully recover. It was the beginning of the Great Divide economically. Politically, the workers in these midwestern towns, whose interests Carter had ignored in appointing Volcker, would later provide a political base for the revolt against the Democratic Party.

For their part, Democrats would never fully recover their reputation as protectors of the average American, and they would also lose any residual public support for the Keynesian view of government and the economy that the party's economists had championed and was the basis for the Second New Deal. New Deal economics rested on the assumption that government intervention in the market could benefit workers and consumers. The Democrats' failures during the Carter administration strengthened the traditional American argument, voiced by Reagan, that "government is the problem not the solution." Government bureaucrats rather than corporate chieftains became the targets of public wrath. In short, by the end of Carter's term, the New Deal economic agenda lay in ruins, as well as the theory behind it. In its place arose a Democratic Party that was competitive but no longer dominant and no longer clearly rooted in the promise of prosperity for the "forgotten American."

The Democratic Rout

Carter and the Democrats were routed in the 1980 election. Carter won only 41 percent of the vote and 9.1 percent of the Electoral College vote. (By contrast, Herbert Hoover had won 11.1 percent of the Electoral College vote in 1932.) Democrats lost 12 Senate seats and 33 House seats. With his references to "welfare queens," Reagan's campaign certainly struck a chord with voters who were still unhappy with the civil rights acts and the Great Society; he also attracted votes from evangelical Protestants angered by the Supreme Court's ruling on abortion and by the feminist campaign for an Equal Rights Amendment. (In the 1978 elections, Democrats had lost a Senate race in Iowa partly because of defections from working-class Catholics in eastern Iowa over the abortion issue.) Reagan benefited from Carter's failure to rescue the hostages in Iran and from a suspicion that Carter could not stand up to the Soviet Union.

But the election was primarily a referendum on Carter and the Democrats' handling of the economy. Reagan succeeded, above all, because he trounced Carter among voters who thought their family finances were "worse off than a year ago." According to the *New York Times* survey, these voters went for Reagan by 72 percent to 28 percent. Many of these Reagan supporters were working-class voters who had backed Carter in 1976. Reagan edged Carter among the blue-collar voters whom Carter had won by 16 percentage points in 1976. Reagan won the voters with a high school diploma by 51 percent to 43 percent and those with "some college" by 55 percent to 35 percent. These voters, who had once made up the core of the New Deal coalition, and most of whom had voted for Carter in 1976, became the "Reagan Democrats." Some would return to the Democratic fold to vote for Clinton or Obama, but many would be lost to the Democrats.

The Reagan years were important in shaping the Democrats' governing and electoral coalitions. In August 1981, Reagan fired and replaced over twelve thousand unionized air traffic controllers who had gone on strike. Reagan's replacement of striking workers, which proved successful, created a precedent that other industries, including Phelps Dodge, International Paper, and Hormel, followed in the 1980s. Reagan's NLRB also ruled repeatedly against unions. The corporate offensive, backed by the Reagan administration, succeeded. From 1980 to 1990, union membership in the private sector shrunk from 20.1 percent to 11.9 percent.

The continued growth of the public employee unions made up partly for the evisceration of the private sector unions, and labor remained a player in the Democratic Party's quest for votes, but it had a diminished role in the party's governing coalition. "There is no chance that Democratic elected officials in the foreseeable future will permit a declining labor movement with little public support to regain the influence and stature it had in Congress in the 1960s," *Washington Post* journalist Thomas B. Edsall wrote in his 1984 book *The New Politics of Inequality*. As

we will recount in the next chapter, that would leave an opening for Democrats who listened to business rather than labor to
redefine what it meant to be a Democrat.

In Washington and in the Democratic Party, labor had to
share power and influence with a host of interest and advocacy
groups, many of which had originated in the sixties and were
seen as being on the left or center-left. They were dubbed the
"New Politics" faction of the Democratic Party. These included
NOW (National Organization for Women), NARAL (National
Association for the Repeal of Abortion Laws), the Environ-
mental Defense Fund, AARP (American Association of Retired
Persons), the Alliance for Justice, the American Civil Liberties
Union, the Vera Institute of Justice, the Institute for Policy Studies, Public Citizen, Common Cause, Friends of the Earth, the
NAACP (National Association for the Advancement of Colored
People), the National Council of La Raza, People for the American Way, the World Wildlife Fund, and the Children's Defense
Fund. Some of these groups, like Nader's Public Citizen, shared
labor's support for New Deal economics and wanted, if anything, to expand its reach, but many of the groups were preoccu-
pied with social or environmental causes or with the welfare of
particular constituency groups.

Some of the groups like NOW and the Sierra Club had genuine memberships that met and elected the groups' officials, but
many of them were Washington letterhead groups that relied on
help from wealthy donors or foundations. The groups' staffs and
their prime constituencies were the college-educated voters who
lived in the big metro centers. They were cut off socially and
politically from much of the electorate, and in particular from
what had been the Democratic Party's older working-class base.
Many of these working-class voters rejected the groups' views on
abortion, the death penalty, gun control, environmental protec-

tion (which was seen as a threat to jobs), and affirmative action. In their priorities and advocacy, the groups tended to deepen the divide between the Democrats and their former working-class base.

Those organizations concerned with social and environmental issues and with constitutional rights enjoyed strong support from the foundations, banks, and corporations whose leaders were part of the Democratic governing coalition. Banks and businesses might have been averse to labor law reform or a new consumer protection agency, but they were highly supportive of abortion rights, the protection of endangered species, freedom of speech and worship, gun control, criminal justice reform, and equal opportunity for minorities. Allied with business, these groups exercised some influence over party platforms, candidate statements, and government. By the 1980s, few Democratic officials or candidates opposed abortion or gun control. The groups and their business allies helped secure during the Reagan years the resignation of James Watt as interior secretary, Anne Gorsuch's ouster at the Environmental Protection Agency, the renewal of the Voting Rights Act, and the rejection of Robert Bork as a Supreme Court nominee.

The 1984 and 1988 presidential elections showed the strengths and the weaknesses of labor and the New Politics groups. In 1984, the AFL-CIO, National Education Association, and NOW, none of whom had ever endorsed a candidate in the Democratic primaries, endorsed former vice president Walter Mondale. The groups sought to exercise their power over who the party would nominate. Mondale, for his part, actively sought their endorsement and later that of the Sierra Club, which had never endorsed a presidential candidate. Mondale assumed that by gaining these groups' endorsement, he would receive the support of the broader constituencies they purported to represent. Sidney Blumenthal wrote in the *New Republic*, "Mondale implicitly accepted the symbolic claims of the interest groups headquartered in Washington. The AFL-CIO was working people, NOW was women, and the NEA [National Education Association] was teachers."

Mondale's strategy worked to some extent in the primary, helping him to win the nomination over Colorado senator Gary Hart. In the run-up to the convention, Mondale doubled down on the strategy by choosing, at NOW's behest, Congresswoman Geraldine Ferraro as his running mate. But the Reagan campaign, branding Mondale as a candidate of the "special interests," destroyed him in the general election. Mondale also became unwittingly identified with all of their most extreme positions on the family (as an instrument of patriarchy), crime (as the pardonable product of poverty), or the defense budget (which should be cut drastically). Mondale suffered the worst defeat of any presidential candidate, winning only one state (his own) and the District of Columbia. The election showed, among other things, how little support labor and the new Washington pressure groups enjoyed in the electorate.

In 1988, the presidential nomination battle was fought primarily between Massachusetts governor Michael Dukakis and civil rights leader Jesse Jackson, who had run third in 1984. Jackson had proclaimed in that election that he was trying to build a "rainbow coalition," but his principal support was among black voters, and his slogan, "It's our turn now," suggested to voters that he meant that it was the turn of black voters and their candidate to govern. "He kept talking rainbow," one white liberal told Bob Faw and Nancy Skelton in their chronicle of the campaign, "but more and more he was embracing one color—black!" That perception haunted Jackson in his 1988 campaign, as did his past as a militant promoter of affirmative action and reparations for blacks.

Jackson sought to attract white working-class voters by supporting major government expenditures for jobs—he championed an industrial and infrastructure program to "rebuild America"—and a single-payer health insurance system. Some of Jackson's economic programs would later be espoused by Democrat Bernie Sanders in 2016 and even by President Joe Biden, but in 1988, Jackson had to contend with the skepticism about ambitious government programs bred during the Carter years and reinforced by Reagan. That, and the view of Jackson as primarily a candidate of and for blacks, drastically limited his appeal among white Democrats. That year, he won 92 percent of the black vote and carried thirteen state primaries and caucuses, but his support among white voters was concentrated among young people with college or graduate degrees. He won, in other words, a slice of what would become the Democrats' new electoral coalition but failed to pick up or bring back the older white working-class vote. If anything, he increased the hostility of these voters to the Democratic Party.

Dukakis tried to avoid any connection to the past or present of the Democratic Party. "This election isn't about ideology; it's about competence," Dukakis declared in accepting the nomination in July. Dukakis's opponent, George H. W. Bush, was seen as a weak candidate and, on the eve of the Republican convention, trailed Dukakis by 17 points in opinion polls, but Bush was able to turn the election around by identifying Dukakis with the New Politics groups' opposition to patriotic displays (including saying the Pledge of Allegiance in schools), support for criminal justice reform, and opposition to capital punishment. Dukakis, like Carter, lost decisively the vote of the white working class. As a result, he lost most of the midwestern industrial states as well as the South.

There were signs of a new Democratic vote in Dukakis's results as well as in Jackson's. For the first time, a Democrat won the vote of professionals. Many of them were repelled by Republicans' growing links to the religious right. But the support of these voters was not enough to overcome the loss of working-class voters. If the Democrats wanted to win back the White House, they would have to recast their appeal. And that's where the Democratic Business Council, the Democratic Leadership Council, and Bill Clinton came in.

Chapter Three

The Successes and
Failures of the New
Democrats

There can be a difference between a political strategy that secures a majority for a candidate and party in one or two elections, and a strategy that leads to the kind of majority Republicans enjoyed after 1896 or Democrats after 1932. To achieve that kind of enduring realignment, a party's approach to policy has to mesh with its approach to politics. It has to advance policies that actually benefit the constituencies that make up its majority. If it doesn't, key constituencies will eventually turn on it.

After the Democratic defeats in 1980, 1984, and 1988, Democrats adopted a new approach. With funding from the Democratic Business Council, which was established in 1981, and leadership from the Democratic Leadership Council, which began in February 1985 after Mondale's crushing defeat, a group of Democrats, dubbed "New Democrats," adopted a new approach that shaped the successful candidacy and the presidency of Bill Clinton. The political strategy worked, and a variation on it also got Barack Obama elected in 2008, but the Democrats' policies didn't create an enduring majority. Instead, by widening the Great Divide, they laid the groundwork for further erosion in Democratic support among working-class voters and for Donald Trump's victory in 2016.

The Business Council and the DLC

Democrats had always enjoyed some support from large and small business. During the New Deal years and their aftermath, as long as Democrats controlled one or both houses of Congress, which they did from 1954 to 1994, Democratic committee or subcommittee heads could count on contributions from the industries they oversaw. California congressman Tony Coehlo, who was put in charge of the Democratic Congressional Campaign Committee in 1981, and who championed Democrats' ties to business, said, "Business has to deal with us, whether they like it or not, because we are the majority."

But there were other businesses that as a matter of history or social commitment had an affinity to the Democrats and whose leaders often constituted part of their governing coalition. As William Domhoff wrote in *The Power Elite and the State*, the Democrats have "always been the party of the 'out-group' within the power elite, of those who in some way differ from the wealthiest WASP bankers, industrialists, and retailers of their day." During the Roosevelt years and the two decades afterward, Democrats got the support of Texas oil, banking and ranching, southern agribusiness and textile firms, the Jewish firms on Wall Street (who also identified with the Democrats' underdoggery), and Hollywood and the entertainment and media industry, in which Jews were prominent. They also got backing from department stores, real estate and construction firms (which depended on government largesse), and the defense industry.

With the corporate offensive against labor and the rise of the New Politics lobbies, southern business and the extractive industries crossed the aisle to back Reagan conservatives. But the Democrats picked up support from Silicon Valley, some of whose firms were run by recent immigrants and who, in spite of their fabulous wealth, saw themselves as upstarts or outsiders. Together, many of the leaders of these industries functioned as part of the Democrats' governing coalition. What they said and did counted with the Democrats in office.

In 1981, the Democratic National Committee set up the Democratic Business Council to marshal support and get money from sympathetic business leaders. With three hundred executives contributing $4 million annually, it became the party's main funding arm. Unlike their Republican counterparts, the Democratic business leaders did not seek to undo the New Deal. They supported a minimum wage and Social Security, they thought government needed to reduce poverty, and some of them dealt with unions in their workplace. Many of them were socially liberal and averse to the growing ties between the Republicans and the religious right. But council members pressed the Democrats not to raise taxes on the wealthy and to retain lower taxes for capital gains. They favored reducing the deficit, which they held responsible for inflation and the reduction in the value of their assets. They opposed any Democratic measures that smacked of managed trade and they favored large-scale immigration.

During his campaign, Mondale had held a meeting in St. Paul in August 1984 with seventy of his financial backers, including Los Angeles industrialist Irvin Kipnes, the head of the council. Kipnes told reporter Robert Kuttner that presidential candidate Mondale had assured them he would quit "knocking the rich." Subsequently, Mondale defied his advisers who urged him to endorse an evenhanded but not pro-business tax reform bill sponsored by Senator Bill Bradley and Representative Richard Gephardt. In his campaign, Mondale also promised to reduce the deficit, another favorite cause of Business Council members. During the decade, the council would continue to attempt to move Democrats toward what they saw as a more friendly pro-business politics and away from the Democrats' growing interest in managed trade policies and tax reform. They found an ally in a new group started in the wake of Mondale's rout.

The Democratic Leadership Council (DLC) was founded on February 28, 1985, in a meeting on Capitol Hill. The group was the brainchild of Al From, an aide to Congressman Gillis Long, who had chaired the House Democratic Caucus, abetted by a group of politicians led by Virginia governor (and later senator) Chuck Robb, Georgia senator Sam Nunn, Tennessee senator Al Gore, and Congressman Richard Gephardt (who would leave the group within two years). The group was composed initially of House and Senate Democrats and governors. It started with 40, mostly from the South and West, grew quickly to 140, and eventually started over a dozen state chapters that local and state officials joined. Its annual conferences attracted several thousand, including the national press. It raised money from some of the same people who contributed to the Business Council. Eventually, its board of advisers and donors would include representatives from Boeing, Bristol Myers Squibb, Coca-Cola, Dell, Eli Lilly, Federal Express, GlaxoWellcome, Intel, Motorola, U.S. Tobacco, Union Carbide, and Xerox. The DLC became a key part of the Democrats' governing coalition.

From's view was that the Democrats needed a strategy and platform that could win back the white working and middle classes and restore Democratic support in the South and West. (The last time Democrats had won California was in the 1964 presidential election.) He blamed Democratic losses on what he called the "single interest and single constituency" groups—in other words, on the New Politics groups and labor upon which Mondale had relied in the 1984 election. In its first years, the DLC attempted at times to mollify its critics in the Democratic National Committee, but after Jackson's strong showing in the 1988 primaries and

Dukakis's defeat in the general election, the DLC sharpened its stand against what it called "liberal fundamentalism."

The DLC's economic stands—articulated by its think tank, the Progressive Policy Institute, and in declarations adopted at its annual conferences—tried to address, and take into account, the skepticism about government and the enthusiasm about the free market that had arisen in the wake of Carter's failure to stem stagflation and Reagan's apparent success in spurring a recovery from the deep recession in 1981–82. The DLC tried to promote the Democrats as a party of business and free markets. It stressed economic growth over redistribution, and market incentives rather than outright regulation to protect the environment or to increase access to health insurance; it promoted free trade and the North American Free Trade Agreement (NAFTA) among the United States, Mexico, and Canada; it urged reducing the budget deficit (which it blamed for slow growth and inadequate investment), and it called for reducing—or "reinventing"— government employment through outsourcing its functions to private industry. The DLC's approach was roughly congruent with the more creative, less dogmatic strands of Republican conservatism that were promoted by groups like Empower America. And it won the praise of business lobbies. Thomas J. Donohue, the head of the U.S. Chamber of Commerce, wrote later about From and the DLC, "With vision and persistence, he helped lead a major political party back to the principles of private sector growth, trade, jobs, personal responsibility, and fiscal stability."

In its social and defense policy, the DLC tried to distance itself from the New Politics groups. "We believe in preventing crime and punishing criminals, not in explaining away their behavior," it declared in its New Orleans Declaration in 1990. "We believe the United States must maintain a strong and capable defense," the declaration said. Nunn, Robb, and other DLC leaders were "New

South" Democrats who opposed racial segregation and discrimination, but they did not support the explicit or implicit imposition
of quotas favored by New Politics groups in the name of affirmative action. "We believe the promise of America is equal opportunity, not equal outcomes," the group stated. They opposed "welfare
paternalism" and thought the system should be reformed to discourage dependency. If queried by a journalist, From and the DLC
leaders would say they favored abortion rights and gay rights, but
they didn't think these positions should be headlined by Democrats or serve as litmus tests for politicians. The DLC limited its
stand on these issues to saying, "We believe government should
respect individual liberty and stay out of our private lives and individual decisions." In the Progressive Policy Institute's most notable
publication, *The Politics of Evasion*, by William Galston and Elaine
Kamarck, which came out in 1989 after the Democrats' third
straight presidential defeat, the authors urged Democrats to convey "a clear understanding of, and identification with, the social
values and moral sentiments of average Americans."

The DLC's ultimate objective was to win back the White
House. From tried to get Nunn or Robb to run for president in
1988. When they did not, the group backed Tennessee senator
Al Gore, who had not yet become a climate activist and who
ran as a DLC and New South centrist, but who ran behind both
Dukakis and Jackson. Afterward, From set his sights on Bill
Clinton, whom he convinced to become the DLC's chairman
in 1990. That proved to be a better bet for winning the White
House, although not in the long run for regaining the Demo-
crats' working-class majority.

Bill Clinton's Campaign

Bill Clinton had exactly the right attributes the Democrats
needed in 1992 to attract its new voters while retaining enough

of its old New Deal base, including white southerners. He also managed to please the different components of the Democrats' governing coalition. By the fall, he was enthusiastically backed by the DLC, the New Politics groups, and the AFL-CIO.

Clinton grew up Hot Springs, Arkansas, and later, after law school, returned to run for attorney general and then governor. He had a feel for Arkansas's Southern Baptist culture and also for the nostalgia that many Arkansas Democrats felt for the New Deal, which had brought electricity and a thriving poultry industry to the countryside. He had an instinctive blend of economic populism and social conservatism that he could invoke with spectacular success during elections. But he was also a product of the new left. Clinton went to high school when Arkansas was in the throes of the civil rights revolution. He went to college at Georgetown and studied at Oxford on a Rhodes scholarship, where he met liberal intellectuals Robert Reich, Strobe Talbott, and Derek Shearer. He got a law degree from Yale where he met Hillary Rodham. In 1972, he worked on the McGovern campaign.

In his first term as governor from 1978 to 1980, he ran afoul of the state's timber, poultry, and tobacco industries, and in 1980, he was defeated for reelection by a Republican they supported. When he ran again and won in 1982, Clinton was careful to cultivate the Tyson and Stephens families—doyens of Arkansas business—and he would retain their support. Don Tyson of Tyson Foods would lend Clinton his corporate jet for his campaigns. As he prepared to run for president, Clinton had touched all the right bases. He had the right political instincts and the right contacts. As Derek Shearer later recounted to us, the only group conspicuously missing from Clinton's collection of admirers and associates were labor activists and leaders, but that, too, reflected what had happened to the Democrats' electoral and governing coalitions.

In the fall of 1991, as Clinton's campaign was beginning, the country was in the grips of a recession, to which the Bush administration appeared oblivious. The recession itself was not deep or prolonged, but it revealed the growing inequality and the loss of industry created by footloose corporations and Reagan's and Volcker's overvalued dollar. With the Cold War over, Clinton didn't have to address defense and foreign policy. Clinton, echoing Roosevelt during the Depression, focused his campaign around winning the "forgotten middle class," to which he promised a tax cut.

Clinton's campaign manifesto, *Putting People First*, was drafted by Reich, business consultant Ira Magaziner, and Shearer, the coauthor of a provocative new left book entitled *Economic Democracy*. The manifesto was redolent with populist appeals. "America is the greatest nation on earth," the manifesto wrote. "But for more than a decade our government has been rigged in favor of the rich and special interests. While the very wealthiest Americans get richer, middle-class American pay more taxes to their government and get less in return."

The manifesto promised a raft of proposals that targeted the "rich and special interests." It would "eliminate deductions for outrageous executive pay" and end "tax breaks for companies that shut down their plants here and ship American jobs overseas." At the same time, it promised a national health-care program that would provide "universal access to basic medical coverage" and it promised "cracking down on drug manufacturers and insurance companies." George Bush, Clinton said in accepting the nomination, "won't take on the big insurance companies and bureaucracies to control health costs and give us affordable health care for all Americans. But I will."

Clinton also appealed to the New Politics social constituencies. Clinton backed abortion rights in the wake of the Supreme Court's restrictive *Webster v. Reproductive Health Services* decision. At the Democratic Convention, the campaign heralded "the year of the woman." Clinton declared his support for civil rights and ending racial discrimination. But at the same time, he carefully followed the DLC's strategy of "inoculating" himself from the white working-class backlash and from the penumbra of issues about welfare and crime that surrounded it and from the skepticism about "big government" that dated from Carter's presidency.

Clinton defined his constituency as Americans who "do the work, pay the taxes, raise the kids, and play by the rules." He promised to be tough on crime: he refused during the primaries to stop the execution in Arkansas of a mentally retarded black man convicted of killing a policeman and he denounced an African American rap singer, Sister Souljah, who had lauded black rioters for violence against white people. And he ran on a promise to "end welfare as we know it." Anyone who watched the convention, or who got one of the thousands of copies of *Putting People First*, saw Clinton the economic populist in action. But the first ads that began airing in the Midwest after the convention promised to "end welfare as we know it."

Clinton the candidate also charmed Wall Street and Hollywood. He wooed Wall Street with his support for NAFTA and free trade and for curbing the deficit. A *Los Angeles Times* study in July 1992 on the eve of the convention found that Clinton's single greatest source of money had come from corporate lobbyists and lawyers. The next in line were big securities firms, and leading these was Goldman Sachs, whose chairman was Robert Rubin. Rubin, who had already become one of the DNC's biggest donors and a key member of the Democratic governing coalition, would become the most influential person in guiding the Clinton administration's economic policy.

Clinton's First Missteps

In Clinton's first two years, he abandoned the carefully nuanced strategy of his campaign—with disastrous results for the Democrats' links to the "forgotten middle class." At Clinton's very first event after winning the election in November, a Veterans Day celebration in Little Rock, he put aside the DLC's strategy of soft-pedaling controversial social stands. He announced his support for lifting the ban on gays in the military. That provoked a furious rebuttal not just from Republicans but from Nunn and other Democrats and from the popular Colin Powell, the chairman of the Joint Chiefs. "Because it was the first controversial issue facing the administration," From later wrote, "it took on more of a definitional character than it might have if Clinton had raised it a year or two later, after he had cemented his reputation as a different kind of Democrat."

Over the next twenty months, Clinton punctuated his presidency with appointments and initiatives that provoked the kind of backlash he had avoided during the campaign. In April 1993, he nominated a former Yale Law classmate, Lani Guinier, to be in charge of the Justice Department's civil rights division. Guinier's stands on racial justice ran counter to Clinton's and the DLC's on equal opportunity over equal outcomes. She advocated subjecting judicial appointments to racial quotas and requiring supermajorities for bills that affected minorities. In 1994, Clinton and the Democrats attached a ban on assault rifles to a tough anti-crime bill, provoking a Second Amendment clash that carried into the 1994 campaign and doomed several Democratic candidates. Except in the case of Guinier's appointment, where he admitted her stands ran counter to his own, Clinton was expressing his moral convictions, and two decades later, Clinton's stand on gays in the military looks far less controversial. But at the time Clinton ended up miring the Democrats in the bog of post-sixties cultural controversy.

Clinton also abandoned his economic populism. His two top economic appointments were business-oriented Democrats: Goldman Sachs chair Rubin as head of the newly established National Economic Council and Texas senator and Finance

Committee chair Lloyd Bentsen, a favorite of Wall Street and Texas oil, as secretary of the Treasury. Rubin was a typical Wall Street Democrat, concerned about the poor and supportive of social issues, but convinced that what was good for Wall Street and America's multinationals was good for the country. Like Clinton, Bentsen and Rubin had taken little interest in labor unions.

In a March meeting, Rubin and Bentsen successfully opposed Clinton's proposal to remove the tax deduction of executive salaries over a million dollars. They convinced Clinton that companies should be allowed to deduct performance bonuses—often in the form of stock options—that companies could bestow upon their executives. Their intercession actually led to ballooning wealth for Wall Street and Silicon Valley executives, facilitating the rise of the superrich.

With their backing, and at the urging of Federal Reserve head Alan Greenspan, Clinton also focused on cutting the budget deficit, even at the expense of public investments, and reneged on his promise of a middle-class tax cut. The budget cuts probably prolonged the downturn that had begun in 1991 and particularly affected what had been the Democrats' working-class base. From 1992 to 1994, wages for workers without college degrees declined by 2 percent, while those for workers with degrees increased by a percent. And Clinton steamed ahead with the NAFTA agreement that would widen the class and regional divide. That showed again the supremacy of the business elite within the party and the growing irrelevance of labor.

Clinton came under intense pressure from business lobbies led by the Business Roundtable, which spent $5 million in September 1993 on ads, and a newly formed lobby of businesses and business lobbyists, USA*NAFTA, which had twenty-three hundred corporate members and forty-six trade associations, to get the agreement signed and ratified by Congress. The agreement lowered tariffs among the three countries, but it was primarily devoted to easing Mexican regulations on foreign investment and eliminating the threat of expropriation. The labor-backed think tank the Economic Policy Institute (EPI) warned that NAFTA would widen the existing small trade deficit with Mexico and result in a net loss of jobs, particularly in manufacturing. EPI's estimates were countered by those from the Institute for International Economics, which Peter Peterson, a former Nixon commerce secretary turned billionaire investment banker, had founded, and which enjoyed lavish support from both American and foreign corporations and from the Ford Foundation.

The institute's first director and cofounder was a former Democratic official, C. Fred Bergsten, who remained at the helm for twenty-one years. With Bergsten, the institute functioned as part of the Democrats' governing coalition. Its economists predicted that NAFTA would lead to a $9 billion trade *surplus* over the decade and a net increase of 171,000 jobs. The AFL-CIO didn't buy the argument, and the general public remained skeptical about the agreement's benefits. A poll taken on the eve of the vote showed that voters thought NAFTA would encourage U.S. companies to move to Mexico (60 percent to 33 percent), hold down wages in the United States (58 percent to 32 percent), and eliminate jobs (48 percent to 32 percent). Working-class voters were particularly opposed to the agreement.

Consistent with these sentiments, most Democrats in the House opposed the bill. But Clinton, with the help of USA*NAFTA, recruited enough Republicans to get the bill through. He signed it on December 8, promising that it would provide "200,000 jobs by 1995 alone." EPI's and the AFL-CIO's predictions turned out to be far more accurate. Over the next twenty-eight years, the United States ran a trade deficit with Mexico every year except for two. In 2006, EPI toted up the job gains and losses under NAFTA from 1994 to 2004. It estimated that the United States had lost a net 1,015,241 jobs, of which 660,000 were in manufacturing. Its trade deficit with Mexico in that period totaled $107.3 billion.

NAFTA had also widened the Great Divide. The job losses were concentrated in states like Michigan, Wisconsin, Ohio, and North Carolina, which would go Republican in 2016. Clinton won his agreement but further alienated working-class voters and undermined whatever support he and Democrats had gained during the election from his espousal of economic populism. The AFL-CIO felt betrayed. In response to Clinton signing the agreement, the federation declared that it would suspend any contributions to the Democratic National Committee for six months. That came just at the time when the administration was trying to mobilize support for an initiative that it hoped would unify the party and the country behind it.

ClintonCare

In the early 1990s, there was widespread support for some kind of a national health insurance plan, as the number of uninsured in the country spiked from twenty-five million to forty million. In the 1992 campaign, voters ranked health care among the top three issues of concern. Two-thirds of voters said they favored tax-financed national health insurance.

In response to these sentiments and reflecting a long-standing party priority, Clinton and the Democrats had promised a plan during the campaign. Once in office, Clinton set up a task force, headed by Hillary Clinton and Ira Magaziner, to devise a plan. In September 1993, Clinton announced that the plan was done. Evoking the highly popular Social Security and Medicare programs, Clinton held up a model "health security card" before television cameras that would entitle every American to insurance coverage. Clinton's speech was greeted enthusiastically. "The Clinton plan is alive on arrival," the *New York Times* declared. But the plan was very different from Social Security or Medicare.

Social Security and Medicare had been based on the idea that government would collect premiums from individuals to fund health-care expenditures and pensions for senior citizens. The programs were based on a one-to-one relationship between citizens and their government. But the Clinton plan, described in a 1,342-page bill, set up "regional healthcare alliances" in each state that would purchase insurance from competing private companies. Citizens and companies would then be offered a choice of plans. The price and scope of the coverage would be set by the alliances. Big companies would be required to offer coverage to their employees; individuals who didn't receive coverage through their employer would be required to purchase insurance from one of the alliance offerings. The plan was devilishly complex. A poll taken in February 1994 found that only one in four Americans knew what a "health alliance" was.

The plan's structure, which retained private insurance companies and employer-based insurance, was constructed in order to retain business support. Big companies including Ford and Bethlehem Steel had intimated that they might support a plan as a way of lowering their costs. But on the Business Roundtable, they were outvoted by the big insurance companies, which didn't want their coverage regulated by the alliances, and by companies like General Mills and Woolworth, which didn't provide insurance to many of their employees, and didn't want to have to do so. The plan was killed by the united opposition of Republicans and business lobbies, led by the Chamber of Commerce and Business Roundtable. Michigan Democratic congressman John Dingell, the head of the key health-care committee in the House, said Clinton's failure to win over the Business Roundtable was the "defining event" in the bill's defeat.

But the bill also fell prey to the public's fear of "big government," which dated back to the American Revolution, but which had been aroused by the failures of the Carter administration to contain inflation. Clinton's complex mix of the private and public in the alliances sowed doubts among the public about whether the plan would actually benefit them. In fact, it probably would have—more than the later Affordable Care Act that the Obama administration passed. It included controls on prescription drug prices and widened Medicare to include drug prices. And it might have done better about holding down health-care costs, but few people understood that. The plan itself was a product of health-care professionals and business consultants who lacked—absent strong input from below—any sense of what kind of program would prove comprehensible and acceptable to the public and who were unable to explain and justify it afterward. The plan's formulation and politics reflected the triumph of the metro center professionals in the Democratic Party.

The 1994 Elections

As the 1994 election approached, the carefully calibrated approach with which Clinton had conducted his successful 1992 campaign was in tatters. The populist strategy of Putting People First had been transmuted into a very conventional strategy of promoting business confidence and hoping the continuing economic expansion would eventually lift all the boats; the promise to protect American jobs and the "forgotten middle class" had been transformed into the free-trade-at-all-costs commitment to NAFTA; and the culturally moderate New Democrat profile Clinton had so strenuously sought to cultivate had been compromised by perceived social liberalism and a seemingly bureaucratic approach to solving social problems.

Plagued by declining wages and stagnating incomes in the midst of economic growth, the Democrats were extraordinarily vulnerable to a Republican counterattack based on populist anti-government themes—the very themes likely to resonate with the working-class voters Reagan had won over. The Republicans argued, in essence, that the Democrats were more interested in promoting big government and social liberalism than in solving the public's problems, and they made the case that very little good had come from the first years of Clinton's term. Working-class voters were highly receptive to this argument.

Voting patterns from the 1994 election confirm how successfully these Republican attacks landed with elements of the Reagan coalition. They were able to mobilize this coalition on the congressional level, something they had hitherto not been able to do. Working-class voters deserted the Democrats in droves. From 1992 to 1994 Democratic congressional support declined 10 percentage points among high school dropouts, 11 points among high school graduates, and 12 points among those with some college. In contrast, Democratic support among the college-educated held steady at 1992 levels.

Almost all this 1992–94 decline in Democratic support occurred among the white working class. The drop was particularly sharp among men. Democratic support among white men with only a high school education declined a whopping 20 points (to 37 percent); among white men with some college it dropped 15 points (to 31 percent).

The cratering of Democratic congressional support was spectacularly evident among voters who had supported H. Ross Perot's populist campaign for president in 1992. These voters were predominantly white working class and populist in orientation. White working-class Perot voters in particular moved massively against the Democrats: down from 52 percent in the 1992 congressional elections to just 25 percent support in 1994. Moreover, Perot voters who voted Republican in 1994 were from groups under the most economic stress, with estimated post-

Declining Democratic Support, 1992–1994

Democratic congressional support among key subgroups.

	1992 (%)	1994 (%)	Shift
Not a high school graduate	67	58	-10
High school graduates	58	47	-11
Some college	53	41	-12
College graduates	46	46	0
White men, only high school	57	37	-20
White men, some college	46	31	-15
White working class, supported Perot in 1992	52	25	-27

Data rounded to nearest whole number.
Source: 1992 and 1994 exit polls.

1979 wage losses more than double those of the Perot voters who voted Democratic. In other words, just those voters one might have most expected in the past to vote for a Democrat voted for a Republican.

The desertion of the white working class was the real story behind the Democratic congressional debacle in 1994—a pattern of desertion that parallels the decay of the Democratic presidential coalition in the 1970s and 1980s. In this sense, the 1994 election merely played out on a different stage the political sentiments these voters had expressed at the presidential level for decades. No more special dispensation for congressional Democrats anymore, these voters seemed to be saying. As a result, a GOP wave, powered by a 7-point advantage in the nationwide popular vote, swept over the country. Republicans gained control of both the House (for the first time since the 1952 election) and the Senate, picking up 8 seats in the Senate and 54 in the House. They also took 10 governorships from the Democrats.

The Senate seats Republicans picked up included both Tennessee seats, plus open seats in Arizona, Maine, Michigan, Ohio, and Oklahoma and incumbent Harris Wofford's seat in Pennsylvania. Republicans gained 19 House seats in the South, giving them a majority of the seats in that region for the first time since Reconstruction. Republicans were aided by an alliance with the Congressional Black Caucus and black state organizations to guarantee black congressional representation by concentrating African American votes. The effect of this was to sacrifice other districts where moderate Democrats had had an edge. Nonetheless, the results ratified on the congressional level what had already happened to the region on the presidential level.

The losses were, however, truly all over the country, reflecting the nationalized nature of the election. Democrats lost 15 seats in the West and 12 seats in the Midwest. The midwestern losses were a harbinger of the Democrats' future problems in Trump country, as Republicans successfully ran their anti-government populist playbook throughout the region. Ohio was a particular locus of this upsurge; Republicans picked up 4 House seats in the state. Mike DeWine easily won the Senate seat vacated by Democrat Howard Metzenbaum. And Ohio voters reelected Republican governor George V. Voinovich with 72 percent of the vote, the highest share for any Ohio gubernatorial candidate since 1826. Clinton and Obama would go on to win Ohio in the presidential elections, but the 1994 results foreshadowed the state's turn toward the Republicans.

The Political Rebound

Republican conservatives deemed the results of the 1994 election "revolutionary," and even sober pundits talked of a Republican realignment. But what the election really established was an unstable equilibrium between the parties. Once in power, the Republicans gave vent to policies that had been nourished in talk radio and in conferences at the Heritage Foundation. These included closing down the Departments of Education and Commerce, defunding the EPA, and cutting social programs, including Medicare and Medicaid, while using the cuts to fund new tax cuts for businesses and investors. Bill Clinton, chastened by the Democrats' defeat in November, knew how to take advantage of these vulnerabilities while attempting to minimize his own.

Clinton reaffirmed the social conservatism of the 1992 campaign. In 1996, he signed a Republican-drafted welfare reform bill that limited the time and size of benefits. (Even the DLC was critical of some of its provisions.) The Republican bill was based on the assumption, popularized by Charles Murray's *Losing Ground*, that the growth of welfare payments was due to the unwillingness of many recipients to find work. In September 1996, Clinton also signed a Defense of Marriage Act that gave states the right to refuse to recognize gay marriages. Clinton signaled that he had abandoned any effort, epitomized by his health-care plan, to expand the scope of the New Deal's social programs. "The era of big government is over," he announced in his January 1996 State of the Union. He focused instead on smaller bite-size executive actions on student loans and home buying.

In the 1996 election, Clinton successfully targeted the Republicans for their radical assault against what became referred to as "M2E2"—Medicare, Medicaid, education, and the environment. Buoyed by the belated recovery from the 1991 recession, and enjoying the widespread support of business from his stands on trade and deficits and his 1996 bill deregulating the telecommunications industry, Clinton easily won reelection. Clinton's rebound was testament to his political skill. But his reelection, coming on the heels of the 1994 Republican triumph and continued Republican majorities in Congress, was also a clear sign that American politics was suffering from an unstable equilibrium between the parties that would lead over the next decades to an alternation in power and repeated gridlock between Congress and the White House.

China and the WTO

Clinton governed during his second term as a business Democrat. He did get Congress to pass in 1997 an act extending Medicaid coverage to children, but his principal concern was in promoting the "new economy" at home and globalization around the world. The new economy was to be powered by semiconductors (dubbed the "new oil") and the internet, and globalization would allow goods, services, capital (including factories!), and even labor to move freely across what were seen as artificial national boundaries. Clinton described globalization as "the economic equivalent of a force of nature, like wind or water." Rubin and his successor in 1999, Larry Summers, enchanted by the work of a young Federal Reserve economist, Daniel Sichel, even became convinced, as stock prices soared and unemployment fell, that the new economy had tamed the business cycle.

Clinton's main accomplishments during his second term were laying the groundwork for China's accession to the World Trade Organization in 2001 and, under Rubin's and then Summers's leadership, furthering the deregulation of finance that had begun under Carter and Reagan. Both efforts were lauded at the time by Democrats and Republicans. The only dissenters were consumer groups, the left-leaning unions like the United Auto Workers, and a few labor and left-wing Democrats like Congressmen Dick Gephardt and Senator Paul Wellstone, along with independent Bernie Sanders. These initiatives signified the Democrats' growing subordination to Silicon Valley and Wall Street and to the mores and sentiments of upscale professionals who lived in the big metro centers. These initiatives would, in the end, put the economy at risk and accelerate the flight of the working class from the

Democratic Party, but Clinton, unlike Carter, didn't have to suffer the electoral consequences of his actions.

In his 1992 campaign, Clinton had denounced Chinese leaders as "tyrants" for the massacre of protesters at Tiananmen Square in 1989 and promised not to renew annually "most favored nation" (MFN) trading status—extending to China the same favorable terms of trade it extended to other countries—unless it turned a corner on human rights. But after the November election, Clinton was besieged by business lobbies and prominent former officials calling on him to grant MFN to China and not to link it to China's human rights record. The National Association of Manufacturers and the Business Coalition for U.S.-China Trade, a group of 334 companies, lobbied him to take advantage of China's "booming market." By 1994, the coalition had over eight hundred companies. Clinton, whose reproaches to China over human rights had been rebuffed by its leadership, gave in and approved MFN for China. But the biggest battle was to come.

In January 1995, the World Trade Organization (WTO) was formed. It established global rules for the world's nations and businesses, lowering tariffs and removing barriers that barred entry by certain foreign businesses. In effect, each nation would enjoy MFN with each other as long as each adhered to the WTO's rules against government subsidies and nontariff barriers. China sought membership, but to gain it, it would have to obtain support from the United States on the terms of accession. For the United States to agree, it would have to grant China "permanent normal trading relations" (PNTR) to avoid the annual vote on MFN. Business Roundtable members donated $68 million to members of Congress and the Democratic and Republican parties in the months before the vote on PNTR and the WTO. Boeing and Motorola and other top companies pressured legislators in each congressional district.

Robert Kapp, the president of the U.S.–China Business Council, argued for passing PNTR and welcoming China into the WTO. "Opening China's markets to U.S. products and services under this agreement is the biggest single step we can take to reduce America's growing trade deficit with China, a problem we have faced for a decade." The lobbies' arguments were reinforced by those from corporate-funded think tanks, including Brookings and the Institute for International Economics (now renamed after its billionaire funder and founder, Pete Peterson, to the Peterson Institute for International Economics [PIEE]). PIEE's experts argued that China's imports would merely displace those from South Korea and other Asian countries and not threaten American firms. They predicted an immediate $5.4 billion jump in exports from China joining the WTO.

Clinton, who had been the recipient in 1996 of over a million dollars in illegal donations from foreign businessmen allied to China, argued for the agreement to admit China on economic and geopolitical grounds. In a speech defending the agreement in March 2000, Clinton called it "the equivalent of a one-way street. It requires China to open its markets—with a fifth of the world's population, potentially the biggest markets in the world—to both our products and services in unprecedented new ways. All we do is to agree to maintain the present access which China enjoys. . . . We'll be able to export products without exporting jobs."

Clinton continued, "By joining the WTO, China is not simply agreeing to import more of our products; it is agreeing to import one of democracy's most cherished values: economic freedom. Now of course, bringing China into the W.T.O. doesn't guarantee that it will choose political reform. But accelerating the progress—the process of economic change will force China to confront that choice sooner, and it will make the imperative for the right choice stronger." Speaking at the Woodrow Wilson

School at Princeton that year, Clinton boasted that the agreement brings the world "closer than ever to redeeming the vision of Woodrow Wilson, of reaching his dream of a world full of free markets, free elections, and free peoples working together."

Many critics of the agreement focused on China's human rights record, but some pointed out that the agreement might actually cost American jobs. One of the first critics was Robert Lighthizer, who had served as deputy trade representative in the Reagan administration and would later head USTR under Trump. Writing in the *New York Times* in 1997, he warned that "it is not an exaggeration to say that if China is allowed to join the W.T.O. on the lenient terms that it has long been demanding, virtually no manufacturing job in this country will be safe." At EPI in 2000, Robert Scott warned that the agreement could cost the United States 872,000 jobs over the decade and cause the trade deficit with China to nearly double in ten years. (Two experts from the Peterson Institute termed Scott's prediction "an absurd extrapolation.") But outside of a few private sector unions like the United Auto Workers, the AFL-CIO was relatively silent about the trade agreement. In 1995, John Sweeney, who came out of the Service Employees International Union, had taken the helm of the federation. For Sweeney and his immediate circle, trade was not a big issue, and the federation was eager not to alienate Clinton and his vice president, Al Gore, who was running for president that year.

When the vote occurred in May, the Clinton administration, the business lobbyists, and the corporate think tanks prevailed. PNTR passed by 83 to 15 in the Senate. Only 7 Democrats opposed it. In the House it passed by 237 to 197 with 138 Democrats opposing it. The bill's passage showed the business lobby's power over the Clinton administration and Congress and over the Democratic Party. The bill's passage had no immediate effect on the country's politics—it was not an issue in the 2000 presidential election—but its longer-term economic and political effects were devastating to the Democratic Party and to the working-class voters it hoped to win over. It reinforced the trend toward seeing the Democrats as a party of coastal elites indifferent to what had been its working-class base.

Economically, Clinton and the corporate think tanks were proven to be completely wrong and the small, labor-backed EPI correct. Scott discovered that he had underestimated, if anything, the number of jobs lost. These totaled 2.7 million (2.1 million in manufacturing) between 2001 and 2011 from Chinese import competition (much of it initially from American firms that in the wake of China's accession and the absence of fear of tariffs transferred their production to China, where wages of manufacturing were approximately 5 percent of what American workers were being paid). Three economists, David Autor, David Dorn, and Gordon Hanson, writing in 2016, estimated that 2.4 million jobs were lost to Chinese competition from 1999 to 2011. The trade deficit with China, which the administration had promised would shrink, went from $28 billion in 2001 to $349 billion in 2008. The story is similar in geopolitics. Entry into the WTO failed to encourage economic freedom and a steady passage toward liberal democracy. Instead, under China's president Xi Jinping, political autocracy and control of enterprises by the Chinese Communist Party increased.

The political effects in the United States of China's WTO agreement played out over the next two decades. What Autor, Dorn, and Hanson called the "China shock" widened the Great Divide between the prosperous metro areas, which specialized in finance and high technology (most of the material products of which were produced abroad), and the small and midsize towns of industrial America. Many of the jobs lost were unionized jobs in manufacturing, whose workers still had ties through their unions to the Democratic Party. The first presidential candidate to recognize the

China shock and campaign against it was a Republican, Donald Trump, and he won many of the states and regions that had been most affected by Chinese export competition and by American factories leaving for China. Indeed, Autor, Dorn, Hanson, and Kaveh Majlesi calculated that if Chinese import penetration had been 50 percent less in Michigan, Wisconsin, Pennsylvania, and North Carolina, Hillary Clinton would have won those states.

But there was also a subtler effect of the China shock and of the jobs lost to Mexico under NAFTA. Republicans, of course, had played a prominent role in boosting both trade treaties, and the Great Divide had opened up under Reagan and Volcker, but the people who lived in middle America felt betrayed by the Democrats' role in championing these treaties. They saw the Democrats as a party of Hollywood, Wall Street, and Silicon Valley that no longer cared about the welfare of the "forgotten middle class." It was evident in part in the clash over family, nation, faith, and Democratic support for the minorities and immigrants who lived in the big metro centers, but it was also evident in the party's support for NAFTA and China and the WTO. Autor and his coauthors had looked not only at the 2016 election but at political trends from 2002, after China entered the WTO, to 2016, and they found that Republicans had gained over Democrats in those congressional districts that had suffered from Chinese import competition. In other words, the support for Republicans predated Trump's attacks against the Democrats' "bad trade deals" and expressed a deeper disenchantment with the Democratic Party and what, in the wake of NAFTA and the WTO, it was seen to stand for.

Financial Deregulation

Under Rubin and then Summers, the Clinton administration's Treasury Department also became a willing accomplice of Wall

Street. In 1998, Rubin, Summers, and Greenspan nixed a proposal from the Commodities Future Trading Commission to regulate financial derivatives. Having the CFTC oversee these unregulated over-the-counter transactions, Rubin wrote, would "create uncertainty over trillions of dollars of transactions." Sarah Rosen, White House senior adviser to the National Economic Council, cautioned, "Without better justification, it sounds like Treasury wants to protect the traders from regulation." A decade later, the failure of the Clinton administration to regulate derivatives would play a role in the financial crisis.

In 1999, with Rubin having left for the chairmanship of Citigroup, and Summers in charge of Treasury, the Clinton administration backed the Banking Act of 1999, which was sponsored by three Republicans. The act overturned the New Deal's Glass-Steagall Act, which walled off commercial banks, which collected people's savings and made loans, from investment banks, which bought and sold stocks, and might also sell insurance and other financial products. The corruption encouraged by the lack of separation had been blamed for the crash of 1929. But the banks and brokerage houses, including Rubin's Citigroup, which had started an insurance business, wanted to be able to branch out, and they lobbied energetically for the Banking Act.

Democrats joined Republicans in voting for the repeal. It passed the Senate by 90 to 8. Only seven Democrats voted against it. Senator Paul Wellstone, one of the seven, warned that Congress had "seemed determined to unlearn the lessons from our past mistakes." But Nebraska Democratic senator Robert Kerrey countered, "The concerns that we will have a meltdown like 1929 are vastly overblown." The House voted 362 to 57 in favor of the legislation. A total of 155 Democrats favored the bill, and only 51 plus independent Bernie Sanders opposed the legislation. Summers was exultant about the results. "Today Congress voted to update the rules that have governed financial services since the

Great Depression and replace them with a system for the 21st century. This historic legislation will better enable American companies to compete in the new economy." But, as Wellstone warned, the bill demonstrated the administration's and Congress's ignorance of history. It also demonstrated the hold that business had gained over the Democratic Party and the utter lack of influence of labor and of those New Politics groups that took an interest in the economy.

In sum, during the end of Clinton's first term and during his second term, the Clinton administration coupled the opening to China on trade with financial deregulation. This was combined with Rubin's and Summers's defense of a strong dollar, which penalized American exports. Rubin's support for a strong dollar did boost the American financial industry during Clinton's second term and George W. Bush's presidency. It accelerated what critics called the financialization of the American economy. From 1980 to 2000, the financial assets of American banks rose from 55 percent to 95 percent of GDP. In 1980, manufacturing had accounted for 21 percent of American GDP and finance for 14 percent. By 2002, 21 percent was devoted to finance and 14 percent to manufacturing. The numbers, as Michael Lind observed in *Land of Promise*, his economic history of the United States, had exactly reversed.

Manufacturing was, of course, based in the Midwest and South and finance in the big metro centers, so the trend toward financialization was mirrored in the widening of the Great Divide. And the reinforcing spiral of a strong dollar, rising trade deficits, and financialization, which began under Reagan and accelerated under Clinton, would continue into the twenty-first century. The resulting growth of this economic divide would be mirrored in the growing political divide between blue-collar workers and the Democrats.

Buoyed by the high-tech and internet boom, Clinton retained

his popularity through the end of his second term. He overcame a sex scandal and the Republican attempt to impeach him. In an odd way, his sexual transgressions may have actually helped him among working-class voters, as Trump's may have done in 2016. They proved he was a normal guy, not a sneering elite. In interviews we conducted in West Virginia in 2004, voters who planned to support George W. Bush and viewed Kerry as effete and upper class fondly recalled Clinton, who they had supported, as a "rascal." In that sense, the DLC strategy of avoiding the extremes of social liberalism had worked. But Clinton's neoliberal policies on trade and finance set a trap for the nation and the Democrats that Barack Obama would be unable to elude.

Chapter Four

Obama and the Lost Opportunity

The trends that we saw emerging in the 1990s—the turn to the Democrats among professionals and women, the growing numbers of minorities who were voting Democrats—contributed to 2000 Democratic presidential candidate Al Gore's numerical, but not Electoral College, majority over George W. Bush. In May, Vermont senator Jim Jeffords left the GOP, giving the Democrats a Senate majority. But Bush's initially strong response to the September 11 terrorist attack from al-Qaeda rallied the country around him and his party, and led to Republican victories in 2002 and 2004. Bush was able to rekindle the public's trust in the Republicans as the party of national security. But in 2006, in the wake of continued setbacks to Bush's ill-conceived invasion of Iraq, the president's bungling of the response to Hurricane Katrina, and a bevy of Republican scandals, the Democrats won back the House and Senate for the first time in twelve years.

The battle for the Democratic presidential nomination in 2008 came down to two candidates representing parts of the post–New Deal Democratic Party: Clinton—women, especially liberal professional women, and Hispanics; Obama—blacks, millennials, and college graduates. In the primaries, Obama had the advantage of appealing to both the working-class black vote that Jackson had carried in 1988 and, as the eloquent and inspiring University of Chicago law professor and Iraq War opponent, to the college and postgraduate vote, particularly among the young. Unlike Clinton, who was still identified with what journalist Sidney Blumenthal called the "Clinton wars," Obama could appeal to the growing number of Democrats, independents, and moderate Republicans who despaired of the partisan warfare and division in the country. He had voiced that appeal in his 2004 keynote address to the Democratic Convention.

> There is not a liberal America and a conservative America—there is the United States of America. There is not a black America and a white America and Latino America and Asian America— there's the United States of America. The pundits like to slice-and-dice our country into Red States and Blue States; Red States for Republicans, Blue States for Democrats. But I've got news for them, too: We worship an awesome God in the Blue States, and we don't like federal agents poking around in our libraries in the Red States.

He ran, following the example of Reagan in 1980 and Ross Perot in 1992, against Washington, and implicitly Clinton. He denounced the "dead zone that politics has become, in which narrow interests vie for advantage and ideological minorities seek to impose their own version of absolute truth." He promised to "overcome the power of lobbyists and special interests." He promised to bring "Democrats, Republicans, and independents together." Clinton regarded Obama's promise of political unity as hopelessly naive, and as a political strategy for governing, it proved to be so. But the promise of an America that was neither red nor blue resonated among a growing sector of the electorate and continues to do so.

The way that Obama, who was literally an African American, dealt with race was also essential to his appeal. Where Jackson had promised a "rainbow coalition," Obama promised a campaign and a presidency beyond race; he said he would leave that age-old conflict behind him and the country. There was no hint in Obama's campaign of Jackson's defiant words "It's our turn." Obama ran on "hope," his official slogan, rather than past grievance. To the extent that some white voters might have opposed him because he was black, others voted for him precisely for that reason. One Obama supporter told the *Washington Post* that he hoped "someday we'll erase all this nonsense about race." He described his own support for Obama as "reverse prejudice."

In the general election, Obama was by no means a sure bet to defeat Senator John McCain, a war hero and also someone who was perceived as being above the fray, as being able to unite rather than divide the country. From the Republican Convention in early September through September 17, McCain led Obama in most polls, but Obama took the lead in the next days and held it through the election. The turning point came on September 25, when Bush called Obama and McCain to Washington for a meeting with him and senior lawmakers about the financial crisis that the collapse of the investment bank Lehman Brothers had precipitated. In the meeting, Obama showed himself far superior to McCain in his grasp of the details and in his suggestions for what to do. There were other factors that also contributed to Obama's victory—including growing public doubts about the qualifications of McCain's running mate, Alaska governor Sarah Palin—but Obama's understanding of the crash and what it portended tilted the election in his favor. His professorial mien, his cool intelligence, which might have alienated voters in other circumstances, won them over.

The election was a decisive win for the Democrats. Obama won 53 percent of the vote—the first time since 1976 that Democrats had won a majority—and 365 electoral votes to McCain's 173. Democrats took the Senate by 59 to 41 (including two independents) and, when Arlen Specter switched parties in April 2009, enjoyed a cloture-proof majority. They controlled the House by an overwhelming 257 to 178. Obama's victory reaffirmed the post–New Deal trends among minorities, professionals, and women, to which he added younger voters, and he managed to win back many of the white working-class voters who had abandoned the party in 2000 and 2004.

Obama faced a daunting challenge as president. As he took office in January 2009, unemployment had risen from 5 percent in January 2008 to 7.8 percent. "This is unprecedented," Mark Zandi, chief economist of Moody's Economy.com, told the *New York Times*. "It's coast to coast. It's everywhere. There's really no refuge in this job market. There's no safe place." But the challenge of getting people back to work was an opportunity to restore the Democrats' reputation as stewards of the economy—which had been integral to the party's New Deal majority—and to restore the public's faith in the power of government.

There were, of course, significant differences between Obama's situation and that of Roosevelt in 1933. By March 1933, when Roosevelt took office, the Great Depression had been raging for four years, and unemployment was at 25 percent. Republicans and their business allies were thoroughly discredited. And a desperate public welcomed government intervention. But there were also similarities. Obama enjoyed high public approval. In the last week of January 2009, he enjoyed a 67 percent approval to 13 percent disapproval rating in the Gallup Poll. A total of 41 percent of Republicans approved of his presidency. (By contrast, Reagan enjoyed only 51 percent approval after taking the oath in January 1981.)

At the same time, the public was already blaming bankers for the crisis. According to the Gallup survey, the public's opinion of banks had plummeted from 2004, when 53 percent of Americans had a "great deal" or "quite a lot" of confidence in the nation's banks, to 22 percent. Republicans' reputation had also suffered. According to Pew polls, Republican Party identification had sunk to 23 percent by spring of 2009 and was just 16 percent among moderates.

There was, it seemed to us at the time, an opportunity for Obama to reforge the Democratic majority around its greatest strength by pursuing a politics and policy that would bring working-class voters back into the Democratic Party. But it would take an approach that was at once populist—uniting "the people" against the "malefactors of great wealth"—and that was effective in fostering investment and stemming the rise of unemployment. Obama had to show he was on the side of the average citizen and not the bankers; and he had to stop the economy from hemorrhaging jobs. He didn't succeed during his first climactic years at either. Except when he was running for reelection, Obama balked at populist appeals. Instead, he cautiously settled for half-measures and continued the Democrats' devolution into a party with only a tenuous hold on the working-class voters who had once sustained it.

The Post-New Deal Democrat

Obama, who was born in Hawaii in 1961, was raised by his mother and her parents. He went to a private college preparatory school in Honolulu and to college at Occidental and Columbia. Afterward, he signed on as a community organizer for a Chicago group that had been influenced by Saul Alinsky's populist methods of organizing the "have-nots" to "fight privilege and power." Alinsky saw politicians as the enemy, and the job of organizers as not leading but as getting the organized to fight for themselves.

Obama was assigned an area in Chicago's dirt poor, primarily

black southeast side that had been decimated in the early 1980s
by the closing of the huge Wisconsin Steel plant. In his presidential campaign, Obama would tout his experience as a community
organizer "on the streets of Chicago," but he was a bust at organizing. He got very little accomplished and, disillusioned, quit
after three years to go to Harvard Law School, where he planned
to lay the groundwork for a political career. Obama didn't simply
give up on organizing; he also abandoned the populist framework of Alinsky's methods. Instead of pressuring politicians on
behalf of the people, he decided to become a politician himself.

After getting his law degree in 1991, Obama returned to Chicago, where he worked for a boutique law firm, taught at the
University of Chicago Law School, and lived in Hyde Park, a
tony enclave on the primarily black south side where the university sat. At his first chance in 1997, he ran for the state senate
and won. Obama's approach to politics was that of a liberal and
a pluralist rather than a populist. He was a standard-issue liberal
on civil rights, human rights, the minimum wage, and campaign
finance reform and taxes, but he didn't divide American politics
into the haves and have-nots. He wanted to reconcile rather than
divide.

In 2000, eager to move up, he challenged southside congressman Bobby Rush in the primary, and he got routed. Obama's
appeal was too abstract for Rush's constituents, many of whom
were the same people that as a Black Panther he had once
tried to organize. Afterward, in the 2000 redistricting, Obama
worked with an expert to alter his Hyde Park–based state senate district so that some poor blacks were excluded and some
wealthy whites along Chicago's gold coast, whom he had gotten
to know through his law practice and his service on foundation
boards, were included. A Chicago consultant who had worked
for Obama told the *New Yorker*'s Ryan Lizza that Obama realized "his appeal to, quite frankly, young white professionals was

dramatic." Obama was a post–New Deal Democrat very much attuned to the new constituencies that were shaping the party. He was at home with the Pritzkers of Hyatt Hotels and other members of Chicago's liberal elite.

During his presidential campaign, Obama had displayed at times a combative stance toward the bankers and the financial industry and toward the financial deregulation that had taken place during the Clinton and Bush administrations. Both administrations had created a "market that favors Wall Street over Main Street," Obama said in March 2008. "We let the special interests put their thumbs on the economic scales," Obama declared in September after Lehman Brothers went under. But when he took office, he largely eschewed attacking Wall Street, and he assembled a team of economic advisers drawn from the same governing coalition that had staffed the Clinton administration.

The top appointments went to protégés of former Treasury secretary Rubin, who, after leaving office, had become the chairman of the board of Citigroup, which government had had to bail out in November 2008 because of the high-risk investments it had undertaken. Timothy Geithner, Obama's Treasury secretary, had worked with Rubin and Summers in the Clinton administration. Summers, whom Obama appointed the head of the National Economic Council, had been Rubin's deputy; and Gene Sperling, the deputy head of the NEC, and later its head, had also worked under Rubin and Summers and had worked at Goldman Sachs. Peter Orszag, the director of the Office of Management and Budget, and Jason Furman, Summers's deputy at the NEC, had worked at the Brookings Institution's Hamilton Project, which Rubin had founded.

These appointees shared Rubin's concern with restoring "business confidence" by not rattling Wall Street with aggressive investigations, criminal indictments, and new regulations, which they believed could cause another panic. The Rubin protégés also shared his determination to curb budget deficits, which they advocated even during a recession. (In Obama's closing off-the-record interview with "progressive" members of the press, which was made public through an FOIA suit, he complained of Rubin's calls to Democrats urging them to cut the deficit.) Rubin's protégés were not corrupt; they were not the lobbyists Obama had promised to exclude; but in their outlook, they were oriented toward Wall Street rather than Main Street. Their appointment confirmed the iron grip the country's financial elite had secured over the Democrats' governing coalition.

In Obama's inaugural address that January, he cast blame equally on Main Street and Wall Street for the crash and recession. "Our economy is badly weakened, a consequence of greed and irresponsibility on the part of some, but also our collective failure to make hard choices and to prepare the nation for a new age," he said. During the administration's first year, Obama said he was "outraged" when newspapers revealed that executives at the American International Group (AIG), which the government had given a $173 billion bailout, had received $165 million in bonuses, but the government did nothing about it. While the administration demanded, and got, the chief executive of General Motors to resign as a condition of government aid, they didn't demand the resignation of any banking executives, including those from Citigroup and Bank of America, as a condition of receiving aid.

Even though it appeared that the banks and mortgage giants had been guilty of defrauding their customers—Bank of America and JPMorgan Chase would later settle civil suits against them—the Justice Department failed to prosecute a single one of the bankers who had been at the helm. Geithner also opposed imposing "haircuts"—which were reductions in the amount bank shareholders could get back from Citigroup and AIG. Collectively, the benefits bestowed upon the banks without significant penalty, or even official condemnation, gave the appearance that the administration was firmly on the side of the banks. In his authoritative study of the administration's bailout efforts, *The Escape Artists*, Noam Scheiber wrote that even though the average American only "dimly understood" many of the favors and subsidies to the banks and insurance companies, their "cumulative effect was to trigger a gag reflex." Obama's inaction created the impression, whether warranted or not, that he was really on the side of Wall Street rather than Main Street. It created a political opening on the right for free-floating indignation that the nascent Tea Party movement filled.

Obama did attempt to stem the recession by getting Congress to pass a stimulus bill, but his efforts to do so fell short. Obama and his top economic advisers began discussing what to do soon after the election. The person in charge of estimating how large a stimulus would be needed was Christina Romer, a Berkeley economist whom Obama appointed to head the Council of Economic Advisers. Romer was the one top official who had no connection to Rubin or Wall Street. In December, Romer calculated that it would take a $1.8 trillion stimulus to halt the recession and start unemployment coming down. But Summers, who as head of the National Economic Council was responsible for presenting Obama with options, rebuffed her. At Summers's insistence, she lowered her estimate to $1.2 trillion, but when Summers submitted his recommendations to Obama, it was for a stimulus of between $600 billion and $800 billion. Summers's proposal warned that too large a deficit could upset investors and the financial markets. Obama was also worried about deficits. The administration got Congress to pass a $787 billion stimulus bill, only part of which raised consumer demand. The stimulus failed to halt job loss. From January to October that year, unemployment climbed from 7.8 percent to 10 percent.

As it became obvious in the summer that the economy was worsening, Romer pressed for another stimulus but was rebuffed by Geithner, who had become worried about the deficit, and by Orszag, who, after leaving the administration in 2011, would head to Wall Street for a job at Citigroup. Romer warned that the administration was repeating the error that Roosevelt had made in 1937 when, frightened by his advisers about the deficit, he had imposed budget cuts that halted the recovery, but Orszag countered that growing deficits would harm business confidence. The administration boasted about its plans to reduce the deficit in the budget it submitted the next winter. The president, the budget stated, planned to "cut in half the deficit."

Foreclosures also continued apace in 2009—a record high 2,824,674, up 21 percent from 2008. In addition, a total of 10.7 million homes, or 23 percent of all residences, were "underwater"— meaning that the homeowners were paying out more in mortgages than the houses were worth. The administration decided against helping the homeowners who were underwater—it was deemed too expensive—and settled for a complex program to help people who faced foreclosure. It involved banks splitting the cost with the government, but the banks balked at processing the applicants. During the program's first year, less than 10 percent of those facing foreclosure benefited. All in all, the administration's program to speed the economy into recovery looked like an abject failure.

Some liberals criticized the administration for not spending enough, but many voters had exactly the opposite reaction. Imbued with traditional American anti-statism, they saw rising unemployment and foreclosures as proof that the stimulus money had been wasted, or had even cost jobs by crowding out private investment, and they called for the administration to cut its expenditures. That became one of the rallying cries of the Tea Party, a national collection of right-wing populist groups that sprung up in 2009 in protest of the administration's stimulus.

Administration defenders later argued that Obama could not have possibly gotten a larger stimulus programs or a housing program through Congress. That might have been the case, but after Republican Arlen Specter switched parties in April 2009, the Democrats enjoyed a cloture-proof 60–40 majority in the Senate and a huge margin in the House. The Obama administration was not prepared to try. They were leery of any larger stimulus program because of fears about the deficit. Obama and his political advisers were also averse to waging political struggles outside of Capitol Hill and the White House. Obama was determined to create bipartisan support for his programs, and when that failed, he backed off.

During the campaign, Obama had created a huge grassroots army, Obama for America. After the campaign, ten thousand organizers volunteered to become Organizing for America. But Obama and his campaign aides decided to fold OFA into the Democratic National Committee where it eventually expired. Obama's approach bore out his rejection of Alinsky-style populism as an approach to building support. Marshall Ganz, a former aide of Cesar Chavez, who had helped the Obama campaign create a grassroots organization, lamented in an interview with us Obama's failure as president to build upon what he had created.

Alinsky said you have to polarize to mobilize and depolarize to settle. Obama was depolarizing when he needed to be mobilizing. It's galling to remember how Republicans have come in with a one-vote majority or no majority at all, and they have treated their election as a mandate, and Democrats have come in with a solid majority and they have treated it like something they have to prove they are entitled to. Obama's whole approach was to minimize opposition rather than to maximize support.

Obama had run against Washington, but as president, he had become captive to its inner circles. His "organizing" was confined to Pennsylvania Avenue. That included his contact with the labor movement. He would confer with Andrew Stern, the head of the Service Employees International Union, but he largely ignored labor as a political force that could help his legislation on the ground and as a potential bulwark for the Democratic Party. As a senator he had voted for the Employee Free Choice Act. The act would have allowed unions to gain recognition by gathering a majority of signatures in cases where corporate management might try to undermine a union election. Obama had a cloture-proof majority and a Democratic House that might have passed it, but during the discussion of whether to urge Congress to pass it, Obama was warned against doing so by three Chicago billionaires to whom he had been close: Penny Pritzker, who had been the finance chair of his campaign and whom he would appoint secretary of commerce, Lester Crown, chairman of Henry Crown and Company, and Neil Bluhm, a partner in Walton Street Capital LLC. Obama dropped the bill as a priority and, by doing that, forfeited any chance to alter the Democrats' increasingly narrow governing coalition and to create a genuine counterweight to the influence of business and Wall Street.

Obamacare as Welfare

During the 2008 campaign, Obama had promised that if he were elected, he would promote a national health insurance program. The plan Obama outlined resembled the one that Massachusetts had adopted under Governor Mitt Romney. It was an approach also favored by the Business Roundtable. It rested on companies and individuals being required to purchase private insurance. As president, Obama asked the relevant Senate and House committees to come up with a detailed plan along those lines. He correctly assumed that with the proper incentives, he could get the drug companies, hospitals, and insurance firms that had opposed the Clinton administration plan to sign on.

The Senate committees had to come up with a plan that sixty senators would vote for. With the Republicans united against the plan, that meant getting support from everyone in the Democratic Caucus, including two independents, which forced the Democratic leadership to drop several aspects of the plan that might have won public support. These included a "public option"—a government plan that would compete with the private plans that were offered in each state's exchanges—and the right for people over fifty-five to buy into Medicare. The former approach was supported by two-thirds of the public and the latter by 80 percent. Independent senator Joe Lieberman of Connecticut, where Aetna and Cigna are headquartered, rejected these proposals that would have bypassed private insurance. Geithner and Orszag, backed up by the deficit hawks in the Senate and House, also insisted that the proposal be revenue neutral. That cut down drastically on the subsidies that the bill could offer people who might have difficulty buying insurance or would have to settle for a minimal plan.

Democrats rejoiced at the passage of the Affordable Care Act in March 2010. "This is what change looks like," an exultant Obama declared on television. But the bill proved to be very unpopular outside of the most liberal Democratic areas. In January 2011, three months after the Affordable Care Act was passed, the public was 50 percent unfavorable to 41 percent favorable to the bill. In October of that year, it was 51 percent unfavorable, just 34 percent favorable. Many Americans opposed a bill that required that they purchase insurance. The subsidies for purchasing insurance stopped at about $46,000 a year. Those who made more, and were not insured through their employer, would have to pay whatever the insurance companies were charging on the exchanges. That accounted for a lot of working-class Americans. And the bill included $716 billion in Medicare cuts over ten years. The bill's sponsors insisted these cuts would not affect coverage for seniors, but many older voters were not willing to take their word for it.

Taken together, these provisions were seen by many working-class voters and senior citizens as requiring them to pay for subsidies to people who made less than $46,000. These voters were therefore likely to view the Affordable Care Act as a welfare bill in disguise. In the summer of 2009, as Obama was still mired in an effort to win bipartisan support for his plan, the Tea Party groups, funded by Charles and David Koch's Americans for Prosperity and by another Republican business group, FreedomWorks, mounted a national campaign against the bill that continued up to the 2010 midterm elections. The Tea Party won widespread support among Republicans and independents. In her survey of Tea Party supporters, Emily Ekins found that to them "the ACA seemed like another transfer program, giving people something they need at the expense of people who have earned." By passing the Affordable Care Act, Obama and the Democrats had inadvertently revived the working-class objection to welfare that the DLC and Clinton had attempted to address.

Eight years later, when Republicans sought to repeal the law without replacing it, many of the voters who opposed it in 2010 realized that it did have important benefits—such as the prohibition on denying coverage either outright or through exorbitant premiums to people with preexisting conditions—but over the next elections, these benefits would be ignored. In the 2010 midterm elections, Obama and the Democrats had to contend with opposition to the ACA as well as a huge public backlash from their failure to punish Wall Street and to stem the recession. The result was an electoral disaster that rivaled that of the 1994 election.

The 2010 Election Debacle

As early as April of that year analysts could see the Democratic debacle shaping up. Nate Silver of FiveThirtyEight predicted a 50+ seat loss for the Democrats in the House. It turned out that Silver's assessment, which many Democrats resisted, was actually too optimistic. In the election, they actually lost 63 seats in the House and, with that, control of the chamber. In doing so, Democrats lost the House popular vote by 7 points, inverting Obama's 7-point lead in the 2008 presidential election. They also lost 6 Senate seats, 6 governorships, and control of 25 state legislative bodies.

Democratic losses in the nationwide popular vote showed clear signs of the emerging Great Divide between the dynamic postindustrial metro areas of the country and the working-class areas in the small towns, rural communities, and midsize cities scattered across the Heartland that were still dependent on manufacturing, farming, and resource extraction. Democrats lost the white working class by a hefty 23 points, rural areas by 25 points, and white working-class men by 31 points. And their advantage in the overall working-class vote completely reversed, going from an 8-point lead in 2008 to a 7-point deficit.

2010 Democratic Margin

Working class	-7
White working class	-23
White working-class men	-31
Rural areas	-25

Source: Yair Ghitza, "Revisiting What Happened in the 2018 Election," Catalist, May 2019.

Democratic House losses were particularly brutal in the upper Midwest. Michigan's House delegation went from 8 to 7 Democratic to 9 to 6 Republican; Ohio's from 10 to 8 Democratic to 13 to 5 Republican; Pennsylvania's from 12 to 7 Democratic to 12 to 7 Republican; and Wisconsin's from 5 to 3 Democratic to 5 to 3 Republican. The political complexion of the Midwest literally changed overnight.

Reflecting these changes, the statewide House vote in Great Divide states saw massive shifts against the Democrats. The Democratic margin in Michigan swung 16 points toward the GOP; in Minnesota the shift toward Republicans was 18 points; in Ohio and Pennsylvania it was 16 points; and in Wisconsin there was a 15-point shift, driven by a brutal 26-point decline in Democrats' margin among white working-class voters. In West Virginia, Democrats had carried the statewide House vote by 34 points in 2008 but lost it by 11 points in 2010, an astonishing 45-point shift. Swept out in the wave was Democratic control of West Virginia's First District in the Rust Belt area of the state's northern panhan-

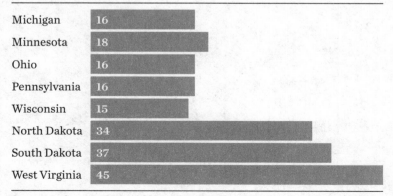

Republican Swing, 2008–2010
Statewide House vote shift

Michigan	16
Minnesota	18
Ohio	16
Pennsylvania	16
Wisconsin	15
North Dakota	34
South Dakota	37
West Virginia	45

Source: Authors' analysis of 2008 and 2010 Federal Election Commission data.

dle. That seat had been occupied for forty-two years by the father and son team of Bob and Alan Mollohan.

South Dakota's lone representative, Democrat Stephanie Herseth Sandlin, who easily carried the state by 35 points in 2008, saw the state swing 37 points Republican and lost to Republican Kristi Noem. And in North Dakota, Democrat and "prairie populist" Earl Pomeroy, incumbent since 1992, lost to Republican Rick Berg by 10 points after having carried the state easily by 24 points in 2008.

Falling Off the Fiscal Cliff

In the wake of the Democrats' rout, Obama and his top political adviser David Plouffe concluded that in order to win over independent voters, Obama would have to move to "the middle" by proposing sharp spending cuts that would lower the deficit and the national debt. That, as it turned out, was a misunderstanding of what concerned independents. A varied group, independents' most common complaint at the time was that government was controlled by "special interests." They also recoiled at the fractious party politics in Washington.

Obama's economic advisers also contended that deficit cuts would benefit the recovery and the economy's long-term prospects. Orszag had left but had been replaced at the Office of Management and Budget by Jacob Lew who had served under Rubin at Citigroup and was also active in the Hamilton Project. Chief of Staff Rahm Emanuel had also left and been replaced by another ex–Wall Streeter, William Daley, fresh from employment at JPMorgan Chase. Romer, who would have dissented, had left in September 2010. The result of these policies would be to prolong the downturn and make Obama and the Democrats even more unpopular.

During the winter, Obama and his economic staff began

negotiations with the new Republican Speaker of the House, John Boehner. Boehner demanded $60 billion in budget cuts to approve a resolution that would keep the government running after March 4. Obama agreed finally to $38 billion in cuts. Obama boasted of having negotiated "the largest annual spending cut in our history." Boehner and the Republicans upped the ante. They demanded that if the House were to vote to raise the debt ceiling by $2.4 trillion, upon which the government's payment of its debts depended, then the Obama administration must agree to budget cuts equivalent to the increase in ceiling.

Instead of calling the Republicans' bluff, Obama once again agreed to negotiate. Obama proposed a "grand bargain" of $4 trillion in cuts spread out over twelve years that would include major cuts in Medicare and Medicaid but would also include about $1 trillion in tax increases. Obama's willingness to cut these programs, as Geithner had strongly urged, signaled how far he and his administration had moved away from the promise of New Deal liberalism. These programs, passed in Johnson's administration, had been integral to the Democrats' appeal to the ordinary American and to senior citizens. But the House Republicans turned down Obama's offer. They balked at *any* tax increases.

Obama and the Republicans finally agreed on August 2 to $900 billion in cuts over a decade and to $1.5 trillion in additional cuts the specifics of which would be set by a new joint committee of three Republicans and three Democrats. If they couldn't agree, then cuts in defense and social spending would occur automatically. In a speech, Obama justified the deal by resorting to the kind of household metaphor popular among conservative economists. "Now every family knows that a little credit card debt is manageable, but if we stay on the current path, our growing debt could cost us jobs and do serious damage to the economy."

The budget deal did not restore Obama's hold over the electorate. In early August, Obama's approval rating, as measured by Gallup, plunged to a new low of 40 percent approval and 52 percent disapproval. In addition, Obama faced a revolt from the liberal intelligentsia. *New York Times* columnist Paul Krugman labeled Obama "President Pushover." In an article in the *New York Review of Books*, Elizabeth Drew wrote:

> Someday people will look back and wonder, *What were they thinking?* Why, in the midst of a stalled recovery, with the economy fragile and job creation slowing to a trickle, did the nation's leaders decide that the thing to do—in order to raise the debt limit, normally a routine matter—was to spend less money, making job creation all the more difficult?

Young activists took exception as well. Writing on Web pages, they charged that both the Democrats and the Republicans had been taken over by an "economic elite." Inspired by the occupation that year of Tahrir Square by Egyptian demonstrators, they called for a similar occupation—Occupy Wall Street—to be held in a park near the stock exchange. "We are the 99 percent that will no longer tolerate the greed and corruption of the one percent," the demonstrators declared in September. Over the next months, new occupy movements sprung up in scores of cities. The occupations eventually petered out, but they sent a message to Obama similar to the message that Huey Long's Share Our Wealth clubs had sent to Roosevelt seventy-five years before.

Obama's Populist Moment

Obama and his political advisers got the message. Facing reelection the next year, Obama pivoted from conservative centrism to progressive populism and economic nationalism. In November, Obama picked a fight with the House Republicans over extending the Social Security payroll tax cut for workers. Boehner said they would only agree to do so if Obama agreed to repeal the Affordable Care Act. In response, Obama took to the road, giving speeches in New Hampshire and Pennsylvania "What does it say about us that we're willing to cut taxes for people who don't need it and raise taxes on folks who do need a tax break?" he asked in Scranton. Boehner and the Republicans gave in.

On December 6, Obama gave a major address at Osawatomie, Kansas, where in 1910 Theodore Roosevelt had joined forces with Republican progressives against his successor, William Howard Taft, to proclaim "the new nationalism." Obama's speech was equally reminiscent of Roosevelt in 1936 and Bill Clinton in 1992.

> Long before the recession hit, hard work stopped paying off for too many people. Fewer and fewer of the folks who contributed to the success of our economy actually benefited from that success. Those at the very top grew wealthier from their incomes and their investments—wealthier than ever before. But everybody else struggled with costs that were growing and paychecks that weren't—and too many families found themselves racking up more and more debt just to keep up.

This time Obama didn't confer equal blame on Wall Street and Main Street for the Great Recession but pointed to the "breathtaking greed of a few." He positioned himself as the defender of the "innocent, hardworking Americans who had met their responsibilities but were still left holding the bag." The *New York Times* described the speech as "being infused with . . . the moralistic language that has emerged in the Occupy protests around the nation."

In Obama's campaign the next year against Republican nominee Mitt Romney, he criticized Romney as a "plutocrat" who, as the head of Bain Capital, had closed factories and sent jobs overseas. In May, Obama began running ads in Pennsylvania, Iowa, and Ohio that featured laid-off steel workers from a company bought by Bain. In Ohio and Michigan, the campaign attacked Romney for opposing the popular bailout of the auto companies. *Mother Jones* published a video in September of Romney telling wealthy donors of the "47 percent of the people who will vote for the president no matter what . . . who are dependent upon government, who believe that they are victims . . . who believe that they are entitled to health care, to food, to housing, to you-name-it." The Obama campaign put up an ad immediately attacking Romney for having "callously written off veterans, the elderly and the disabled." When Romney selected Paul Ryan, a champion of "entitlement" cuts in Medicare and Medicaid, as his running mate, Obama, who had proposed major Medicare cuts, accused Romney and Ryan of favoring a plan that could "force seniors to pay as much as $6400 more a year for their health care."

In the final tally, Obama got 332 electoral votes to 206 for Romney. He carried all of the industrial Midwest and Pennsylvania except for traditionally Republican Indiana. This was because Obama won back many white working-class voters. In Wisconsin Obama improved Democrats' margin among these voters by 18 points, coming close to an even split and erasing most of the catastrophic drop in white working-class support in 2010. Similarly, in Iowa Obama managed an even split among white working-class voters after Democrats lost these voters by 16 points in 2010.

Obama's success in the 2012 campaign showed that a populist politics that positioned the Democrats as the party of the "innocent victims" of the "greedy few" could win back many of the working-class voters who had deserted the Democrats, and it could also provide support for policies that would actually promote rather than undermine economic growth. Unfortunately, this lesson from 2012 was lost on many Democrats.

The Election of 2014

In Obama's second term, he had to contend with a Republican House for four years and with a Republican Senate after the 2014 election. He had to fight rearguard battles against House Republicans and got very little accomplished in domestic policy. Like other second-term presidents, Obama concentrated on foreign policy, where he enjoyed executive power. There was a brief, instructive period in 2013 where it looked like the Democrats would be able to build on their political success in 2012, but it didn't last.

In the summer of 2013, Obama and the Democrats got into another pitched battle with the House Republicans who threatened to shut down the government on October first when the budget expired if Obama and the Democratic-led Senate didn't accede to Republican demands to block or delay implementation of the Affordable Care Act. This time, Obama put his foot down, and from October first to seventeenth, the government shut down. Just as in 1995, the Republicans had overplayed their hand. The public sided with Obama and the Democrats. According to a *Washington Post*/ABC poll, 81 percent of Americans disapproved of the shutdown, and in the generic congressional poll for the 2014 election, Democrats led Republicans by 45 percent to 37 percent, suggesting that Democrats stood a good chance in the next year's midterm of winning back the House and retaining the Senate.

But the Democrats' political advantage created by the shutdown didn't last. In a speech in September, Obama had previewed the rollout of the Affordable Care Act the next month. "Most of the stories you hear how Obamacare can't work is just not based on facts," he declared. But the program's rollout turned out to be disaster. The government's website kept crashing. Waiting times were interminable. People couldn't understand the choices. Their existing plans were getting canceled. On November 15, Obama admitted, "We fumbled the rollout."

By March, according to a Pew poll, voters were preferring Republicans on the generic ballot by 47 percent to 43 percent. Obama's popularity had plummeted. And in the same poll, respondents said by 65 percent to 30 percent that they wanted the new administration elected in 2016 to pursue different policies from those of the Obama administration. In the 2014 elections, the Democrats got routed again. The Republicans won 247 House seats and flipped 9 Senate seats, attaining a majority in that body. Democrats won only 36 percent of the white working-class vote. And they lost middle-income voters by 55 percent to 44 percent.

In the House elections, Republicans thoroughly dominated the industrial belt from Pennsylvania to Iowa and Missouri. They also picked up a seat along the Texas border in a majority-Hispanic district, foreshadowing future Democratic challenges among Tejanos. Also in Texas, Republican Greg Abbott easily defeated Democrat Wendy Davis in the governor's race, losing Hispanics by only 55–44 and carrying Hispanic men. Nationally, Democrats still had a big advantage among Latinos but it was 10 points lower than in 2012.

There were three main factors in the Republican success. The first was the unpopularity of the Affordable Care Act. There was the botched rollout, but when people became able to enroll in 2014, many from the working and middle class discovered that their premiums were rising. Administration supporters explained that their premiums would have risen anyway without the Affordable Care Act, but that was scant consolation. The increases in premiums reawakened complaints that the ACA was a disguised program transferring income and benefits from the middle to the bottom of the income scale. In addition, many

Americans discovered that contrary to Obama's promise that "if you like your doctor, you can keep your doctor," they could not necessarily do so under the new program. In 2016, while on the campaign trail, Bill Clinton summed up the problems with the plan:

> So you've got this crazy system where all of a sudden 25 million more people have health care and then the people who are out there busting it, sometimes 60 hours a week, wind up with their premiums doubled and their coverage cut in half. It's the craziest thing in the world.

Clinton's characterization of the Affordable Care Act was personally unfair given the opaque complexity of the plan Hillary Clinton and Ira Magaziner devised in 1993, but it got at the political problem with Obamacare. Both plans suffered in the end by having to design coverage to overcome the opposition of powerful business interests.

The second factor was the continuation of the downturn. The unemployment rate had dropped since it had peaked in 2010, but it was still over 6 percent for most of 2014. Obama's failure to secure the larger stimulus program and his acquiescence in budget cuts after 2009 had subverted the recovery. In 2013, in the wake of spending cuts, GDP rose an anemic 1.8 percent.

And the third factor was that in contrast to 2010 when the Republicans had nominated extreme right-wing Senate candidates who had lost, this time they nominated for Senate and governor mainstream conservatives like Colorado's Cory Gardner or Maryland's Larry Hogan who defeated Democratic liberals. The 2014 election hammered the final nail into the coffin of the inevitable Democratic majority thesis. It didn't show that the Republicans had acquired a permanent majority, but it did show that the Democrats could not assume that political history was on their side. American politics was caught in a seesaw, and that would become even more apparent in the elections to come.

The Last New Democrat

The Democratic Leadership Council closed its doors in 2011, but Obama governed for two terms very much according to the playbook the DLC had developed in the late 1980s. That was particularly noteworthy in his social policies and contributed to his political success. He was the first African American president, but he steered clear of policies that specifically benefited black Americans. Georgetown University professor Michael Eric Dyson accused Obama of a "reluctance to highlight black suffering." During his campaign and first years, Obama refused to endorse the idea of gay marriage. He finally did so in May 2012 after it had lost the sting of controversy for Democrats.

Obama endorsed immigration reform that would have allowed illegal immigrants to stay and work in the United States, but set up an arduous path to their obtaining citizenship. He aggressively deported illegal immigrants who had committed crimes, earning him the reputation among the pro-immigration lobbyists of the "deporter-in-chief." He favored strengthening border security. In 2012, Obama established the DACA (Deferred Action for Childhood Arrivals) program that allowed the children of illegal immigrants who had graduated from high school or were enrolled in school or who had served in the armed forces to be safe from deportation for two years, after which they could apply for work permits. The limited program, which targeted children who could not be blamed for crossing the border, was popular.

Obama bemoaned the killing of black teenager Trayvon Martin in Miami Gardens, Florida, in 2012 by an armed resident, George Zimmerman, who believed Martin looked suspicious. Obama also praised the role of the Black Lives Matter organization, which led the protests in Ferguson, Missouri, in 2014, after a policeman, Darren Wilson, killed a black teenager, Michael Brown, whom he suspected of robbery. But Obama's attorney general Eric Holder cleared Wilson of the charge that he had illegally used force against Brown, who at one point had grabbed Wilson's gun. Obama also refused to echo the BLM call for "defunding the police." Obama made a serious effort to distance himself from the radicalism of the movement—to be supportive of both the issues raised by BLM *and* of law enforcement.

> [I]f we paint police in broad brush without recognizing that the vast majority of police officers are doing a really good job and are trying to protect people, and do so fairly and without racial bias, if our rhetoric does not recognize that, then we're going to lose allies in the reform cause.

In other words, Obama, like Clinton after 1994, carefully followed a path of moderation on social issues that the DLC had advised. It was a factor in preventing an even greater loss of working-class votes during both of their presidencies. Through his socially moderate outlook, he was able to make his race a political advantage rather than disadvantage.

But Obama, like Clinton, also followed the DLC's playbook on economics. His economics was a form of market liberalism, a third way, as Clinton would put it, between New Deal liberalism and Reagan conservatism, solicitous of the poor and unemployed, but also of business confidence and of the danger of deficit spending even during a recession. He periodically voiced discontent with China's trade practices, but up until the end followed Clinton's approach. He established an annual Strategic and Economic Dialogue with China that got nowhere. In an interview with us, Michael Wessel, a commissioner of the congressionally created

U.S.-China Economic and Security Review Commission, said that China used the talks "to stall and delay any action on any of the critical issues that had arisen in the bilateral context." Wessel described Obama's approach as "naive." America's trade deficit with China grew from $227 billion in 2008 to $347 billion in 2016.

To his credit, Obama did rescue the American auto companies, but he failed to halt the widening of the Great Divide. Brookings found that 64 percent of the nation's economic output in 2016 was produced by the fewer than five hundred counties that voted Democratic and just 36 percent by the more than twenty-six hundred counties that voted Republican. During the Obama administration, income inequality reached heights not seen since 1928. And there was a net loss of 300,000 manufacturing jobs during his presidency.

Obama, like Clinton, also consistently failed to address the massive hole in the Democratic electorate and governing coalition that had been caused by the labor movement's decline. During his administration, the conservative American Legislative Exchange Council, backed by the Koch brothers' business network, launched a campaign to further weaken the labor movement by getting states to restrict collective bargaining and political participation for public employee unions and to pass right-to-work laws.

The key battle occurred in Wisconsin. The Republican governor and state legislature attempted in 2011 to pass Act 10, drastically limiting collective bargaining for public employees, making union dues voluntary, and forcing the unions to seek recertification each year. Unions and Democrats in the state staged massive protests in Madison against passage of the legislation. But in the words of the *Milwaukee Business Journal*, "Obama stayed largely above the fray." The measure passed and led to a sharp decline in public union membership in Wisconsin. The American Federation of State, County and Municipal Employees (AFSCME) lost two-thirds of its members, and the Wisconsin teachers' union went from 98,000 to 36,000 members. Other midwestern states, inspired by Wisconsin's example, passed right-to-work laws.

Obama himself remained popular to the end. According to Gallup, his approval rating was 59 percent and disapproval rating only 37 percent as he was leaving office. But Obama left the Democratic electoral coalition in a shambles. Democrats had not had so few seats in the House of Representatives since 1928. Republicans controlled 32 governorships and Democrats only 17. Republicans controlled both houses of 30 state legislatures and Democrats only 11. Some of this, of course, was the result of Republican money and organizing efforts, and over the longer run, it was the result of the erosion of the Democratic Party's local organization, which had been centered around the labor movement. But Obama did nothing to arrest the erosion of the Democratic organized base. And his neoliberal economics drove many working-class voters into the arms of the Republican Party.

Chapter Five

Hillary Clinton, Donald Trump, and the Deplorables

In 2012, Obama won the presidency by striking a populist chord against Mitt Romney in the industrial Midwest and by winning working-class votes in Ohio, Wisconsin, Michigan, and Iowa. But Washington's Democratic consultants and the party's wealthy donors drew an entirely different conclusion from Obama's success. They insisted that Obama had won the election by summoning up what they variously called "the rising American electorate," "the rising American majority," and "new American majority."

In 2013, consultant Celinda Lake foresaw a "new American electorate" of "women, minorities, the young, and the unmarried." It was similar to what we had foreseen in *The Emerging Democratic Majority*, but with the white working class entirely absent and professionals or postgrads concealed in other identities. In 2015, unchastened by the Democratic rout in the 2014 elections, Stanley Greenberg described a "rising American electorate of African Americans, Hispanics, millennials, and unmarried women [that] will constitute 54 percent of the electorate in 2016." "History is on the side of the ascendant revolutions," Greenberg declared.

Greenberg's and Lake's convictions were echoed by Gara

LaMarche, the director of the Democracy Alliance, a group of ultra-wealthy Democratic donors. In September, as the general election between Hillary Clinton and Trump was unfolding, he wrote:

> There is one sure path to a progressive victory in the 2016 election, and that is to excite, mobilize, and turn out at the polls the communities of what have been called the "new American majority"— African-Americans, Latinos, Asian-Pacific Islanders and other communities of color, young people and women, as well as progressive white voters.

Their views ended up guiding the Clinton campaign. As a person close to Clinton remarked to us in the spring of 2020, she was going to run a campaign against Trump based on "identity politics," attempting to optimize the Democratic vote among each of these constituencies in order to secure a majority. Clinton focused on women voters. Her campaign slogan was "I'm with HER," and at the convention, she burst through a simulated glass ceiling. In the general election, she aimed ads at respective parts of the "new American majority" depicting Trump as bigoted toward each of them. "Donald Trump wants to see us disappear," a Clinton ad told Hispanic voters. Another ad that was aimed at women voters had Trump saying "Putting a wife to work is a very dangerous thing."

When the results came in, however, Trump had defeated Clinton, and Democrats had lost both the Senate and the House. While she had won different parts of the "new American majority," she had lost, and lost decisively—by a greater margin than any Democrat since 1984—the white working-class voters who made up a significant part of the industrial states that Obama had carried in 2008 and 2012. By losing these voters and these states, she lost the election, and the Democrats lost the House and the Senate. Clinton and the Democrats had drawn exactly the wrong conclusions from Obama's victory in 2012. Instead of affirming the "new American majority," that election had reaffirmed the importance to the Democrats of the working-class voters who had once made up the core of its majority coalition.

Some of Clinton's supporters later blamed Bernie Sanders's primary challenge for disrupting her path to the nomination and sowing doubts about her candidacy. There was a certain truth to this. By criticizing Clinton's subordination to neoliberal, third way, or Wall Street economics, Sanders had exposed a flaw in Clinton's and Democrats' promise to voters. The policies that had begun under Bill Clinton and been followed, more or less, by Obama had not delivered prosperity, particularly to those towns and regions that depended on manufacturing or mining. And there was no reason to believe that Clinton would diverge from those policies. Trump was able, in effect, to piggyback on the case that Sanders made against Clinton's and the Democrats' economics. And that challenge was an important reason for Trump's political success against her in the industrial Midwest.

But Trump's campaign also targeted the cultural divisions that Bill Clinton, following the DLC's playbook, and Obama had tried to evade in their campaigns. Controversial views on social issues had begun to surface during Obama's second term—not so much in Washington, but on college campuses and social media and in the foundations, publications, and groups that were aligned with the Democratic Party—in what could be called the "shadow Democratic Party." By focusing on identity politics and on Trump's character, Clinton had opened wide a Pandora's box of cultural strife. Trump was able to appeal to both the economic and cultural grievances that Americans on one side of the Great Divide held against the other.

The Sanders Challenge

As the Democratic and Republican primaries were beginning in the summer of 2015, Washington's political experts believed that the general election would be between Clinton and former Florida governor Jeb Bush—a reprise with the first names changed of the 1992 election. But it quickly became apparent that Clinton faced a stiff challenge from Vermont senator Bernie Sanders and that Bush would be unable to stand up to Trump's jibes. Sanders focused on the difference between his economic stands and those of Hillary Clinton, Obama, and Bill Clinton and on Clinton's own ties to Wall Street.

Sanders had told talk show host Stephen Colbert that he preferred to be described as a "progressive," but he didn't back away from having described himself for decades as a "democratic socialist." Sanders's version of socialism was European and Canadian social democracy, not Soviet or Chinese socialism. He wanted to contest the power that the "billionaire class" had over American politics and the economy by strengthening unions and creating a popular movement. As a House member in the '90s, Sanders had opposed NAFTA, PNTR for China, and the repeal of Glass-Steagall. As a senator during Obama's presidency, he had staged a one-man filibuster against Obama's deal with the Republicans in December 2010 to cut spending and preserve the Bush-era tax breaks for the wealthy. He also opposed the Trans-Pacific Partnership trade agreement that Obama had negotiated and that Clinton had enthusiastically supported.

In his campaign against Clinton, he reiterated his stand against the trade deals Democrats had backed. "I don't think it is appropriate for trade policies to say that you can move to a country where wages are abysmal, where there are no environmental regulations, where workers can't form unions," he said. He wanted Wall Street firms to pay a transaction tax that could be used to fund free tuition to public colleges. He called for reinstating Glass-Steagall. He wanted to replace the Affordable Care Act with a Canadian-style single-payer health-care system. He represented, in other words, a rebuke to the policies that the last two Democratic administrations had embraced.

Sanders also called for Clinton to make public the speeches she had given for a minimum of $225,000 each to Goldman Sachs and other financial firms prior to launching her campaign. Clinton refused—and her supporters later blamed Sanders's request for undermining her presidential bid—but as it turned out, Sanders was on firm ground in demanding that the public have access to these speeches. In these speeches, which WikiLeaks published during the general election, Clinton had assured bankers of her support for free trade and for appointing Wall Streeters to oversee financial regulation. She had also declared her support for cutting the deficit, including by cutting Social Security, and for eventually creating "open borders" with Latin America. She dismissed attempts to blame the banking system for the crash and the Great Recession as an "oversimplification" and a "misunderstanding and really politicizing of what happened."

Sanders carried on his campaign up until the convention, but he couldn't overcome the misgivings, especially among black and older voters, about his credibility as a general election candidate. Sanders's avowal of "democratic socialism," no matter how anodyne in its details, was anathema to older voters who grew up during the Cold War and to many Latinos who identified socialism with that practiced in Castro's Cuba and Maduro's Venezuela. In a general election, Sanders probably would have had trouble justifying the huge tax increases that would have been required to finance his health plan. But the surprising success of a septuagenarian socialist from Vermont should have constituted a warning signal to Clinton and the leading Democrats about their third way, neoliberal outlook.

Sanders's campaign proved particularly successful among younger (eighteen- to twenty-nine-year-old) voters. He won these voters by 71 percent to 28 percent over the months of primaries and caucuses. In total, he got more of these voters than Trump and Clinton combined. Many of these voters, who had come of age during the Great Recession, expressed dissatisfaction with income inequality and economic opportunity and even with capitalism itself. Since 2010, the popularity of capitalism among members of the millennial generation and Gen Z had declined sharply by 10 points and was now about matched by the popularity of socialism. If they had attended college, many of these voters were burdened with student debt, and were not gaining the kind of employment they had hoped a college degree would secure. Three-quarters of those with student debt thought it was harder for their generation to get started in life than previous generations. An NBER study has confirmed that, along with student debt being more common and higher than among previous generations, college graduates from the millennial generation are more likely to live at their parents' home. They also have a higher rate (52 percent) of working at "mismatched" jobs— jobs that do not require a college education.

In a deeper sense, many of these younger people suffered from a kind of existential anxiety from which earlier generations of young people, particularly before the sixties, had been spared. It manifested itself not only in left-wing views of capitalism, but in mental illness and in experimentation with different sexual and social identities.

Sanders also did better than Clinton among white working-class voters and rural and small-town voters—three constituencies that had been fleeing the Democrats. Sanders won two key industrial states, Michigan and Wisconsin. These voters were responding in part to Sanders's criticisms of neoliberal economics but the voters also saw Sanders as a more sympathetic figure than Clinton. In the telling question of which candidate cares more about people like you, Sanders bested Clinton.

Some commentators and later Clinton herself attributed Clinton's electoral difficulties to misogyny, but in Maryland, for instance, white working-class voters had no trouble supporting Senator Barbara Mikulski. As would become even clearer in the general election, Clinton reflected culturally one side of the growing class divide that was defining the Democratic Party and limiting its appeal to working-class voters. These voters could detect her indifference or, in some cases, hostility to their concerns.

The Key to Trump's Defeat of Clinton

In the general election, Trump bested Clinton in states that included four different kinds of economies and populations.

- Southern states that had been solidly Democratic but had begun turning Republican in response to the civil rights acts and the counterculture. These states had few union members and many white evangelical Protestants. Typical of them would be Mississippi or Alabama.
- Farm states that had been traditionally Republican even during the New Deal. They had relatively little heavy industry, few unions, and many white evangelical Protestants. Typical would be Kansas and Nebraska.
- States dependent on resource extraction for jobs and state revenues that were threatened by Democratic support for regulations to cut carbon emissions in response to climate change. West Virginia had voted for a Republican presidential candidate only three times between 1932 and 1996 but became solidly Republican after that.
- Industrial states that depended heavily on manufacturing

for jobs and revenue, were significantly unionized, and had been dependably Democratic, but had suffered serious losses in manufacturing from 2000 to 2016 and went for Trump in 2016 after voting for Bill Clinton and Obama. These include Pennsylvania, Wisconsin, and Michigan. Michigan went from 921,000 manufacturing workers in 2000 to 628,0000 in 2016; Wisconsin from 605,000 to 482,000; Ohio from 1,047,000 to 716,000; and Pennsylvania from 879,000 to 591,000.

There are clearly overlaps in these categories. Louisiana and Texas are southern states that are also dependent on resource extraction. North Dakota is a farm state increasingly dependent on its oil and gas industry. Iowa and Indiana are farm states that also have suffered significant losses in manufacturing. Pennsylvania contains large postindustrial metro areas, but also manufacturing and mining, especially in the west, that led to its joining the formerly dependably Democratic industrial states that went for Trump in 2016.

What was significant about Trump's victory was the inclusion of these industrial states. Without them, he could not have won the presidency. He won those states mainly because he drastically increased Republican support among the white working class, particularly in those places that suffered from deindustrialization. A postelection study by political scientists J. Lawrence Broz, Jeffry Frieden, and Stephen Weymouth compared support for Romney in 2012 with Trump in 2016 and found that support for Trump had particularly increased "in counties with larger declines in manufacturing employment." There were two reasons for that: first, many of these voters backed his challenge—which was very similar to Sanders's—to neoliberal positions on trade and on factories moving out of the country; secondly, many voters in these states supported his challenge to the culture of the heavily Democratic postindustrial metro centers and college towns. The 2016 election saw the return of the culture wars of the 1980s with the Democrats again on the losing side.

The Cultural Clash

The division over economics and culture more or less ran along the lines of the Great Divide that began to arise in 1980s between the postindustrial metro regions and the parts of America that were threatened by the loss of manufacturing and mining jobs. But it created economic and cultural differences *within* states as well as between them. In Ohio, for instance, Columbus's Franklin County, where Ohio State University is, was on one side of the divide and Youngstown's blue-collar Mahoning County on the other. In Maryland, Dundalk, a small town on the outskirts of Baltimore, is on one side and Baltimore on another. But in those industrial states like Ohio and Wisconsin, where the voters in the small towns and midsize cities outnumbered those in the big postindustrial metro centers, the Great Divide led to the states going Republican rather than Democratic in 2016.

There were differences in economic perception on either side of the divide that led to different political perceptions. The voters in the big metro centers had not felt threatened by NAFTA or the China trade; if anything, these trade agreements had meant cheaper consumer goods and also outlets for expansion for their financial and business services. They did not worry about immigrants taking their jobs or raising the local tax burden for social services. The voters in Youngstown, Dundalk, or Hazleton, Pennsylvania, did. Many of the voters in these towns that suffered from deindustrialization blamed the Democrats for their woes, even though the economic difficulties these areas faced had begun with Reagan and Volcker and continued under the two Bush presidencies. They welcomed Trump's attack on the Democrats' "bad trade deals." These economic differences underlay and reinforced cultural differences that helped to differentiate Trump from Clinton voters and, more broadly, Republicans from Democrats.

People's sense of their own self-worth depends on the ways in which they can think of themselves not as isolated collections of cells destined to disintegrate but as people having multiple identities that transcend their own biological individuality. They need affirmation from others, and they need to feel they are part of not only families or neighborhoods but also larger communities. The college-educated professionals who set the tone for the culture of the postindustrial metro areas can think of themselves as Chicagoans or New Yorkers, for instance, but also (for those who have lived in numerous places, including abroad) as being cosmopolites, citizens of the world. They can feel part of a larger national or international community with whom they commune at conferences or conventions. They can identify with the college they attended and with the firm they work for, as well as with their family and neighborhood.

They are often secular in their outlook and define themselves by having a certain lifestyle—as being "into" certain things or even having unorthodox sexual preferences or family arrangements—and they regard these as the basis for new cultural norms for which they demand respect and recognition. They live, in other words, amid a plentitude of identities that define what matters and what is moral behavior. With the young college-educated who find themselves lacking the kind of employment they expected, this search for new identities and lifestyles veers off into a search for new sexual lifestyles. Young people in colleges or in the big metro centers might introduce themselves, "I'm Jana Jones, I'm queer, and my pronouns are they/them." Of course, not everyone who lives in New York or Chicago thinks this way, but through the representation of college-educated professionals in the media, politics, the arts, and business, these norms became the leading edge of the culture in these areas.

By contrast, many of the people in the deindustrialized towns and small cities of middle America have been stripped of essential elements of their identity. They used to enjoy lifetime employment for a big corporation at which they expected their children could also work. They belonged to a union. They would go to the same bars after work and play on the weekends in softball or bowling leagues, which were often connected to their jobs. They and their children would go to the same high school and follow the fortunes of the school's sports teams. They would go to the same churches. If they were men, they would have gone into the military and identify as veterans. They will take pride in having lived in the same place or region all their life. Much of that common life is gone.

In Mansfield, Ohio, for instance, where Senator Sherrod Brown grew up, most of the big factories have closed. What used to be a huge General Motors plant is now a huge empty field. The United Auto Workers' union hall across from the plant became a Jews for Jesus assemblage. Many of the neighborhood pubs are gone. The high schools are dogged by low test scores and are a source of strife rather than civic pride. Many of the people who worked in the factories have moved to the suburbs where they work—usually for less pay than before—as part of the office or sales economy. They have been thrown back on the most basic elements of their identities: nation, family, and faith, the cars they drive, or the guns they own, which protect the home and family.

Where college-educated professionals welcome an influx of low-skilled immigrants as a source of inexpensive childcare and landscaping, the people in middle America may see them not only as a tax burden but as a threat to what had been a common culture. They feel threatened, and looked down upon, by the upscale denizens of the postindustrial cities. They resent what they regard as the special attention given to the plight of racial minorities, some of whom are doing better than they are. They are put off by many of the lifestyles practiced and extolled on college campuses and big metro centers. They think calling someone "queer" is an insult. Katherine J. Cramer has documented these sentiments in her book on Wisconsin, *The Politics of Resentment*, as has Andrew J. Cherlin in *Labor's Love Lost*. In England, David Goodhart made a similar point about the division over Brexit in *The Road to Somewhere*.

A lot of these cultural differences revolved in 2016 around what was called "political correctness." In the sixties' new left, political correctness was seen as a virtue—as the possession of a "correct line" on race, class, or imperialism. But the term began to be used in the eighties as a criticism of left-wing campus culture, and reemerged as an issue in the 2010s as the college-educated young attempted to impose social conformity on their superiors and peers. Students accused faculty or each other of committing "microaggressions." At Harvard Law School, students petitioned the school not to teach rape law. Faculty at the University of California campuses were warned by administrators that saying "America is the land of opportunity" or "I believe the most qualified person should get the job" was a microaggression. Teachers were also told to issue "trigger warnings" before airing works such as *The Great Gatsby* that might trouble students.

These practices spread to the business world where employees received extensive lists of terms not to use. These included any "gendered language," such as policeman, mailman, chairman, and mankind. That was followed by the vogue for pronoun specification and use of terms like "pregnant people" instead of pregnant women. Corporations and schools hired experts in what was called "diversity, equity, and inclusion" who subjected employees to training sessions in avoiding a range of "isms," including sexism, racism, and ableism. For those in postindustrial areas and in college towns, these new norms became part of a new moral lifestyle; for those on the other side of the divide, they represented a lack of appreciation, and even scorn toward, their views of family and sexuality and toward their own economic difficulties.

Immigration became a special area in which political correctness reigned. Liberal publications aligned with the Democrats regularly replaced the term "illegal immigrants" with "undocumented" or "unauthorized" immigrants, as if to suggest that an unlawful act had not been committed. During the years leading up to the November 2016 election, concerns about illegal immigration fused with fear of terrorist attacks by immigrants— particularly by Muslims from the Middle East and South Asia. There was a spate of terrorist incidents. These included the Boston marathon bombing in April 2013, the massacre in San Bernadino, California, in December 2015, and the Orlando, Florida, nightclub killings in June 2016. As a result, opposition to illegal immigration became an even sharper dividing line in the country's politics and became central to the contest between Trump and Clinton, who, on this issue as on the others, represented the cultural outlook of the postindustrial metro areas.

The cultural divide also opened up over race and police brutality. The police killing of suspected thief Michael Brown in Ferguson in August 2014 sparked several months of demonstrations and calls to defund the police. In April 2015, demonstrators rioted for days in Baltimore over the death of a suspect, Freddie Gray, in a police van after his arrest. During this same period, police officers were gunned down—apparently in retaliation—in New York City, Dallas, and Baton Rouge. The controversy over these incidents provoked opposing reactions that mirrored the Great Divide: on one side, charges of "systemic" or "structural" racism, particularly in the police and prison systems, and of "white privilege" being baked into American institutions; on the other side, charges of hostility to the police and to white people in general. These opposing views were identified, respectively, with Democrats and Republicans and with their candidates.

The Shadow Parties

American political parties are different from European parliamentary parties. They don't have platforms that bind their members. Politicians are accountable in theory and often in practice to the primary voters who nominate them. But they are also influenced by donors, lobbyists, trade associations, foundations and labor organizations, policy groups and think tanks, activist organizations, private and social media, and politically aligned powerful individuals like Robert Rubin or Charles Koch who can either speak directly to politicians and officeholders or speak through the groups and media of the shadow party. Up until the 1990s, this assemblage of powerful groups and individuals was relatively narrow. It consisted of people who could meet directly with high officials. We described it as the party's governing coalition. But with the rise of the internet, cable news, and talk radio, the means of communicating with and pressuring high officials widened. We call this wider assemblage the shadow party.

Seventy years ago, when the AFL-CIO was formed, it had an oversize influence in the governing coalition along with what remained of the urban political machines like Richard J. Daley's Chicago party organization. Labor and the machines kept the party rooted in the culture of the working class. But the labor movement is no longer a dominant voice, and by Bill Clinton's election, the machines were gone. In their place are the big donors from Wall Street, Hollywood, and Silicon Valley, think tanks like the Center for American Progress and the Peterson Institute, foundations like Ford and George Soros's Open Society, political groups like the Working Families Party, the Human

Rights Campaign, and Black Lives Matter, publications like the *New York Times*, *Washington Post*, and *New Yorker*, media networks like MSNBC, substackers, bloggers and tweeters, and hundreds of smaller groups headquartered in the postindustrial metro centers and college towns who often communicate through social media. Some of these groups say they are nonpartisan, but they are sympathetic to the Democratic Party and speak primarily to its voters and politicians. Together, they make up the Democrats' shadow party.

Rescuing a useful term from the old socialist lexicon, one could describe this shadow party and its groups and influentials as representing the *vanguard* of the college-educated professionals in the postindustrial metro centers. Their views are not representative of everyone who lives in Evanston, Illinois, or Mountain View, California, or Austin, Texas, but they represent the most concentrated, best organized, most extreme, and most highly publicized expression of what many people in these places and in college towns think about the economy, race, immigration, and the family. In many of the media organizations and foundations, young staffers determine the political direction. Richard Healey, a founder of the Grassroots Power Project and a longtime adviser to foundations and political groups, told us, "The young people on social media have a dense network of righteousness. The senior staff are too often cowed by it."

Faced with gridlock in Washington and a divided electorate, and lacking in the popular power that labor once possessed, the young people, Healey argues, are driven to focus on politically correct language and on diversity and inclusion. "If we have no power, we will argue about words," he says. "If we have no power, we'll worry about hiring policies because it's the only power we have. We can't actually change homelessness. We can't change poverty, we can't change bad health care. But, man, we sure can control something. What is it? Hiring practices, firing practices, and words." The result is an aura of moral censoriousness—of neo-Puritan religiosity—that surrounds much of the Democrats' shadow party groups.

Unlike her husband, who had never entirely shed his southern small-town roots, Hillary Clinton was a perfect representative of the social elite and political vanguard of new postindustrial metro centers. She voiced their preoccupations with breaking through the glass ceiling and with diversity and inclusion. Her campaign slogan, "Stronger together," depicted a collage of races, sexes, and ethnicities. At the same time, she appeared cold, cerebral, and snooty to people on the other side of the Great Divide. Her attempts at empathy appeared contrived.

In the 2000s, the Republicans' shadow party continued to consist of major business groups like the U.S. Chamber of Commerce and the Club for Growth, the Koch Network of donors, the religious right media, megachurches and organizations, gun clubs, Fox News, talk radio, and other media, conservative think tanks and policy groups and, after 2009, the activist network around the Tea Party groups. As was the case with the Democrats' shadow party, where there were big differences between Sanders and Clinton followers, there were clear differences over candidates and outlooks within the Republicans' shadow party. Most of the Washington-based business and policy groups scorned Trump, but he was a hit with activists and their groups.

Trump, of course, was anything but a product of middle America. But he had the mentality of an outsider and a kind of man-in-the-street grasp of politics uncluttered by briefing books and by policy memos from thinktanks. And his years as an entertainer taught him how to speak to people who were different from him. He voiced the particular fusion of cultural and economic concern that characterized middle America. He wanted to build a wall to keep out illegal immigrants but, unlike business Republicans, he wasn't eager to privatize Social Security or put people at the mercy of big health insurance companies.

In his campaign, Trump was able to bypass the business Republicans and speak to the voters in middle America with the help of the new social media that had developed in recent years. While Clinton's campaign was chaired by John Podesta, the head of the Center for American Progress, and a veteran member of the Washington establishment, Trump's campaign chairman was Stephen Bannon, who was the executive chairman of Breitbart .com, a widely read conservative website that most liberal Democrats had never even heard of. Trump could also rely on the network of Tea Party activists who had themselves been organized through the internet. His campaign virtually absorbed the Tea Party groups and other similar groups like right-wing TV host Glenn Beck's 9–12 Project. He spoke to their preoccupations with American nationhood and illegal immigration—two subjects that were foreign to Clinton and to that part of the Great Divide that she represented. By November 2016, these groups no longer existed independently of the Trump campaign.

Making America Great Again

Most Democrats as well as many Republicans underestimated Trump as a candidate. They saw him simply as a fast buck operator and a buffoon. The *Huffington Post* (subsequently renamed *HuffPost*) declared that it was going to cover his candidacy under entertainment rather than politics. But Trump, while ignorant of and uninterested in thorny details about economic or foreign policy, had an extraordinarily shrewd grasp of how the Great Divide was affecting not only the economy but also politics and culture. By playing to one side of that divide, Trump succeeded in winning the electoral votes of older industrial states that the

Democrats had assumed to be part of their impregnable "blue wall."

In the general election, Trump attacked Clinton's economic and cultural views in a way that resonated among working-class voters in middle America. Trump would often begin his speeches by criticizing corporations that shipped their jobs overseas or to Mexico and promising to bring the jobs back. He would also attack the Democrats' "bad trade deals" and threaten to put tariffs on Chinese imports. And he promised to replace the Affordable Care Act with a plan that "will take care of everybody." In Trump's closing ad, he attacked the "corrupt political establishment" and "the global structure" for destroying America's greatness.

> It's a global power structure that is responsible for the economic decisions that have robbed our working class, stripped our country of its wealth and put that money into the pockets of a handful of large corporations and political entities.

Clinton largely ignored Trump's challenge to her economics. According to a study by the Wesleyan Media Project, only about a quarter of her ads were about policy, and few of those were directly about economics. By contrast, over 70 percent of Trump's ads were about policy. Clinton might have felt that she could rely on the Washington Democratic establishment to discredit Trump's economics. The Peterson Institute, which had earlier promised huge job gains from NAFTA and from the PNTR with China, claimed that Trump's trade policies were sure to cause a recession. The *Washington Post* suggested that Trump's closing ad, because it flashed the faces of George Soros, Lloyd Blankfein, and Janet Yellen, among many others, on the screen, was anti-Semitic. Soros is probably the largest individual contributor to Democratic candidates; officials from Goldman Sachs played a huge role in the economic policy of the Clinton, George W. Bush, and Obama administrations. And few people (including ourselves) knew Yellen, who was the head of the Federal Reserve, was Jewish. The *Post's* response showed the degree to which the liberal press was determined to ignore the economic challenge of Trump's campaign. Clinton and the establishment Democrats' response to Trump's economic views testified to their utter failure to understand the poverty of their own approach to trade and multinational corporations.

The heart of Trump's appeal fused economics and culture. Trump's campaign slogan, borrowed from Reagan, was "Make America Great Again." Many older voters from industrial states understood Trump to be promising to bring back prosperity to their region. They remembered, too, a time when as consumers they would look for the "Made in the USA" label as a sign of superior quality in goods. Others saw Trump's slogan as a promise to reverse moral decline or to end the "forever wars" or to stop the millions of illegal border crossings.

In response, Clinton dismissed the promise of "make America great again." "Despite what you hear, we don't need to make America great again. America has never stopped being great," she told voters in South Carolina. In an interview with the executive editor of the Silicon Valley–based LinkedIn, Clinton scoffed at the idea. "'Make America Great Again' is really code for, 'Hey, I can turn the clock back. And I can make you feel good. And I can get you the job that you used to have and even at more money.'" Clinton was heard correctly to be voicing the snobbery of the postindustrial metro areas toward the victims of deindustrialization.

Trump's promise to end illegal immigration was both economic and cultural. He charged illegal immigrants with taking jobs from Americans and with raising social welfare costs in cities and states. He also claimed that many of them were "rapists" and "criminals." Clinton pointed to the "ugliness" and "bigotry" of the latter appeals, but she ignored the issue of border security. Instead, her platform and her speeches focused on creating a path to citizenship for illegal immigrants. Referring to Trump's promise to "build a wall" preventing illegal immigrants from entering the country, Clinton said, "Instead of building walls, we need to be tearing down barriers." She was tone-deaf to an issue that vexed millions of working-class voters. Like other leading Democrats, Clinton assumed that by championing the cause of illegal immigrants, she was winning the support of Latinos, even while angering working-class white voters. Democrats, as it turned out, were completely misreading the attitudes that many Hispanics had toward illegal immigration.

Before running for president, Trump had questioned whether Obama had been born in the United States. That was an implicit racial appeal to conservative voters, but in his 2016 campaign, Trump made few George Wallace–like appeals. The closest Trump got to the controversies swirling around race and police brutality was to condemn the action of San Francisco 49ers quarterback Colin Kaepernick who kneeled rather than stood during the national anthem in protest of police brutality. "Maybe he should find a country that works better for him," Trump said. But Trump's comment was as much about Kaepernick's lack of patriotism as about his stand on police brutality. Trump's sentiment was widely shared on one side of the economic and cultural divide in the country. According to one poll that fall, Americans disapproved of Kaepernick's kneeling by a two-to-one margin.

Clinton, on the other hand, echoed the rhetoric of Black Lives Matter and its supporters in her speeches. Whites, she told the NAACP during a campaign speech, "need to recognize our privilege." And Clinton was dismissive of Trump's supporters as racist and nativist. She told a rally of LGBT supporters in New York in September, "You know, to just be grossly generalistic, you could put half of Trump's supporters into what I call the basket of deplorables. Right? They're racist, sexist, homophobic, xenophobic, Islamophobic—you name it." Clinton's remarks put her squarely on one side of the cultural divide. In our interviews after the election with working-class Trump voters in Ohio, they particularly cited this remark of Clinton's in explaining their support of Trump and their dissatisfaction with the Democrats. "I would say that the single biggest factor in her defeat was her deplorable comment. She insulted us," one steelworker said.

A lot of this culture war between Trump and Clinton was encapsulated in the debate over political correctness. Clinton repeatedly criticized Trump for his derogatory remarks about women and Mexican Americans and for proposing a ban on Muslim immigrants in the wake of the terrorist attacks. In one of her closing ads, Clinton ran Trump's voice saying "she ate like a pig" and "she has a fat ass." In response to these and other attacks, Trump said, "I think the big problem this country has is being politically correct. I've been challenged by so many people and I don't, frankly, have time for total political correctness."

Many voters who backed Trump did not agree with his derogatory statements about women or about Mexican immigrants. According to a Quinnipiac poll in August 2016, 29 percent of Republicans thought "the way Trump talks appeals to bigotry." In the same poll, a third of Republicans said they liked his policies but didn't like Trump as a person. In interviews after the election, we repeatedly heard voters saying that they voted for Trump in spite of disliking some of the incendiary language he used. In supporting Trump against Clinton, they were not so much voting *for* him so much as voting *against* the elites who were trying to dictate how they talked about race, gender, immigration, and a host of other subjects.

According to one survey, agreement with the statement "there is too much political correctness in this country" was second only to "I am a registered member of the Republican Party" in predicting whether someone would vote for Trump. An experimental

study by three psychologists in the fall of 2016 found that expos-
ing subjects to "norms that are designed to increase the overall amount of positive communication can actually backfire by
increasing support for a politician who uses extremely negative
language that explicitly violates the norm," in this case Trump. In
layman's language, injunctions to be politically correct inclined
the psychologists' subjects to favor Trump over Clinton.

By highlighting Trump's genuine moral failings and ignoring
the actual issues about trade, globalization, immigration, and
health insurance, Clinton may have damaged her own campaign
more than Trump's. After poring over the studies of the 2016
campaign, Michigan State political scientist Matt Grossman
concluded on Twitter:

> voters can simultaneously: 1) dislike Trump's loud bigotry 2) dis-
> like Dems' harping on it 3) perceive that Dems used to care about
> white working class, now only care about minorities 4) mistrust
> Republicans on class, but perceive Trump as different. In fact,
> pattern seems dominant.

Clinton had hardened the economic and cultural divide in
the country into a political divide and in the process lost Pennsylvania, Ohio, Michigan, Wisconsin, and Iowa—states that
Obama had won twice.

In our interviews with Ohio voters, they voiced similar sentiments to other midwestern voters who chose Trump over Clinton. They included a steelworker, a machinist, an unemployed
salesman, and two office workers. The machinist had lost his first
factory job when, after NAFTA, the company had moved its plant
to Mexico. Some of what they said about the economy sounded
like Bernie Sanders. "In the '50s companies considered themselves successful. We would measure our success in who had the
most employees and could still turn a profit. Now it's all about

making money for the stockholders." Here are some samples of what they said about Trump, and Clinton and the Democrats.

- I felt Hillary was nothing but a puppet. I like Trump. Sometimes he speaks too much, but he speaks just like us. He is a real person, not just trying to sell a party politics.
- [The Democrats] are more interested in being politically correct, playing it close to the vest, and not [in] taking care of the people. I think Trump spoke to that. And a lot of people thought that, too.
- What does patriotism mean? Is it a sin to love your country as people believe today? You have people taking a knee. Sure, there have been bad things that have happened, but you can't blame the Constitution or our entire system on that. It's people that are evil. Not this country.
- The main reason I voted for him was his immigration policy. I thought that was the single most important issue in the country. And I knew he was going to build the wall. That was his whole campaign. Other than the tax reform, I pretty much agree with everything people said.
- A very good example of [political correctness] is the gun control intervention. It's amazing how much farther the liberals would get if they would just leave that issue alone. But they harp on it and harp on it. And this makes us feel threatened. Not because we are afraid of a tyrannical government, but just because we want to protect our households. We want to have the ability to do that. We are citizens not subjects, and that's the largest issue.
- Anything you say that somebody else doesn't agree with anymore is racist. It has become a code word.

After the election, Clinton and her loyal supporters did everything they could to avoid blaming themselves and decades of Democratic politics and policies for losing the election to a candidate who, even after his election, when most presidents-elect enjoy a honeymoon, remained unpopular with voters. They blamed her defeat on Sanders, on FBI director James Comey, and on the Russian disinformation campaign; and they blamed the voters themselves for being racist and misogynistic. In a speech in March 2018, Clinton summed up the campaign in terms that perfectly echoed the Great Divide.

> So I won the places that are optimistic, diverse, dynamic, moving forward. And his whole campaign, 'Make America Great Again,' was looking backwards. You know, you didn't like black people getting rights, you don't like women, you know, getting jobs, you don't want to, you know, see that Indian American succeeding more than you are, whatever your problem is, I'm going to solve it.

While some Trump voters in 2016 were highly reactionary, political scientists Justin Grimmer, William Marble, and Cole Tanigawa-Lau have shown that Trump's improvement over Romney was primarily attributable to increased support among voters with racially moderate views. Trump's voters were actually less xenophobic, less sexist, had lower levels of racial resentment, and were more tolerant on average than Romney's supporters.

Clinton's loss revealed the weakness in the Democrats' vision of a "new American majority." In losing the support of the white working class and in abandoning much of small town as well as rural America, the Clinton Democrats had abandoned not only any hope of an enduring majority but also of representing the many against the few, the powerless against the powerful—the vision that had animated Roosevelt and the New Deal liberals. Instead, they had enabled the Republicans to reignite the culture war that had helped doom the Democrats a quarter century before.

Chapter Six

Trump, the Shadow Democrats, and the 2020 Election

Donald Trump's victory, along with Bernie Sanders's strong showing in the Democratic primaries, revealed the vast discontent that had simmered under the surface of American politics and that had taken the Clinton campaign, with its claim that "America is already great," by surprise. The discontent was the product of forty years of deindustrialization, which accelerated during the "China shock" of the early 2000s, and of the Great Recession. It manifested itself in manifold ways, some of which seemed to have little to do with the economic experience of the prior decades: anger at illegal immigration, resentment of the coastal elites, and at football players "taking a knee," on the one side; a frantic search for identity, pangs of guilt and shame at America's evils, and apocalyptic fears of climate catastrophe on the other. During Trump's presidency, these fears and anxieties intensified, and then exploded in 2020 as the pandemic raised the specter of death and isolation.

Trump had an opportunity to speak to the discontent on both sides of the Great Divide. In his 2016 campaign, he had, after all, appealed directly to Sanders's voters and an estimated 12 percent of them had backed Trump. But Trump proved to be a much more capable campaigner than a president. If anything, he widened the Great Divide through his incendiary ranting. Democrats, too, had a chance to reorient their politics after Clinton's defeat, but like the country itself, they became obsessed with Trump's excrescences. But they lucked out. In 2020, after a tumultuous primary that brought out the worst in their candidates, and an explosive summer that brought the party's most radical elements to the fore, they nominated a candidate who, like Clinton, ran a race centered around the flaws of his opponent, but who, unlike Clinton, did not convey indifference or contempt toward the people on the other side of the Great Divide.

Trump's Sound and Fury

As president, Trump did respond at least in part to the economic discontent his own voters had voiced. Under Bill Clinton, the United States had acceded to a global trading system that the Chinese and other Asian countries were able to game to their advantage by using currency manipulation, government subsidies, technology transfer, and covert trade barriers to create huge, damaging trade surpluses with the United States. American multinational corporations had benefited initially, often at the expense of American workers, but by the time Trump took office, they had found themselves the victim of technology theft that the Chinese used to build competing firms. Trump sought to use tariffs to protect American manufacturers from being undercut by government-subsidized Chinese exports. He encouraged American firms to return their production facilities from abroad. He renegotiated NAFTA on terms that were more favorable to American workers and American-based companies. He tried to protect American patents from technology theft.

Trump also sought to stem the huge tide of illegal immigration on the southern border. He tried to complete an impenetrable border wall, he increased funding for border enforcement, and he pressured Mexico into retaining asylum seekers and refugees that were traveling to the United States from Central America. These efforts helped him to retain his support in the white working class and actually to create inroads among Hispanics in South Texas who, contrary to the Democrats' assumptions, disliked illegal immigration and wanted strong border enforcement. But Trump's constructive responses to the country's social and economic ills were overshadowed by his gaping flaws as a president.

Trump did not follow the centuries-old script of American presidents. The American Constitution endows presidents with the responsibilities of prime minister and monarch, and as monarch, presidents are supposed to act as suitable representatives of the nation as a whole. Trump failed miserably at the latter responsibility. Instead of attempting to govern as the president of all the citizens, Trump conducted his presidency in the same no-holds-barred divisive manner in which he had conducted his campaign. He aired false and incendiary charges against his political rivals.

He attributed Clinton's margin in the overall popular vote to millions of votes by illegal immigrants. He courted fringe right-wing elements. He initially refused to condemn the neo-Nazis who marched in Charlottesville and gave succor to groups like the Proud Boys and Oath Keepers. He caged the children of illegal immigrants. He and his cronies were enmeshed in financial scandals. His administration was a revolving door of aides and cabinet officials. His approval rating was 46 percent during his inaugural and was down to 41 percent at the time of the November 2018 elections.

When the protests against police brutality in the summer of 2020 descended in major cities into rioting and looting, Trump had a chance to win over the public, but in the midst of police dispersal of a peaceful protest down the street from the White House, he chose to stage a photo op holding a Bible in front of a church. He sowed discord and violence by calling on his perfervid supporters to "liberate Michigan" and other states that had imposed lockdowns during the first months of the pandemic when masks and vaccines were unavailable.

To the extent that he tried to carry out the agenda of his 2016 campaign, he lacked the support in official Washington or among Republicans in Congress. Trump had promised to rein in American multinationals and remove loopholes in the corporate tax code. In the Senate, however, Trump faced business Republicans concerned mainly with deregulating business and lowering taxes on business and the wealthy. As a result, his major legislative accomplishment would be the regressive Tax Cuts and Jobs Act of 2017, the proceeds from which corporations would use to increase their asset values and enrich their stockholders through stock buybacks, and which encouraged rather than discouraged companies to keep their capital abroad.

In the House of Representatives, Trump had to contend with Tea Party Republicans who had no interest in a huge infrastructure bill or in replacing Obamacare with a cheaper, more accessible national health-care program. Trump's own promise to repeal and replace the Affordable Care Act quickly fell by the wayside. He ended up supporting a bill merely to replace Obamacare, which failed because of the opposition from three moderate Republican senators. The Republicans' attempt to repeal rather than amend or improve Obamacare—imperiling, for instance, its guarantee of insurance to people with preexisting conditions—became a major issue for Democrats in the 2018 elections. Trump's character, his divisiveness, along with the Republican attempt to repeal Obamacare, doomed the House Republicans in the 2018 election.

Trump might still have won reelection based on the economy's performance, but when facing his first real challenge in office—the outbreak of the COVID-19 pandemic in early 2020—

he proved incompetent as a chief executive. Trump's behavior during that year became wildly erratic. He assured the public that COVID-19 was no more a threat than the usual winter flu. When it became clear that it was killing thousands, he promoted unproven and even crackpot remedies including the anti-malaria drug hydroxychloroquine and household bleach. He dispensed aid to states according to whether they supported his reelection hopes. Trump's failure became an overriding issue in the 2020 campaign and made him vulnerable to a Democratic challenger. The question was whether the Democrats could avoid the kind of political appeal that had doomed Clinton and earlier Democrats. They almost failed to do so, leaving longer-term questions about the party's future.

One Step Forward, Two Back

In the years leading up to the Democratic presidential elections, the Democrats did show that on one very important issue they had learned their lesson from past defeats. To the extent that a candidate like Clinton had still held illusions about the promise of globalization, few Democrats who took office in 2017 did so. Like Trump, they now saw China as an unfair competitor that threatened jobs rather than as an outlet for investment and trade. Democrats also abandoned the neoliberal faith in markets and aversion to government intervention. They favored what had been called an "industrial policy" to boost American industry and jobs through targeted government spending.

The Democrats also no longer fretted, as Obama officials had, about "entitlements" and deficit spending. They wanted to redo the tax code to end breaks for hedge fund operators and incentives for multinational corporations to invest abroad. When George W. Bush and the Republicans had introduced their regressive tax plan in 2001 that rewarded big business and the wealthy, twelve Democratic senators, a fourth of the caucus, had voted for it. Not a single Senate or House Democrat voted for the very similar Republican Jobs and Tax Cuts Act of 2017. Wall Street did continue to enjoy influence. In March 2018, seventeen Senate Democrats backed Trump and the Republicans' bill to water down the 2010 Dodd-Frank banking regulations. The bill was later blamed for the collapse of the Silicon Valley Bank five years later. But no one in the party's Senate leadership and no House Democrat backed the bill. Many Democrats were moving away from economics of Bill Clinton and Robert Rubin and his protégés.

But as the Democratic presidential candidates jostled in the two years leading up to the primaries and caucuses, it became clear that in other respects, the Democrats were determined to repeat mistakes they had made in the past. As Barack Obama and Bill Clinton had discovered, working- and middle-class voters were suspicious of big new programs that required higher taxes, even if it could be argued that they would benefit from them in the long run. In 2019, however, the seventy members of the House based Congressional Progressive Caucus (augmented by the arrival of four left-wing members, dubbed "the Squad") and fifteen Democratic senators backed Sanders's Medicare for All plan. The senators included four presidential candidates, including Kamala Harris and Elizabeth Warren. Sixty-three organizations from the Democrats' shadow party endorsed the plan.

Some experts in health-care economics have acknowledged that a single-player plan like Medicare for All would, if enacted, be superior to the cumbersome Affordable Care Act, which leaves citizens at the whim of private companies more concerned with profit than care, but establishing Medicare for All would have initially required very large tax increases, which would have been anathema to middle-income voters who already had insurance, and would have caused large dislocations in the health-care and insurance industries. Abstract polling (that didn't cite potential drawbacks) showed public support for Medicare for All, but when some Colorado Democrats, with Sanders's active support, put a single-payer plan on the state ballot for November 2016, the state's voters, leery of higher taxes, defeated it by 80 percent to 20 percent.

Many leading Democrats also endorsed a plan, put forward by Alexandria Ocasio-Cortez, the best-known member of the Squad, and Massachusetts senator Ed Markey for a "Green New Deal." By replacing fossil fuels with renewable energy in order to completely decarbonize the economy by 2030, Ocasio-Cortez and Markey contended, the Green New Deal would create "millions of good, high wage jobs" and "unprecedented levels of prosperity and economic security."

That, too, although highly implausible, won the immediate support of six future presidential candidates as well as a host of Democrat-leaning activist groups and think tanks. It became the cause célèbre of the party's shadow left. But voters were likely to fear the plan's price tag—$10 trillion by Ocasio-Cortez and Markey's estimate and $16.3 trillion by Sanders's estimate—and to doubt whether it would replace the jobs lost by the cessation of fossil fuel production. To them, it had the earmarks of a white and not a green elephant.

Many of the Democrats also drew the wrong lessons from Trump's unpopularity and from their own success in the 2018 House elections. The four left-wing congresswomen who formed the Squad had won seats in that election, but they were replacing Democrats in safe Democratic districts. The key victories that had brought the House back under Democratic control had come in suburban districts, where voters disliked Trump's callous bigotry and divisiveness but were not necessarily fans of Medicare for All and didn't necessarily support the shadow groups' social agenda on immigration, race, or gender.

Many voters, for instance, objected to the administration practice of separating the children of illegal immigrants or asylum seekers from their parents, but they wanted policies that would stem the tide of illegal immigration. Nonetheless, many Democrats joined Ocasio-Cortez and the shadow left in calling for the abolition of ICE, the agency for Immigration and Customs Enforcement, and for decriminalizing illegal border crossings. They denounced Obama for deporting illegal immigrants who had committed crimes.

Many of the Democrats also now backed the demand for a commission on racial reparations making its way in Congress. Within the shadow left, support for reparations grew and for policies that would, in effect, reinstitute racial quotas—dubbed creating "equity" rather than "equality"—in admissions and employment. In California in January 2019, Democrats sponsored a plan to put a proposition on the November 2020 ballot that would do away with the state's prohibition on using race, color, and national origin in school admissions and government policy. All the state's prominent Democrats backed the initiative.

Many of the Democrats' shadow groups and activists embraced the idea that America had a deep-seated problem of "systemic racism" or "structural racism" that underlay its other ills and required a frontal assault, even if that meant subordinating other concerns. In August 2019, the *New York Times* published a special issue titled "The 1619 Project." In its introduction, the magazine claimed that the American Revolution had been fought in order to preserve slavery and that "anti-black racism runs in the very DNA of this country."

The Shadow Party vs. Actual Voters

Fifty years ago, aspiring presidential candidates began campaigning at the earliest in the fall before the year of the elections, but since then, the presidential primary campaign has been moving back toward the beginning of the year before the elections. There is now a long pre-elections season centered around debates that are supposed to winnow down the field. In that period, the shadow Democratic groups have enormous influence over what the candidates say. The candidates worry about pleasing their donors, who in the case of some Democratic candidates like Hillary Clinton or Biden consisted of big money from Wall Street, Hollywood, or Silicon Valley, or in case of others, like Sanders and Warren, thousands, or even millions, of small donors who contribute over the internet.

Some of the shadow groups worry about winning in the final November elections, but some policy groups and lobbies are most interested in pleasing their own followers by pressing insistently for their pet causes, even if a candidate's support of those causes might risk his or her losing in the general election. The latter groups contributed to the candidates' willingness to back huge programs like the Green New Deal and to take radical stances on social issues. As a result, much of the Democrats' debates in 2019 were taken up with the candidates putting forth strong positions that put them at odds not only with the overall electorate but also with the ordinary voters of their own party.

A telling incident occurred in February 2019. A far-right website, angered by Virginia Democratic governor Ralph Northam's judicious refusal to ban all late-term abortions, exploited the Democrats' penchant for political correctness by reproducing a page from Northam's 1984 medical school yearbook that showed a photo of someone in a Klan costume standing next to someone in blackface. After a confused initial response, Northam denied that he was in the photo, but he was unable to explain how the photo got there and apologized for its existence.

In spite of the fact that the photo was thirty-four years old, and that Northam, as a pediatric neurosurgeon and public official, had done nothing that smacked of racism, Democratic activists and media clamored for his resignation. The NAACP, the ACLU, MoveOn, and Planned Parenthood called for Northam's resignation, as did the *Washington Post*. They were joined by *all* the leading Democratic presidential candidates. The furor began to subside, however, when the *Washington Post* conducted a poll that showed that by 58 percent to 37 percent, Virginia's black voters wanted Northam to remain in office. The incident bore out the yawning gap between the political priorities and moral judgment of the shadow Democrats and those of the actual electorate.

Most of the Democratic candidates advocated abolishing ICE and decriminalizing illegal border crossing. In a June 2019 debate sponsored by NBC, one of the moderators asked the ten candidates to raise their hand if their "government plan would provide healthcare to undocumented immigrants." Every Democrat raised their hand. Nine of ten candidates raised their hand to support "decriminalizing" border crossings. They also backed the Green New Deal and—until embarrassing questions about funding began to be raised in the fall—Sanders's plan for Medicare for All.

In the debates, the Democrats went out of their way to burnish their anti-racist credentials. California senator Kamala Harris attacked Biden for opposing school busing in Delaware in the 1970s, and several Democrats criticized Biden for supporting the 1994 crime bill, which two-thirds of the Black Caucus had endorsed. (The bill included an assault weapons ban, and its passage was followed by a decline nationally in crime rates.) Several presidential candidates, including Harris and Warren, also came out in favor of the commission to study racial reparations for slavery. Reparations, polls showed, had little support in the electorate, but the candidates were responding to pressure from groups that were not thinking of policies that would appeal to a majority in an election but were pressing their own priorities. (See chapter eight.)

In the 2020 primaries, Biden initially succumbed to political correctness and radicalism—he called for Northam's resignation and raised his hand in favor of providing government health care to illegal immigrants and decriminalizing border crossings—but after he was warned by House Speaker Nancy Pelosi that he was endangering his chances of defeating Trump, he began distancing himself from the other candidates' more radical stances. He argued that Medicare for All was not feasible and that the Green New Deal's goal of net zero carbon emission by 2030 was unrealistic. (He advocated the Paris Agreement objective of 2050, which is also unrealistic, but less so.) Biden defended Obama's deportation policies, rejected the demand to abolish ICE, and demurred on reparations. He ran primarily on his own electability. He led in the polls on that basis, but he had no support among the shadow Democratic groups that were at the forefront of the party's radicalism.

In early January 2020, the *New York Times*, which had become a key institution of the shadow party, ran its own "primary"—a televised interrogation of the candidates by the editors' staff, after which the staff convened to endorse a nominee. Warren and Minnesota senator Amy Klobuchar got the endorsement. In their statement explaining their endorsement, the editors dwelled on Sanders, businessman Andrew Yang, South Bend mayor Pete Buttigieg, and former New York mayor Michael Bloomberg as alternatives, and only at the end briefly dismissed Biden's candidacy.

They attributed Biden's lead in opinion polls to "familiarity as much as voter intention." In other words, voters were just choosing him because they had heard of him. His agenda, they complained, "tinkers at the edges of issues like national health care and climate." In other words, he doesn't have a plan for ending emissions in 2030 that will also create full employment. "What's more," the editors concluded, "Mr. Biden is 77. It is time to pass the torch to a new generation of political leaders." Their statement was dismissive not only of Biden but of the political impulses of ordinary Democrats. It, too, would bear out the gulf between the Democrats' shadow party and the electorate.

Biden stumbled in the first two caucuses (where activist groups had significant clout) and in the New Hampshire primary, where Sanders enjoyed favorite son status, but with Congressman James Clyburn's endorsement, he won the South Carolina primary easily and went on to win forty-five subsequent primaries. Sanders's backers credited Clyburn and Obama with engineering Biden's nomination, but what Biden's victory in South Carolina did was to reestablish his credibility as the most electable Democrat. And the voters were right. As Obama's vice president, he had the stature to compete with Trump. And unlike his leading rivals, he was not committed to radical programs that would divert voters' attention away from Trump's bilious character and his mishandling of the virus.

Biden vs. Trump

Soon after securing the nomination, however, Biden and the Democrats faced another challenge that could have easily derailed his election chances. The police killing of suspect George Floyd in Minneapolis in May, which was recorded in a video and circulated worldwide, sparked a summer of protests against police brutality that, as other instances of police brutality against black suspects occurred, spread nationwide, and descended into riots and mayhem. Small businesses, many of them minority owned, were burned down. Downtowns were ravaged. In two cities, Portland and Seattle, protesters took over the downtown. Black Lives Matter promoted the slogan "Defund the Police" as the central demand of the demonstrators, and a wide array of groups took up these demands. These included local politicians in several cities who actually voted to defund their police departments. The slogan became identified with the Democratic Party and with its candidates.

Groups and prominent individuals aligned with the Democrats also took up the idea, already expressed in key shadow Democratic publications and institutions, that America was a racist nation whose culture was dominated by "white supremacy" and "systemic racism." In the wake of the furor created by Floyd's killing, demonstrators toppled statues and renamed schools and buildings. They didn't limit themselves to Confederate generals but went after Thomas Jefferson, Theodore Roosevelt, and even Abraham Lincoln. It was as if in the minds of the young protesters, many of whom were college students who had had to spend the year away from school, the political plague of white supremacy and privilege had displaced the threat of COVID-19.

Biden was under pressure to embrace Black Lives Matter and its demands, but as he had done in the debates, he hewed a careful path between the Democratic activists (and the obvious injustice of Floyd's death) and the electorate, which was very divided about the protests, especially as they devolved into violent riots and became linked to a growing crime wave. He condemned the killing of Floyd and of other blacks and commended the protests as "a cry for justice," but he strongly condemned the violence and rejected the call for defunding the police. "Rioting is not protesting," Biden said in Pittsburgh on August 31. "Looting is not protesting. Setting fires is not protesting. None of this is protesting. It's lawlessness, plain and simple. And those who do it should be prosecuted."

Biden also rejected the activists' view of America as riven by racism. Instead, he promised to "restore the soul of America" and to re-create a "*United* States of America." He echoed the rhetoric of Obama's promise to bring the red and blue states, the Democrats and Republicans, together. Biden was determined to run against Trump's divisiveness and bigotry and his handling of the pandemic. He attacked Trump for botching the country's response to the pandemic. Trump, he charged, "has waved the white flag, abandoned our families and surrendered to this virus."

With the assistance of Trump, who under the shadow of the pandemic had become, in author Andrew Sullivan's words, like one of Shakespeare's mad kings, Biden succeeded in making the election a referendum on Trump's behavior and not on his own or his party's political views. He was probably the only one of the leading Democratic candidates who could have pulled it off. He was not a polarizing figure. He still bore his middle-class roots in Scranton. His father had been a car salesman. He was empathetic rather than cerebral. He still genuinely believed in a bipartisan America. He made a serious effort to dissociate himself from his party's cultural radicalism and bloated initiatives. When Trump tried to berate and bait him during their first debate, the audience sympathized with Biden, not Trump. In the end, many voted against Trump rather than for Biden, which in 2020 proved to be a winning formula.

The 2020 Election

Biden succeeded in winning the 2020 election, and the Democrats took back the Senate and retained the House, but in all these cases by the narrowest of margins. The Democrats also did little to reverse their decline among working-class voters or to bridge the Great Divide. Their greatest gains were among white college-educated voters, particularly men, who lived in the suburbs of the big metro centers. Their improved margins among them mostly accounted for Biden's victories in Georgia and Arizona, two crucial swing states, and solidified the Democrats' hold on Colorado and Virginia.

Biden's attacks against Trump's mishandling of the pandemic

and against his divisiveness showed in the results. In the exit polls, the 23 percent of these voters who said that the coronavirus was the most important issue preferred Biden by 85 percent to 14 percent over Trump. The 10 percent who said health policy was the most important preferred Biden by 86 percent to 12 percent. The 21 percent who looked for a candidate who could "unite the country" preferred Biden by 86 percent to 14 percent, and the 24 percent who wanted someone with "good judgment" preferred Biden by 64 percent to 35 percent.

As a result of his campaign's focus, and his own personal traits, Biden did reduce Trump's advantage among white working-class voters nationally by 2 points from 2016. These shifts, though small, helped Biden carry the key Rust Belt states of Michigan, Pennsylvania, and Wisconsin, but they were not enough to reverse Clinton's losses in Ohio and Iowa, two states that Obama had carried. Overall, too, Biden still lost these voters by 27 points. In interviews with these voters, we found special appreciation for Trump's trade policy and his rejection of "globalizers," whom these voters identified with the Democrats.

Contrary to expectations, Biden did not benefit from increased support among nonwhite voters in 2020. His margin among these voters actually declined by 11 points compared to Clinton in 2016. This included a 6-point decline among Black voters and, remarkably, a 18-point decline among Hispanic voters, with this decline being heavily concentrated among working-class voters.

Democratic Margin Shift, 2016–2020

Nonwhite	-11
Black	-6
Hispanic	-18

Source: Catalist, "What Happened in 2022 National Crosstabs,"
  May 2023, two-party vote.

There is no single explanation for Biden's and the Democrats' fading advantage among Hispanic voters. In Florida, the party's association with socialism—through Sanders, but also through the Obama–Biden renewal of relations with Cuba—particularly hurt it among Cubans and among Venezuelan immigrants. In South Texas, it suffered, too, from the association with socialism, but also from Tejano support for Trump's tough border policies, Democratic hostility to police and border agents, and Democratic support for eliminating oil and gas production. In some cities like Chicago, where Hispanic precincts shifted toward Trump, the voters might have been reacting to Democratic identification with black rioters and support for Defund the Police, which Hispanic voters nationwide overwhelmingly opposed. Overall, too, there seems to have been a feeling among many Hispanics that prior to the pandemic, the country had fared well under Trump and would do so again. Over half of Hispanic voters were very or somewhat confident in Trump's ability to make good decisions about economic policy.

Biden held his own from 2016 with Asian American voters probably at least in part from their feeling that through terms like the "Kung Flu" virus, Trump had encouraged anti-Asian sentiment. But there were signs of defection in congressional races in California and in other local races. Like Hispanics, Asian voters were concerned about public safety and rejected demands to defund the police. Asian voters in California, New York, and Virginia were also upset by the Democrats' support for aggressive affirmative action policies that would be at their expense, since in gifted and talented high schools and in top-tier colleges, they were enrolled at percentages well above their percentage in the population and would be harmed by the imposition of the kind of quota systems Democrats were supporting. Partly in reaction to this, Asian neighborhoods in New York City swung by double digits toward Trump in 2020. In California, Asians, as well as Hispanics, played a large hand in the defeat of the affirmative action referendum, which lost by 57 percent to 43 percent.

Democrats won a fifty-fifty tie in the Senate (which the vice president could break) after both Democratic candidates won a runoff in Georgia in January 2021. But without Trump's brazen intervention in the election, one of those Republicans, who came within a whisker of a majority in November, probably would have won, allowing the Republicans to retain control of the Senate. In Senate and House elections in closely contested states and districts where Trump did not intervene, Republicans were able to use the Democrats' identification with cultural radicalism against them. In South Carolina, Democratic Senate candidate Jaime Harrison was running ahead of incumbent Republican Lindsay Graham until Graham began running ads linking Harrison to demands to "defund the police." "Jaime Harrison started to plateau when 'defund the police' showed up with a caption on TV across his head," Clyburn said afterward. Congresswoman Abigail Spanberger, who represented a suburban Richmond, Virginia, district that she had won from a Republican Tea Partier in 2018, lashed out after the 2020 election. "Don't say socialism," Spanberger said angrily. "Don't say defund the police when that's not what we mean."

In all, the elections suggested that while the Democrats had succeeded in 2020 where they had failed in 2016, it was largely because of voters' attention to Trump's misdeeds. If the Republicans had run their own version of Biden, the results might have been very different. The Democrats had still not established their credibility as stewards of the economy. And the shadow party's attachment to cultural radicalism posed an extreme danger to the party, not only among the general electorate but among its own less ideological voters. As for Biden, he really had no mandate except not to be Trump. Like Warren Harding in 1920, he had run as the candidate promising a "return to normalcy." But with the pandemic still raging, and the economy still in arrears, and the culture war still being fought across the Great Divide, it was unclear, to say the least, what a return to normalcy would consist of.

Chapter Seven

Joe Biden's New
New Deal

Everything about Biden's earlier record as a senator and as vice president suggested that he would be a cautious president and would, like Obama in his first term, squander opportunities in a vain attempt, as he put it in his campaign, to end "the never-ending war between the parties." As a senator from Delaware, an affluent state with a predominately white electorate that had until 1992 tilted Republican, he had hewed carefully to the political center. He had been, for instance, one of the few Democrats to vote for a balanced budget amendment to the Constitution. A report from early in his campaign had strengthened that impression.

In June 2019, at a private meeting in New York, Biden had assured wealthy donors, who feared Sanders's and Warren's economic populism, that if he were elected president "no one's standard of living will change, nothing would fundamentally change." "I need you very badly," he said. But a year later, in May 2020, after Biden had already secured the nomination, he told former rival Andrew Yang privately that the country needed "a new New Deal." In accepting the nomination in August, Biden invoked Roosevelt publicly.

Nearly a century ago, Franklin Roosevelt pledged a New Deal in a time of massive unemployment, uncertainty, and fear. Stricken by disease, stricken by a virus, FDR insisted that he would recover and prevail and he believed America could as well. And he did. And so can we.

Biden had not emphasized economics in his fall campaign. He had appointed transition teams to develop policy as a sop to the left of Sanders and Ocasio-Cortez, but their proposals didn't make it into his campaign speeches or ads. He ran on "restoring the soul of America" and combating COVID-19, but in the economic statements Biden did make, he sounded more like Sanders and Warren than like the man who had assured Wall Streeters that nothing would change. He repeatedly invoked the Democrats' historic commitment to the average American. "Why should a firefighter, an educator, a nurse, a steelworker pay a higher tax rate, and this is the God's truth, a higher tax rate than the super wealthy?" he asked in one speech. "Folks, I believe we should be rewarding work not wealth in this country. Do you all realize that just as the pandemic started, the listed billionaires in America made another $300 billion? Not a joke, $300 billion they made in the middle of the pandemic," he said in the same speech.

Still, few, including ourselves, could have predicted that as president, Biden, with a tenuous majority in the Senate, would dare mimic what Roosevelt had done and try to create a "new New Deal." Yet that is what he tried to do. He broke sharply with the neoliberal economics of the Clinton and Obama administrations—the obeisance to balanced budgets, the reluctance to protect domestic manufacturing, the accession to business tax breaks, and the paeans to the global economy. He took a page from Trump's appeal and invoked economic policies that put America first. In contrast to Trump, who had turned the NLRB into a lobby for anti-union business, and even to his Democratic predecessors, he unabashedly supported labor unions. And as a former senator, he succeeded in securing some Republican support. He got Republicans to go along with two of his major initiatives—testimony to the value of electing a president with extensive legislative experience in Washington. Biden's initiatives were not without considerable flaws. They were hobbled by powerful industry lobbies who commanded loyalty from many Republicans and some Democrats. But his efforts represented a dramatic departure from Democratic policymaking and politics from Carter through Obama.

Industrial Strategy

In 1982, liberal economist Robert Reich, who would later serve as Clinton's secretary of labor, authored a controversial proposal for an "industrial policy" that would "favor business segments that promise to be strong international competitors while helping to develop the industrial infrastructure and skilled workforce to support those segments." It would also "defuse the resistance to economic change by balancing regional growth and by assisting workers to retrain and relocate." Reich's proposal was not anti-business, but it attempted to subordinate the priorities of individual companies to those of the national interest.

Reich's proposal was rejected by Reagan and the Republicans who were averse to government intervention in the economy; Clinton and Obama attempted to carry out small parts of Reich's program under another name but met resistance from Republican Congresses and business lobbies. Trump actually promoted something like an industrial policy but couldn't convince Republicans in Congress. With a 50 to 50 tie in the Senate that had to be broken by the vice president, Biden seemed to stand little chance of getting much accomplished, but he actually managed to make significant strides toward Reich's idea.

Biden and his advisers proposed what they called an

"industrial strategy." At a talk in Washington in May 2021, Brian Deese, the head of the White House National Economic Council (a position once occupied by Robert Rubin), outlined "a vision for a twenty-first-century American industrial strategy—a strategy to strengthen our supply chains [and] rebuild our industrial base across sectors, technologies, and regions of this country." Over the course of the next sixteen months, it was put into effect in three large bills that Congress passed—two with bipartisan support. The first was the Bipartisan Infrastructure and Jobs Act, which Biden finally signed in November 2021, after a lengthy delay caused by the House's Congressional Progressive Caucus that ended up diluting its political impact. It put money into roads, bridges, clean drinking water, ports and airports, trains, the expansion of broadband, and electrical transmission lines and charging stations—the kinds of internal improvements that government alone had to make but that previous administrations and Republican Congresses had balked at making.

In July 2022, Congress passed the CHIPS and Science Act. It triumphed in the Senate by 64 to 33. Reminiscent of earlier government funding for research and development, it was driven by national security concerns—in this case, by the threat of China rather than the Soviet Union. The program put $80 billion into promoting semiconductor production in the United States and $200 billion into science, technology, and workforce development, including $80 billion for the National Science Foundation. As the program neared passage, and then in the aftermath of its passage, major American semiconductor companies, including Intel and Micron, announced plant expansions in the United States, and Taiwan Semiconductor Manufacturing, the global leader, announced plans for two factories in the United States.

The misleadingly named Inflation Reduction Act—the name itself was a concession to West Virginia senator Joe Manchin—

was passed in September 2022 on a party line vote. It was designed to meet another need that the market could not accommodate on its own—the reduction in carbon emissions to ward off climate change. It was centered on tax credits to businesses for investing in clean energy, especially renewables and batteries, and to individuals who would buy electrical vehicles or green home improvements. The bill flouted objections from climate groups and encouraged existing nuclear energy plants and research in nuclear energy. S&P Global reported that in the wake of the bill's passage on August 16, "at least five major EV manufacturers and battery minerals suppliers, including Toyota Motor Corp., LG Energy Solution Ltd. and Piedmont Lithium Inc., have announced billions of dollars' worth of investments in the domestic production capacity encouraged by the legislation."

There were three features of these bills and of related White House actions that indicated clearly that Biden and the Democrats had learned something from the policy failures of the prior three decades. First, the bills had strong "buy America" provisions in them. As we noted, by the 1970s, America's post–World War II "free trade" strategy had begun to run aground in the face of competition from rebuilt economies in Japan and western Europe. Even after China had begun to take advantage of America's open markets and footloose multinational corporations, successive administrations had failed to do anything about the damage to American industry. Biden's "buy America" provisions were meant to revive American manufacturing. They appealed to an American nationalism and patriotism scorned by many of the shadow Democratic groups.

On taking office, Biden had signed an executive order, "Ensuring the Future Is Made in All of America by All of America's Workers," calling on the federal government to buy American-made goods. In his first two years, Biden signed three bills with "made in America" provisions. The infrastructure bill required that "all iron, steel, manufactured products, and construction materials used in covered infrastructure projects are produced in the United States." The Inflation Reduction Act limited tax credits to businesses that use American-made products and individuals who buy American-made goods—provisions that sparked protest from the European Union. And the CHIPS and Science Act was specifically focused on promoting semiconductor production in America and penalizing semiconductor production in China.

While allowing exceptions, Biden maintained the Trump administration tariffs on steel and aluminum imports, which the Trump administration had justified on national security grounds. The Chinese had complained to the World Trade Organization dispute panel about the U.S. use of a national security justification, and in December 2022, the WTO ruled in favor of the Chinese. The administration responded that the WTO dispute settlement process had "no authority" to review national security issues. "The Biden administration is committed to preserving U.S. national security by ensuring the long-term viability of our steel and aluminum industries." In other words, the United States would now manage its trade relations with China, which was the actual target of the tariffs, without reference to the WTO. Biden had repudiated the heart of the Clinton administration's trade strategy.

The second feature of the Biden bills was their attention to workers' wages. The infrastructure bill made federal aid for infrastructure projects contingent upon contractors paying the prevailing wage benefits under the Davis–Bacon Act, which protects construction workers and their unions from being underbid by nonunion contractors who had sometimes used low-skilled legal and easily exploitable illegal immigrant labor. The Inflation Reduction Act also required that in order to receive tax credits, businesses would have to adhere to Davis–Bacon.

Third, all the bills contained provisions that were intended to aid regions that had suffered from deindustrialization and the loss of mining jobs. As the Brookings Institution's Mark Muro, an economic geographer, noted, the CHIPs Act "contains numerous place-based programs aimed at combating the nation's uneven economic development. These spatially targeted initiatives seek to promote a more equitable geography of growth across the country." The act included $10 billion to create geographically dispersed technology and innovation centers. The Inflation Reduction Act contained special provisions for rural communities. The infrastructure bill included money to bring broadband to small towns and rural areas where private companies are unwilling to build. Like the administration's political appeal to "made in America," these measures recognized that a political and economic divide exists among Americans and attempted to do something about it.

Biden's policies addressed the damage that Democratic and Republican trade and free market policies had done to the country's industrial base, which had been highlighted by the supply-chain crisis provoked by the pandemic. In that respect, too, they addressed the political damage that deindustrialization had done to the older Democratic coalition. But Biden's efforts were only a down payment on the kind of policies that would be needed to close the divide economically and politically. Industry lobbies succeeded in convincing Republicans and some Democrats to weaken key provisions of the bills.

There were obvious steps not taken. In the original bills, Biden and leading Democrats had included tax reforms that would have discouraged more industries from leaving the country and incentives for companies to bring their factories back to the United States, but to get bipartisan support for the infrastructure and chips bills, Biden had to drop these provisions. To get fifty Democratic votes for the Inflation Reduction Act, the

Democrats had to excise a provision that would have removed a special tax loophole for hedge fund managers. Arizona senator Kyrsten Sinema, who was then a Democrat and had been heavily funded by financial lobbies, made the provision's removal the price of her vote.

Industry lobbies also succeeded in watering down provisions in the bills that barred companies from using federal subsidies to buy back and increase the price of their own stock. As Senator Warren pointed out in the Senate debate, the bills would not have prevented the companies from using the subsidies to free up other funds for stock buybacks. Even the provision of the Inflation Reduction Act that subsidized purchases of American-made electric vehicles contained a telling loophole that allowed companies to buy foreign vehicles and then lease them out.

All in all, Biden's foray into industrial strategy was just that. It was an important first step, but its limits reflected the degree that the decline of the labor movement had ceded ultimate control of American economic policy to business and financial lobbies. The Democrats had yet to carry out fully the principle that was at the heart of Reich's original concept—that in exchange for government assistance, the government will be able to require that these firms act in the public and national interest.

There is also a dangerous temptation latent in Biden's appeal for an industrial strategy. To the extent Biden succeeded in winning Republican support in the Senate, it was by focusing on the threat of China. In the case of the Chips Act, that focus, highlighted by the supply chain crisis during the pandemic, was certainly justified, but in the future, Democrats, in search of a bipartisan consensus on industrial policy, could be tempted to hype the threat of China to the detriment of broader foreign policy objectives.

Over the last two years of Biden's term, the administration is unlikely in any case to go beyond what it accomplished in the first two years. With the House back in the hands of Republican majority hostile to any government intervention in the market, it is doubtful that Biden and Democrats could get agreement on new initiatives. To take new steps, the Democrats would need to create an enduring majority.

The Labor President

The other part of Biden's industrial strategy was to encourage the countervailing power of unions. Biden said he intended "to be the most pro-union president leading the most pro-union administration in American history." In one sense, that is less hyperbole than one might think. Roosevelt was not an enthusiastic supporter of the National Labor Relations Act of 1935. It was a product of Senate liberals led by New York senator Robert Wagner and dubbed the Wagner Act. And Biden faced far greater obstacles than Roosevelt in actually promoting unions.

Biden's main means of aiding labor was by appointing a secretary of labor and a National Labor Relations Board sympathetic to unions. Biden appointed former Boston mayor and former union member and official Marty Walsh to be secretary of labor. Walsh was the first former labor official to serve in that position. And Biden stocked the NLRB with pro-union representatives. He appointed a former lawyer with the Communications Workers of America as its general counsel.

Under the Wagner Act, the NLRB had been designed to promote collective bargaining, but subsequent Republican administrations and Republican NLRB majorities had chipped away at its provisions and at labor's prerogatives. It regulated rather than promoted collective bargaining, and whether it did so on the side of labor or business depended on who appointed its majority. Even under Democratic administrations, the NRLB had been weakened to the extent that businesses had been able to resist unionization either by acting illegally and paying the minimal penalties or by tying NLRB decisions up in court. The AFL-CIO's main objective since the Carter years had been to reform labor law to prevent business from ignoring its rulings.

Under Carter, Democrats had almost passed labor law reform. Clinton had little interest in it, and Obama, pressured by his Chicago donors, had also given labor law reform short shrift, but under Biden, the House passed the PRO Act. Among other things, the act would have upped the penalties on companies for illegally firing labor organizers, cut short company delaying tactics, and repealed some provisions in the anti-labor Taft–Hartley Act. Because of Republican opposition, the Democrats were unable to get the 60 votes for it in the Senate to break a filibuster. But Biden's NLRB and its general counsel adopted rulings that began to accomplish what the PRO Act had intended. For instance, in December 2022, it passed a rule that raised the penalty that companies would have to pay workers that it fired illegally.

Biden also did what his Democratic predecessors had avoided. As Amazon workers in Alabama were voting on whether to unionize at an Amazon warehouse—a vote that ultimately failed—Biden released a video warning their employer that "there should be no intimidation, no coercion, no threats, no anti-union propaganda." In May 2022, he invited labor organizers who were trying to organize Starbucks and Amazon to the White House. While union leaders were delighted, Starbucks protested that Biden should have invited a representative from the company to the meeting. These were merely friendly gestures, but they sent a message that the guy in the White House was supporting the workers on picket lines. None of his Democratic predecessors had gone that far.

Some liberal pundits and labor historians criticized Biden and Walsh for getting Congress to enact as law the agreement they had helped negotiate between the twelve railway unions and management after four of the twelve unions had threatened to strike over the absence of paid sick leave. A retired labor official, who knew all the principals involved, described the contract, which eight of the unions had endorsed, as "the best recommendations" he had seen. If the unions had gone on strike in the weeks leading up to Christmas and paralyzed the economy, they and the labor movement would have incurred the public's wrath. Biden and Walsh did the labor movement a favor by preventing the strike.

But Biden's and Walsh's efforts on behalf of unions were thwarted by the power of the business lobbies over the Republican Party and some Democrats. A provision that would have required companies that received federal funds to maintain neutrality toward union organizing attempts was stripped out of the industrial strategy bills. Like Biden's attempts to bring American factories back home, his efforts to help revive the labor movement were hampered by the absence of organized power to counteract the strength of American business and its Republican allies. In his rhetoric and political appeal, Biden had turned a corner, but in practice, he was still waiting for the light to turn green.

Administration Failings

Some of Biden's other initiatives were less promising than these and contributed to voters' lack of approval of his presidency. Biden promised to improve dramatically upon Trump's handling of the pandemic, but his performance was erratic. He declared the pandemic over before it was over. Biden's Centers for Disease Control and Prevention (CDC) was slow to respond to new variants of the virus, and when it did, it offered confusing advice. His Health and Human Services Department failed to trace adequately the spread of the virus. Trump's one major contribution to fighting the virus had been his Operation Warp Speed, which funded the development of vaccines, but the Biden administration only belatedly, and at a much lower scale, funded the development of new vaccines.

The Biden administration's handling of the withdrawal from Afghanistan in the summer of 2021 dealt a large blow to his popularity by undermining the public's faith in the administration's competence, which had been an important selling point in the 2020 election. Biden also failed to improve on Trump's handling of the southern border crisis. While he actually retained Trump's measures, including Title 42, which allowed the United States to repel migrants on the grounds of a health emergency created by the pandemic, his and other Democrats' rhetoric on immigration encouraged a huge influx of illegal immigrants and asylum seekers. In 2021, 1.7 million migrants sought to cross the border illegally. From September 2021 through September 2022, it was 2.8 million, more than twice as high as during the height of Trump's presidency in 2019. In January 2023, Biden announced a plan to limit surging entrants from Cuba, Nicaragua, and Venezuela to thirty thousand a month who legally apply for asylum and enter through Mexico. Predictably, he was denounced by the shadow party's immigration lobbies. "The proposal is illegal and discriminatory," the Young Center, which is funded by large corporations and by Ford and other foundations, declared.

Biden tried to deal with his party's cultural radicalism the way Reagan had dealt with his party's when he took office in 1981. Biden consigned the most strident advocates to obscure White House offices and to assistant secretaryships where they might not attract public attention. But in 1981, there were no social media and websites tracking government doings, and the national press had little interest in what an assistant secretary of education was cooking up, but Biden has had to contend with Fox News,

Breitbart.com, and numerous websites and Twitter feeds that paid attention to these relatively obscure officials and their departments. In addition, the Democrats' shadow groups were ready to pounce on any administration attempt to draw lines against even the most egregious examples of this radicalism.

The administration also gave its critics ammunition. It incurred credible law suits from conservative legal groups when it announced policies that favored minority businesses in dispensing economic aid or that gave preference to "people of color" in receiving COVID-19 treatments. The administration strongly endorsed "gender affirmative care" for children, which can include drugs and surgery. Some Democrats had to answer for these initiatives during the 2022 elections, and Democrats will have to do so in 2024 as well. They represent the interjection of the shadow party groups' agenda into official party policy. What these groups advocate almost universally widens the Great Divide and alienates working-class voters that the Democrats need to reach.

The 2022 Midterms

Throughout much of 2022, Democrats in Washington feared that they would get routed in the midterm elections. Biden's approval ratings were about where Trump's had been before the 2018 midterms. But Biden didn't inspire the same visceral dislike as Trump did. Instead, he was seen as doddering and ineffective. In focus groups we witnessed, undecided or swing voters (for instance, those who had backed Trump in 2016 but Biden in 2020), when asked to describe Biden in a word or phrase, portrayed him as "old and slow," "old and needs to be stronger," "ineffective," "stuck in the past," "tucked away," and "lost his fastball."

Voters were in a sour mood over how inflation—which had been spurred in part by the administration's $1.9 trillion American Rescue Plan but was caused primarily by global supply chain blockages—was eating away at people's savings and earnings. People were worried about rising crime rates, which in some cases they blamed on activist demands to defund the police or eliminate cash bail, and many were critical of Biden for failing to control the country's southern border.

But three things happened that improved Democratic prospects. First, in key Senate and governor races, the Republicans nominated candidates who were inexperienced, who had been endorsed by Trump, and who shared Trump's conviction that the 2020 election had been stolen. These candidates—like the Tea Party candidates of 2010—repelled voters who were not Trump activists or hard-line Republican partisans. They conjured up images of chaos and disorder. Secondly, in June, the Republican-dominated Supreme Court overturned *Roe v. Wade* in the *Dobbs* decision, setting up battles over abortion rights in many states. Together, these two factors highlighted Republican extremism, allowing it to overshadow what would have been seen as Democratic incompetence or extremism and heavily influencing election outcomes. A third factor was that Biden and the Democrats were able to ward off charges that they "couldn't get things done" by passing two big bills, the bipartisan CHIPS and Science Act and the climate-oriented Inflation Reduction Act. Few in the public knew the details of these bills, but their passage helped dim the image of ineptitude that the chaotic withdrawal from Afghanistan had created. Biden's approval rating ticked upward on the eve of the election.

Together, these three factors turned what could have been a rout into a standoff. Democrats actually increased their functional margin in the Senate by one seat. Republicans did win back the House, but narrowly with a 222 to 213 margin. And Democrats gained 2 governorships. As *New York Times* analyst Nate Cohn has argued, Democrats won crucial races where "stop the steal" and abortion rights were major issues. These would include the races in Michigan and Pennsylvania. But Democrats lost races where these issues did not predominate, and where voters' doubts about Biden or about the party's cultural radicalism predominated. These included races in New York, Florida, and Texas.

As far as the future of the Democratic Party was concerned, there was little reassuring about the midterm results. Democratic success depended primarily on Republican extremism. The Democrats failed to stem or reverse the loss of working-class voters. In the overall House vote, the Republican margin among white working-class voters rose from 20 points in 2018 to 27 points in 2022, a 7-point swing against the Democrats. But the swing among *nonwhite* working-class voters was even larger, reducing the Democrats' advantage by 15 points between the two elections.

Overall, the Democratic margin declined by 11 points among Hispanics, 6 points among blacks, and 19 points among Asians between 2018 and 2022. Democratic losses among nonwhites

Democratic Margin Change, 2018–2022

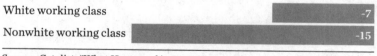

Source: Catalist, "What Happened in 2022 National Crosstabs," May 2023.

were about twice the size of losses among whites and losses among nonwhite working-class voters were about twice the size of losses among corresponding college-educated voters.

Biden's turn away from neoliberal economics and globalization, and his success on Capitol Hill, certainly helped the Democratic cause, but where abortion and "stop the steal" weren't the predominant issues, Democrats' cultural radicalism on race, crime, sex and gender, immigration, and the Democratic groups' apocalyptic fears of climate change continued to hurt the party's cause, particularly among working-class voters. In Wisconsin,

Democratic Margin Change, 2018–2022

Hispanic	-11
Black	-6
Asian	-19

Source: Catalist, "What Happened in 2022 National Crosstabs," May 2023.

an unpopular and vulnerable Republican incumbent, Senator Ron Johnson, was able to defeat his Democratic challenger by pointing to his challenger's support for defunding the police and eliminating cash bail.

In New York, the Democrats' identification with criminal justice radicalism crippled its candidates in the state, with the issue clearly contributing to the Democrats' stunning loss of four House seats. Statewide there was a big shift toward Republicans relative to 2020, with Republican gubernatorial candidate Lee Zeldin running 17 points ahead of Trump among black voters, 18 points ahead among Hispanic voters, and 34 points ahead among "other race" voters, a category that mostly comprises Asians.

In Iowa, which Obama had won twice, and whose congressional delegation had usually been equally divided between Democrats and Republicans, and whose statehouse periodically changed hands between parties, Republicans, campaigning against Democrats' support for defunding the police, inability to police the southern border, support for gun control, and radical views on gender and sex, swept the state. They won the top statehouses, increased their margin in the state legislatures, reelected one of their two Republican senators, and, perhaps most tellingly, ousted the one remaining Democratic House member. As late as 2019–20, Iowa's congressional delegation had been three Democrats and one Republican. Now it is four Republicans.

The Democrats' immigration policies continued to damage its

chances in Texas, where the Republicans once again easily swept all statewide offices. Democrats won the working-class Hispanic House vote statewide by only 6 points. Governor Greg Abbott, in defeating Democrat Beto O'Rourke, ran about 5 points ahead of Trump in 2022. He did even better than that among nonwhite working-class voters, running 15 points ahead of Trump across the state.

Democrats' policies on sex and gender hurt them in Florida. Governor Ron DeSantis, who has strenuously opposed these policies, won reelection in a romp, by 19 points, while Florida House Republicans carried the statewide popular vote by 19 points and picked up 3 seats. Democrats had assumed that Republicans' sponsorship of a law prohibiting instruction in gender ideology for K–3 children would wind up hurting them politically. Clearly it did not.

Democrats had also assumed that DeSantis's involvement in flying migrants to Martha's Vineyard would hurt him among voters, especially Hispanic voters. In fact, Florida Hispanics approved of both the Martha's Vineyard flights and the law restricting the teaching of gender ideology. That's one reason why DeSantis cleaned up among Hispanic voters, carrying Miami-Dade County by 11 points and Hispanics statewide by 13 points.

All told, DeSantis ran 16 points ahead of Trump in his 2022 gubernatorial race. Even more impressively, he ran 27 points ahead of Trump among nonwhite working-class voters. And he did 38 points better among nonwhite working-class voters in 2022 than he did in his initial 2018 gubernatorial race.

As Democrats look toward the 2024 election and beyond, there are a host of factors that could derail their attempt to win Congress and the White House. The public's perception of candidates' age, ability, and experience, the candidate's stated commitments and the candidate's skill as a communicator can all make a difference. In 2024, popular backing for multibillion-dollar support of the war in Ukraine could sour if the war itself drags on without resolution. But the Democrats' failure in Florida has to loom large in their estimation of their prospects. Democrats need only look at the Senate, House, and governor's races in Florida to see what could go wrong, and how the party's identification with cultural radicalism can turn a swing state into a solidly Republican one. We will explore this issue in the next part of the book.

Part II

Cultural
Radicalism

Chapter Eight

Race and Radicalism

In the 1960s, spurred by the Supreme Court's ruling in *Brown v. Board of Education* and the civil rights movement, the United States undertook what has been called a "second Reconstruction." Washington passed the Civil Rights Act of 1964, which forbade discrimination on the basis of race, color, religion, sex, and national origin, the Voting Rights Act of 1965, which required equal treatment of all voters, and the Fair Housing Act of 1968, which prohibited discrimination in home sales and rentals. This legislation, it was hoped, would bring the country closer to fulfilling Martin Luther King Jr.'s dream that his children "will not be judged by the color of their skin but by the content of their character." Over the next half century, however, Americans have heatedly debated whether these bills were sufficient to erase racial inequality and, if not, what else needed to be done.

This debate has often pitted reformers against radicals. In the late 1960s, the radicals won the spotlight, and in the last decade, a radical alternative has once again come to the fore. The leaders of Black Lives Matter and radical intellectuals conceive America as riven with "structural" or "systemic" racism that can only be combated through a sweeping anti-racism that ensures "equity" in wealth and power between blacks and whites. Like the radicals of the '60s, these groups and individuals do not envisage a society in which children "will not be judged by the color of their skin." Instead, they envisage a society in which racial and ethnic groups will have equal shares in the country. This radical view, which we consider to be divisive, has won the support of the major shadow Democratic Party institutions and enjoys support within the Biden administration.

Nationalists and Integrationists

In the sixties, in the wake of the civil rights acts, black intellectuals and political activists recapitulated the historic debate within the movement between integrationists and nationalists. On one side was the NAACP, which had been instrumental in securing *Brown v. Board of Education*, and which was determined to implement the 1960s legislation in order to end discrimination. When school integration stalled, it supported school busing. When companies and areas of employment appeared closed off to blacks, the NAACP supported affirmative action programs. The Johnson administration adopted this approach. It issued regulations requiring that federal contractors expand job opportunities for minorities. Johnson also undertook a "war on poverty" that was ostensibly aimed at the poor of all races and nationalities but was assumed to be of particular benefit to poor blacks.

On the other side was the Black Power movement of Stokely Carmichael's SNCC (Student Nonviolent Coordinating Committee), the Black Panther Party of Huey Newton, and Elijah Muhammad's Nation of Islam. The Black Power movement portrayed blacks as an oppressed colony within the United States. In their original program, the Panthers demanded that blacks receive free health care and full employment, be exempt from military service, and be freed from all jails and prisons. In 1969, James Forman, speaking for SNCC, demanded $500 million in racial reparations, and in 1972, Jesse Jackson's new organization, PUSH, demanded reparations in the form of a $900 million federal "freedom budget." The Nation of Islam demanded that the government carve out an African American nation-state. The Nation of Islam subsequently suffered splits, and the Panthers and SNCC disappeared. But the debate between the reformers and the radicals has recurred.

By the 1980s, it had become clear that the combination of the civil rights acts making discrimination illegal, the Johnson administration's war on poverty and targeted affirmative action programs, and school busing for integration had failed to eliminate racial inequality. A black middle class had grown, but so had an urban underclass that suffered from joblessness, broken families, drug addiction, and violent crime. "By many measures," Shelby Steele wrote in his 1990 book *The Content of Our Character*, "the majority of blacks—those not yet in the middle class—are further behind whites today than before the victories of the civil rights movement." The questions were why that had happened and what could be done about it. There were very different responses among intellectuals, politicians, and activists that would establish the parameters of debate in our time.

Some politicians and political theorists, mainly but not exclusively identified with Reagan conservatism, blamed blacks' failure to progress on a culture that devalued family, education, and work. (Comparisons to the ambition and achievement of Asian immigrants were rife.) While some liberals acknowledged that a culture of poverty had stymied blacks, they saw it as an enduring legacy of slavery and Jim Crow. Conservatives blamed the permissiveness of Johnson's War on Poverty and increased welfare benefits for fostering that culture. Charles Murray's *Losing Ground* became the ur-text blaming welfare; but in *The Bell Curve*, Murray and Richard Herrnstein later suggested that black failings may also be due to a lower average intelligence, some percentage of which might have a genetic basis—a view that echoed older southern arguments justifying slavery and then Jim Crow.

Some left-wing or social-democratic theorists brought a class analysis to bear on continuing racial disparities. They included Robert Allen, Harold Baron, Cornel West, Adolph Reed, and William Julius Wilson. Wilson, a University of Chicago sociologist, was the key figure. In *The Declining Significance of Race* and *The Truly Disadvantaged*, he located rising racial inequality in the emergence of an inner-city underclass. He recounted how economic factors had contributed to the rise of this desiccated underclass.

During the seventies, Wilson wrote, economic and demographic trends converged to create an underclass. Many blue-collar industries, in search of lower wages from a nonunion workforce and less regulation, and wary of the ghetto riots that had shaken major northern cities in the '60s, began moving out of the cities to the suburbs or the South or overseas. In the cities, working- and middle-class blacks, many of whom had begun to benefit from the Second Reconstruction, moved to integrated neighborhoods and to the suburbs, while the ranks of low-income, less educated blacks were swelled by the continued migration from the South of black farmworkers, who had at best a high school education, and who had been displaced by the mechanization of southern agriculture. As the industries moved out, blacks who remained in the inner city had difficulty finding employment. They also faced social and cultural isolation. In the past, the black working and middle classes had "reinforced and perpetuated mainstream patterns of norms and behavior." Its departure to the suburbs contributed to the breakdown of these communities.

What Wilson saw happening in black inner cities was very similar to what would happen later to white working-class communities that suffered from deindustrialization and from the subsequent loss of a cohesive culture centered around neighbor-hood, school, church, union hall, and local pub. In both cases, economic loss fostered a self-destructive culture, which in turn would lead to additional economic loss. Wilson rejected explanations that put the blame entirely on racism for the continued plight of the inner cities. "One does not have to 'trot out' the concept of racism to demonstrate, for example, that blacks have been severely hurt by deindustrialization because of their heavy concentration in the automobile, rubber, steel, and other smoke-stack industries," he wrote.

In line with this class analysis, Wilson rejected affirmative action as a blanket solution to racial inequality. "The race-specific policies emanating from the civil rights revolution, although beneficial to more advantaged blacks (i.e., those with higher income, greater education and training, and more prestigious occupations), do little for those who are truly disadvantaged," he wrote. Wilson was also critical of the approach of the War on Poverty, which, he charged, had incurred political opposition because, unlike the universal programs of the New Deal, it had required middle-class taxpayers to fund programs from which they would not receive any benefit. Instead, he urged government policies that would promote full employment and higher wages, along with universal childcare and family allowance programs. These programs, he argued, would ease the burden of inner-city families without provoking a racial backlash. Criticized for offering "conservative" remedies for poverty, Wilson responded, "I am a social-democrat."

Some politicians, activists, and academics attempted to revive the radicalism of the sixties black power movement. They rejected Wilson's class analysis. They argued that *Brown v. the Board of Education*, the Civil Rights Acts, and affirmative action, which the Supreme Court had circumscribed in its *Regents of the University of California v. Bakke* ruling, had failed to dislodge an underlying racism that affected all blacks. They called this racism "systemic," or "structural." This racism, which was often invisible except to its victims, accounted for the failure of blacks to achieve social and economic equality with whites. It was the reason for cultural deformations and for the growing wealth gap. They called for aggressive affirmative action and reparations.

One important source for this radicalism came from law students and professors who created what they called "critical race theory" or CRT. Its guiding light was Harvard law professor Derrick Bell who argued that major civil rights reforms—from the Fourteenth and Fifteenth Amendments through *Brown v. Board of Education* and the Civil Rights Acts—had occurred not because of concern about black inequality but because whites believed these measures were in their interest. When and if whites failed to see themselves benefiting, they withdrew their support. According to Bell's theory of interest convergence, the Supreme Court had passed *Brown* in order "to counteract the reports of segregation and lynching that received international attention, particularly in the media dominated by communist governments." Bell believed that racism or white supremacy was a permanent fixture of American life. It was an "ideology" that "made poor and working-class whites feel better about their plight" and that the law implicitly recognized. Whiteness, Bell wrote, was a "property right."

In the 1980s, law students, influenced by Bell, developed CRT. They charged that the "civil rights establishment" had ignored the "systemic" roots of racism, which dated from slavery, and which had penetrated American laws and institutions and had made it impossible for blacks to advance. One of CRT's founders, Kimberlé Williams Crenshaw, described blacks' situation at the end of the twentieth century as "American apartheid." The CRT proponents charged that blacks were being denied faculty appointments, school admissions, and employment because of purportedly race-neutral criteria that assessed merit. Referring back to the sit-ins to desegregate lunch counters, Crenshaw wrote that the law students "saw meritocracy as the new lunch counters in the struggle over law, knowledge, and power." The CRT proponents, who were law students at elite schools or junior professors, muted any class differences between the effect of racism on them and on blacks in Chicago's far south side where Obama had tried to organize.

The abiding assumption of racial radicalism was that any ill effects or lack of achievement suffered by blacks was the result of systemic racism that had infected American institutions. In 1998, University of California at Santa Cruz professor Angela Davis, a former Communist, founded Critical Resistance, a group devoted to the abolition of the prison system and the transformation of criminal justice. "We work to prevent people from being arrested or locked up in prison," the group's statement read. Davis and her fellow radicals described themselves as "abolitionists," implicitly comparing their opposition to the racism of the late twentieth century to the opposition to slavery. In *Are Prisons Obsolete?*, Davis described the prison system itself as racist. "Racism surreptitiously defines social and economic structures in ways that are difficult to identify and thus are much more damaging," she wrote. Davis's analysis would become adopted by the leaders of Black Lives Matter.

During this same time, black politicians and activists also revived the call for reparations. In 1987, the National Conference of Black Lawyers and two other groups formed the National Coalition of Blacks for Reparations in America. In 1994, they assembled an all-star cast in Detroit, including Jackson, Representative John Conyers, and Nation of Islam leader Louis Farrakhan, to endorse its demand for reparations and Conyers's bill to set up a congressional commission to "study and develop reparations

184   Where Have All the Democrats Gone?

proposals." In 2000, TransAfrica founder Randall Robinson, who had earlier led the battle to impose sanctions on South Africa for its apartheid policies, endorsed the demand for reparations in *The Debt.*

The conservative approach to racial equality, stressing flaws in black culture traceable to liberal permissiveness, would continue to be influential among Republicans. Wilson the social democrat would receive awards for his books on the economic roots of race relations, but his proposal for labor market strategies that would stem deindustrialization was ignored by subsequent Democratic administrations. Clinton and George W. Bush's neoliberal trade and investment policies would accelerate the flight of manufacturing jobs from inner cities and from small towns and midsize cities, deepening the plight of inner cities, and create what Trump would provocatively call "American carnage." And Wilson's books would disappear from bookstore shelves devoted to race. (The second edition of *The Truly Disadvantaged,* which appeared in 2012, ranks 656,841 in sales on Amazon's site.)

Critical race theory enjoyed popularity among education schools, ethnic studies departments, as well as law schools. In what would become a standard work, *Critical Race Theory: An Introduction,* law professors Richard Delgado and Jean Stefancic wrote in 2001, "Although CRT began as a movement in the law, it has rapidly spread beyond that discipline. Today, many in the field of education consider themselves critical race theorists who use CRT's ideas to understand issues of school discipline and hierarchy, tracking, controversies over curriculum and history, and IQ and achievement testing." But its influence, and that of its underlying perspective, was largely confined to education, where it fueled disputes about tracking and entrance exams, and to ethnic studies departments and law schools. That, of course, would change in the coming decades.

BLM and Defund the Police

In the second decade of the twenty-first century, the radical outlook burst forth. It helped to frame the politics of the huge national and even international protests against police brutality that began in 2014 and reached an apogee in 2020. Its exponents wrote bestsellers. The radical outlook claimed that racism was the fundamental schism in American life. and that every policy or initiative had to be judged on whether it was racist or anti-racist. "There is no such thing as a nonracist or race-neutral policy. Every policy in every institution in every community in every nation is producing or sustaining either racial inequity or equity between racial groups," Ibrahim X. Kendi, one of the most influential new thinkers, wrote.

Why did this radicalism burst forth in the 2010s? It was directly sparked by the killing of Trayvon Martin and the police killings of Eric Garner in Staten Island and, particularly, Michael Brown Jr. in Ferguson, Missouri, in the summer of 2014 and by a spate of police killings and shootings of blacks in 2020, most notably the death of George Floyd in 2020 in Minneapolis. But of course there had been police killings of black people before that had not sparked months of demonstrations or a turn toward political radicalism among whites as well as blacks. There were four features of the time that contributed to the spread of racial radicalism.

First, young black intellectuals and activists had begun to achieve prominence in major publications, organizations, and foundations. Ta-Nahesi Coates had become a staff writer at the *Atlantic*; Nikole Hannah-Jones had been hired by the *New York Times*; Michelle Alexander was a professor at Stanford Law School; Isabel Wilkerson was on the faculty of Emory University and then Boston University; Keeanga Yamahtta Taylor was at Princeton; Kendi was at American University, soon to join Boston University to head up a richly endowed Center for Antiracist Research; Darren Walker was president of the Ford Foundation; Maurice Mitchell became director of the Working Families Party. They had influence over public opinion that earlier generations may have lacked.

The second factor was ferment among the college-educated young reminiscent of the sixties. It had been fueled by the War in Iraq and by the Great Recession, and then by Trump's presidency. It attracted young whites even more than young blacks or other minorities. In his book *Woke Racism*, University of Columbia linguistic professor John McWhorter described the anti-racist fervor among young whites as "the new birth of a new religion." It was an attempt, McWhorter argued, to create what New England parishioners had called a community of the "elect" or of "visible saints," whose predestined salvation was manifested in their irreproachable behavior. Or you could turn McWhorter's argument around and say that the absence of conventional religion and of expected economic opportunity had created among the college-educated young a search for identity, lifestyle, and salvation that had led some into a moralistic radical politics.

The third factor was the ubiquity of social media, which allowed a video of Floyd being killed to circulate worldwide. It created a global virtual community of protest. And the fourth factor, which contributed in 2020 to the prolonged outbreak of violence—from the ransacking of downtowns to the toppling of statuary and the siege of police stations—was the conjunction of the prospect of Trump's reelection and the pandemic. Trump's extremism provoked extreme responses. And the pandemic shaped these responses. By raising the fear of infection and death, the pandemic induced a desire to escape isolation and anxiety by submersion into mass protests. The demonstrations mixed joy and anger, partying and protest. The fears created by the pandemic, like those aroused the September 11 attack and the anthrax scare, also encouraged a moral absolutism, a division of the country into good and evil. These kind of sentiments affected the right as well as the left, and led to the January 6, 2021, "stop the steal" riots by pro-Trump demonstrators as well as prolonged violence in cities like Portland and Seattle.

The group at the forefront of the protests was Black Lives Matter. The massive protests against George Floyd's killing in May 2020 were spontaneous, but as the protests grew, Black Lives Matter members became organizers and spokespeople who defined the objectives of the protests, most notably the demand to "defund the police." The group grew to forty chapters and even established organizations in Europe. It played an important role in dramatizing police injustice toward black people, but the group's unrelenting hostility to the police and the descent of the protests into looting, arson, and violence ended up alienating many Americans.

Alicia Garza, Patrice Cullors, and Opal Tometi, who described themselves as "radical black organizers," were part of the college-educated young living in the Bay Area and associated with the arts and politics. They introduced the idea of "black lives matter" as a Twitter hashtag in the wake of George Zimmerman being acquitted in 2013 for killing Trayvon Martin. John A. Powell, a professor of law and African American Studies at the University of California, Berkeley, and adviser to activist groups, told us that he had warned the organizers that their slogan would invite the question from whites and other minorities "What about *our* lives?" Powell had suggested "Black Lives Matter, Too," but the organizers were insistent on "Black Lives Matter." Then in September 2014, as protests had begun against the shooting of Michael Brown in Ferguson, and as protesters were increasingly invoking the slogan "black lives matter," Cullors and Darnell Moore organized "freedom rides" from around the country to the protests.

In December 2014, the three women created an organization,

the Black Lives Matter Global Network, and an umbrella group, the Movement for Black Lives, that included the new Black Lives Matter chapters and a score of smaller groups such as BYP100 (Black Youth Project 100) and the Million Hoodies Movement. The Movement for Black Lives held a convention in July 2015 to hammer out a platform. This platform, which was issued the next year and was subsequently refined, became the definitive statement of the new radicalism.

The organizers stressed their links to the Black Power movement of the sixties and the Black Panther Party, but they also drew on new cultural trends on gender and sexuality. "We are intentional about amplifying the particular experience of state and gendered violence that Black queer, trans, gender nonconforming, women and intersex people face," the preamble stated. Following in the path of Davis's Critical Resistance, the group demanded defunding of the police and "an end of public jails, detention centers, youth facilities and prisons as we know them." The platform demanded the federal government create a new welfare system specifically for black people. It would include a "guaranteed minimum livable income" for black people, "full and free access for all black people" to higher and technical education, and "corporate and government reparations" that would provide health care and access to "food sources, housing and land."

The program's language and political approach put it on the very fringes of American politics. How many Americans had a clear idea, especially in 2015, of who "queer," "gender nonconforming," and "intersex people" were? Its demands drove a wedge between blacks and everyone else by insisting the latter pay for a sumptuous welfare state that only blacks could enjoy. And its demands for an end to the criminal justice system, if taken seriously, would have struck fear in the hearts of most

Americans, including black Americans, who would have justifiably worried about their public safety.

But in spite of their fringe radicalism, Black Lives Matter and its offshoots won enthusiastic support from liberal organizations, wealthy donors, and liberal foundations. In October 2015, the Democracy Alliance, an organization of liberal Democratic multimillionaires and billionaires, including George Soros and Tom Steyer, recommended that its members fund the groups of the Movement for Black Lives. Soros's Open Society Foundation gave the groups $33 million. In July 2016, the Ford Foundation joined forces with the Borealis Philanthropy to launch a six-year fundraising project aimed at providing $100 million for the Movement for Blacks Lives. "We'll provide long-term support for the Movement for Black Lives so that these visionary leaders and organizations can continue to cultivate and maintain a movement of young black women and men who are pushing through established boundaries as they seek to realize the promise of equality and justice for all," Ford's statement said.

Black Lives Matter chapters played a leading role in many of the protests that took place in 2020. These protests began peacefully, but descended into looting and anti-police violence. According to insurance estimates, the protests against George Floyd's killing led to $2 billion in damage. That included many small businesses that were burned down. Over the summer of 2020, there were 10,000 arrests. Some BLM leaders tried to calm the protests, but others did not. Interviewed during the August riots in Chicago, a Black Lives Matter leader defended the looting "100 percent. That's reparations." But donations continued to pour into the organization—$90 million in the wake of the Floyd killing.

By the end of 2020, the Black Lives Matter Global Network,

now renamed the Black Lives Matter Global Network Foundation, was awash in money. Some money came from small donors, but Black Lives Matter also got donations from Amazon, Gatorade, Intel, Microsoft, and other major corporations. The next year, however, some local chapters and organizers began to question what the foundation, run by Cullors, was doing with the money. Investigative reports from *New York* magazine and the *Washington Examiner* charged that the foundation had secretly bought a house for $6 million in October 2020 whose function did not appear to be clear. The foundation had also made large payouts for services to Cullors's brother, the father of Cullors's child, and a board member. Amazon suspended the group's online fundraising operation. So did the states of Washington and California, but they relented after a few weeks, and the group continued to raise money and to enjoy support among young people for its cause.

Reparations and White Fragility

While Black Lives Matter groups were protesting police violence, a group of intellectuals were writing widely read and highly acclaimed essays and books that refined and advanced the radical arguments that black power advocates and critical race theorists had made decades before. These writings suggested that racism was pervasive and the singular cause of blacks' lack of social and economic progress and that the eradication of racism required whites' abandoning their conscious and unconscious racism and agreeing to reparations and aggressive affirmative action. Three of the key proponents of the radical outlook were Coates, Kendi, and Robin DiAngelo. And the key institution publicizing this outlook was the *New York Times*.

In 2014, Coates, the son of a former Black Panther Party member from Baltimore and a powerful stylist, published "The Case for

Reparations" in the *Atlantic*. Like the critical race theorists, Coates saw whatever ills had befallen blacks as the result of a "trenchant racism" that was a legacy of black enslavement. "The criticism of black family structures by pundits and intellectuals, ring hollow in a country whose existence was predicated on the torture of black fathers, on the rape of black mothers, on the sale of black children," he wrote. For Coates, racism was not only embedded in institutions but in basic patterns of thought. Reparations would require, Coates wrote, a "revolution in consciousness."

Coates's case for reparations was based on viewing America's blacks as victims of their slave and Jim Crow past. He chided whites for thinking that the past could be overcome. "It is as though we have run up a credit-card bill and, having pledged to charge no more, remain befuddled that the balance does not disappear. The effects of that balance, interest accruing daily, are all around us," he wrote. He described whites as naively believing that "if you stab a black person 10 times, the bleeding stops and the healing begins the moment the assailant drops the knife." Columbia University linguist John McWhorter said of Coates's argument, "He writes as if it is 1950," but a panel of judges from NYU's School of Journalism later named "The Case for Reparations" the top work of journalism for the decade.

Kendi published *How to Be an Antiracist* in late 2019 on the eve of the protests. It became an bestseller and made the author a celebrity on the public speaking circuit commanding fees of $25,000. Kendi's argument boiled down to a few assertions about race. First, racism pervades all institutions in America. Secondly, policies and ideas that affect institutions are either racist or anti-racist. There is no non-racist in between. Third, to eliminate racism, policies have to discriminate on behalf of blacks against whites. "The only remedy to racist discrimination is antiracist discrimination," Kendi wrote. It was a brief for aggressive affirmative action—racial preferences—in all areas of life.

Kendi, drawing on what the critical race theorists had written about school admission and meritocracy, advanced a program for racial proportionality. If blacks were not represented in desirable schools or jobs proportional to their percentage of the population, the institution or practice was racist. If they were overrepresented—for instance, in the number of black students a school district suspended or the number of criminals incarcerated—then the institution was racist. If a seemingly objective measure—such as an SAT test or a law against drug sales—resulted in the disproportional representation of blacks, then it was racist. Kendi used the term "equity" rather than "equality" to describe the desired proportional result. "A racist policy," he wrote, "is any measure that produces or sustains racial inequity between racial groups." Kendi's political formulations were ludicrously simple, but they resonated, as did his use of the term "equity." "Equity" became the accepted buzzword to describe equality of outcome rather than opportunity.

Robin DiAngelo, an obscure education professor at Westfield State University, published *White Fragility* in 2018. Like *How to Be an Antiracist*, it became an instant bestseller and turned DiAngelo into an A-list consultant to schools and corporations. DiAngelo argued that white people had a "white frame of reference" and a "white worldview" that "rationalizes racial hierarchies as the outcome of a natural order resulting from either genetics or individual effort or talent." In other words, she attributed to all white people a Jim Crow view of black people. Whites may not even be conscious of this racism, she wrote, and what DiAngelo proposed to do was to make them conscious of their "racist patterns."

The most important institutional affirmation for this racial radicalism came from the *New York Times*. In August 2019, the *New York Times Magazine* devoted an entire issue to "The 1619 Project," conceived, edited, and introduced by a staff reporter,

Nikole Hannah-Jones. The newspaper claimed that the project would demonstrate that 1619, when the first slave ship arrived, and not 1776, when the colonies declared their independence, was "our true founding." In her introduction, Hannah-Jones argued that "one of the primary reasons colonists decided to declare their independence from Britain was to protect the institution of slavery." The project's underlying argument was that white supremacy over blacks was the fundamental fissure in American history that has affected "every aspect" of the country's history and life.

Scores of historians cried foul. Jones's contention about the American Revolution, as numerous historians subsequently pointed out, was based on a misreading of history. Two sets of prominent scholars published open letters criticizing the project's contention about the founding and the American Revolution as well as its derogation of Abraham Lincoln. Another scholar revealed that she had been asked to assess the project's claims, and had expressed reservations about its thesis, but that her doubts had been ignored. The magazine quietly, and without the usual acknowledgment, then fudged its claims. The line about "our true founding" disappeared from the web version. The protection of slavery became the revolutionary motive of "some colonists." But in spite of these errors, which cast doubt on its basic thesis, the Pulitzer Committee awarded a Pulitzer Prize to Jones for her essay. If Hannah-Jones had been a newspaper reporter who had written a shocking exposé of Wall Street machinations, and if it had turned out that she had muffed a central premise of her story, it is doubtful that she would have gotten a Pulitzer. The award reflected the degree that racial radicalism had taken hold among the country's media establishment. The *Times* itself was unfazed by the errors. It put out "The 1619 Project" as a book, which it intended to distribute to schools, and it became a bestseller.

The Institutions Comply

During the last decade, the racial radicalism championed by Black Lives Matter and by Coates and other prominent intellectuals had a huge impact. Its biggest impact was probably on education, where it extended the influence of critical race theory. Many schools and universities bought into Kendi's and CRT's theories about proportionality and meritocracy. Universities including the California state system dropped standardized tests as a criterion for admission. Magnet high schools such as San Francisco's Lowell, New York's Stuyvesant, and Fairfax County's Thomas Jefferson came under attack, and in some cases watered down their admission requirements often at the expense of Asian Americans. School districts hired newly minted experts in equity to reshape their admissions, their curriculum, and discipline rules. In Virginia's Loudon County, an outfit named the Equity Collaborative called for the creation of a nonwhite Equity Ambassador to police the student body and teachers and cautioned against using terms like "color-blind."

Universities, private corporations, and nonprofits enlisted "Diversity, Equity, and Inclusion" officers and their communications staff to put out language guides that would avoid any hint of racist speech. People were advised not to use any words that included "white" or "black" or "brown," including "blacklisting," "blackbox," "brownbag" lunches, "white hat hacker," and "white" papers. The term "master" could not be used in any context. Nor could "grandfather" (which, according to a Stanford guide, "had its roots in the 'grandfather clause' adopted by southern states to deny voting rights to Blacks.") Most significant of all, perhaps, the term "black" was now to be capitalized as "Black," suggesting that blacks were a national group similar to the "French" or the "Chinese" in conformity with the radical nationalism being espoused by Kendi and others. The capitalization of "black" summed up the radicals' abandonment of King's goal of transcending racial division—not as a means to ignore current racial discrimination but as a long-term objective—and its replacement by a fractious racial nationalism.

Employees, teachers, professors, and journalists who dissented from the prevailing radicalism—for instance, by criticizing affirmative action programs or Black Lives Matter itself or simply by using the wrong words—were punished and sometimes fired. One of the most telling examples occurred at the *New York Times*. In June 2020, in the wake of the protests turning violent, the *Times* published an op-ed by Arkansas Republican senator Tom Cotton advocating that if the local police were overwhelmed, the federal government should send in the military to quell the riots. In his op-ed, Cotton drew a distinction between "law-abiding protestors" and "rioters and looters." Staffers at the newspaper, including Hannah-Jones, called for the newspaper to retract the op-ed, even though the piece was by a United States senator and expressed a commonly held position among Americans and had been published in a section of the newspaper devoted to airing different opinions. In response, editorial page editor James Bennet was forced to resign, his deputy was demoted, and the newspaper published an apology to readers for having printed the article without demanding "further substantial revisions."

In January 2021, the *Daily Beast*, a website eager for clicks, reported that veteran *New York Times* reporter Donald McNeil Jr., who was leading the *New York Times'* coverage of the pandemic for which he and the paper would win a Pulitzer Prize, had once been disciplined for using the "n-word" to a group of prep schoolers whom, at the paper's urging, he had supervised on their trip to Peru in 2019. Even though McNeil had used the term purely illustratively as an example of what someone should not say, he was disciplined at the time after one of the teenagers complained. The *Daily Beast's* story provoked another outburst of racial radicalism at the newspaper that resulted in McNeil being forced to resign for using a term that the paper itself had used in its pages in the same manner.

Similar incidents were legion at Ivy League universities, publications of great and small standing, businesses, and foundations. At the Poetry Foundation in Chicago, a major player in the world of literature, its president and board chair were forced to resign because the foundation's statement that it "stand in solidarity with the Black community, and denounce injustice and systemic racism" was deemed "worse than the bare minimum" in an open letter by 30 poets and 1,800 supporters. At the *Philadelphia Inquirer* in June 2020, the editor was forced to resign after he headlined a story about Philadelphia's architecture, "Buildings Matter, Too." The paper issued an apology that read, "The headline offensively riffed on the Black Lives Matter movement, and suggested an equivalence between the loss of buildings and the lives of black Americans. That is unacceptable."

Democratic administrations also took up the new radicalism. In criminal justice, city governments were pressured to cut police budgets, and some major cities, including Portland, Seattle, San Francisco, and New York, complied. City officials and newly elected district attorneys, including San Francisco's Chesa Boudin, advocated a relaxation of arrest and imprisonment rules that they claimed unfairly discriminated against blacks and other minorities. Several cities and counties, including Maryland's Montgomery County, removed a police presence from schools. (After a shooting at a high school, the Montgomery County Council reinstated the police presence.) In the District of Columbia, the city council passed over the mayor's veto a revision of the district's criminal code that would *reduce* the penalties for carjackings (which had become rife), burglaries, and robberies. The district's revision, cheered by shadow party groups like the foundation-backed Justice Policy Institute, reaffirmed the old charge that "progressives" are more sympathetic to criminals than to their victims.

The federal government also got into the act. Upon coming into office, the Biden administration issued an "Executive Order for Advancing Racial Equity." Part of the agenda consisted in enforcing civil rights laws against discrimination—ensuring equal opportunity—but other parts suggested that the administration would favor blacks and other minorities over whites even if the latter had suffered as greatly from the aftermath of the Great Recession and from the pandemic. Over the next months, the administration did exactly that in orders it issued giving special preference to minority small business owners generally, restaurant owners, farmers, and infrastructure contractors. The Food and Drug Administration (FDA) also issued guidance giving minorities special preference in receiving scarce treatments for COVID-19. The FDA's guidance was echoed by a number of states, including New York.

The Backlash

Republican politicians, Fox News, the Manhattan Institute, and various right-wing websites made the most of Democrats' identification with racial radicalism and the violent protests. They grouped all the various ideas about racial justice under the rubric of CRT. In September 2020, Trump issued an executive order barring federal agencies from funding any training in "Critical Race Theory" or "white privilege." Over the next two years, numerous states and counties barred teaching critical race theory. In the Senate, Republicans, including Minority Leader Mitch McConnell, introduced a bill withholding federal funding from any school that taught *The 1619 Project*.

Democrats rightly warned that Trump's and McConnell's

initiatives could be used to discourage any discussion of racism, but they also dismissed the claims against CRT and the protesters out of hand. It was the Fox News Fallacy. If right-wing sites charged X, then there can be no basis whatsoever for X. American Federation of Teachers president Randi Weingarten stated unequivocally that "critical race theory is not taught in elementary schools or high schools. It's a method of examination taught in law school and college." (As we noted, well before the protests over George Floyd, CRT advocates like Delgado and Stefancic had boasted of the doctrine's influence on educators.) Liberals also insisted that the demonstrations had been peaceful. A study from the Crowd Counting Consortium, by treating every protest, even the tiniest, as a separate event, reported that the protests "were overwhelmingly peaceful." But the damage inflicted by the protesters on downtowns was readily visible in many of the larger cases. In Kenosha, Wisconsin, for instance, forty buildings were destroyed and a hundred others were damaged.

In elections, voters turned against the radical racial agenda. In Senate and House races in 2020, Republicans were able to put Democrats on the defensive by linking them to the widespread demand to defund the police. In South Carolina's Senate race, as we noted, Democratic challenger Jaime Harrison was running ahead of incumbent Republican Lindsey Graham until Graham started tying him to the Black Lives Matter slogan. In 2021, in Virginia's gubernatorial race, Republican Glenn Youngkin was able to take advantage of the racial controversies over Thomas Jefferson High School and Loudon County's Equity Collaborative to tie his Democratic opponent to critical race theory. Republicans, who had lost the last two gubernatorial elections, won all the top state offices.

Racial radicalism divided Democrats as well. In New York City, former policeman Eric Adams, who promised more spending on the police and denounced the "young, white affluent people" promoting defund the police, was elected mayor. In the Democratic primary, Maya Wiley, who ran on a promise to defund the police, came in third. Adams ran way ahead of his opponents in working-class and nonwhite, including black, neighborhoods.

In Minneapolis in November, voters reelected Mayor Jacob Frey over two activists who backed a referendum to replace the police department by a Department of Public Safety. Voters turned down the referendum, with opposition particularly strong in working-class black neighborhoods. In overwhelmingly black Detroit, voters reported by nine to one that they would feel safer with more police on the street not less. Voters in Buffalo and Seattle also favored candidates who supported increasing police funding. In San Francisco in 2022, voters at the urging of the Democratic mayor turned ultra-progressive DA Chesa Boudin, who championed a low police profile and less law enforcement, out of office in a referendum.

Most Americans rejected the key demands of racial radicalism. They rejected "defund the police," to be sure, but also the demand for "equity" or equality of outcomes in school admissions and employment. In California in 2020, as we noted, Democratic leaders put an initiative on the ballot, Proposition 16, that would have repealed the state's ban on using affirmative action in school admissions and government contracting and employment decisions. The measure, endorsed by Governor Gavin Newsom and vice presidential candidate Kamala Harris, was widely seen as allowing schools to adjust merit-based admission policies to admit more blacks and Hispanics and less Asian Americans in order to make black and Hispanic enrollment proportional to their share in the population. It was in line with Kendi's view of anti-racism. In spite of its prominent endorsements and generous funding, the measure failed by 57 to 43 percent, with working-class voters, Hispanics, Asians, whites, moderates, and independents all in opposition.

Americans also looked unfavorably on the demand for racial reparations. Poll after poll showed overwhelming opposition to the idea. An October 2021 Pew survey found opposition by 68 to 30 percent, with that opposition running through essentially every demographic group including all nonwhites with the exception of blacks. Even Democrats were split down the middle. Democratic analyst David Shor reported that reparations was the worst-testing message out of 117 his firm tested for reaching voters.

In recent elections, there were indications that the Democrats' identification with racial radicalism was an important factor in Hispanics, Korean Americans, Vietnamese Americans, and Chinese Americans voting for Republicans. From the big swings among Hispanics toward Trump in 2020 to the Asian and Hispanic support for Republican gubernatorial candidates like Glenn Youngkin in Virginia, Ron DeSantis in Florida, and Lee Zeldin in New York to the leading role of Asian voters in ousting radical school board members and Boudin in San Francisco, it's become clear that Democratic acquiescence in the new radical orthodoxy around race is a liability with these voters and an obstacle to gaining majorities that would could adopt programs in housing, health care, employment, and education that would actually benefit lower-income minorities.

A Changed Country

Of course, the demands made by Black Lives Matter, Coates, and Kendi could be morally justified, even if they are currently impolitic, but these demands, and the picture of America painted by *The 1619 Project,* do not reflect the America of the twenty-first century. First of all, America can no longer be divided into white and black. In 1965, when Congress passed the Immigration and Nationality Act, 85 percent of the population was white, 11 percent was black, and 4 percent was Latino. According to the current Census tabulation, about 58 percent are white, 19 percent are Hispanic, 12 percent are black, and 6 percent are Asian, and Asians (a category that comprises wildly different ethnicities) are the fastest growing group. In other words, America is no longer a white and black country, and the conflict between whites and blacks can no longer explain, as *The 1619 Project* claimed, "every aspect" of life.

Some liberals and radicals have tried to finesse this change in the country's composition by dividing America between white people and "people of color," but "people of color" is an awkward grab bag that includes Asian nationalities that have a higher median income than whites. It also includes in the standard Census classification many Hispanics and Asians of mixed parentage who identify as white. And it ignores potential conflicts between the different racial and ethnic groups over public safety, government spending and taxing, and affirmative action. Should a second-generation Mexican American have to pay racial reparations to black Americans? Should the child of a working-class Vietnamese American family be bypassed for admission to a university in favor of the child of an upper-middle-class black family or in the case of *Students for Fair Admissions v. Harvard* by the child of wealthy Nigerians?

Secondly, the radical agenda failed to acknowledge the differences in class and background among blacks. In 2019, according to a Pew Research study, 45 percent of black households earned $50,000 or more, and 18 percent earned $100,000 or more. In 2000, 15 percent of adult blacks had a bachelor's degree; in 2018, 23 percent. Those numbers are less than for whites or Asians, but roughly comparable to Hispanics. The real problem in the black population, as Wilson noted, is the urban underclass, not the growing suburban middle class. And as Wilson argued, the economic and cultural depredations of this underclass could not be simply explained as legacies of slavery and Jim Crow. They were also the effects of the globalization and deindustrialization that began in the 1970s.

There is also a little-noticed division between blacks themselves—between African Americans who can trace their lineage back to antebellum America or even Jim Crow America and those who emigrated from Africa or the Caribbean after 1965. According to a Pew report, about 12 percent of black Americans were born elsewhere and another 9 percent are second generation—meaning more than one in five blacks and their ancestors were not here even in the Jim Crow era. Those percentages are expected to grow. A significant percentage of these immigrants and children of immigrants are in or are entering the middle class. Almost a third have college degrees—a comparable proportion to the general population.

Coates based his case for reparations not only on past injustice but on the wealth gap between blacks and whites. The principal reason for that gap, however, is the concentration of wealth among whites at the very top of the income scale. About half of Americans of all races and ethnicities possess no net wealth. Between low-income whites and blacks, there are negligible differences in wealth. In fact, according to a St. Louis Federal Reserve study of whites without college degrees, their median income, rate of homeownership, rate of cohabitation, and life expectancy fell between 1989 and 2016, while the comparable measures of blacks and Hispanics without college degrees rose.

There are tragic similarities between the fate of low-income urban blacks and working-class whites in small towns that suffered from deindustrialization and the closure of mines. Both are victims of neoliberal economics and of the trajectory of postindustrial America. The racial radicals who champion a guaranteed annual income for blacks, but no one else, don't acknowledge this in their platforms. A program of revitalization directed at all the different communities, small towns, and cities affected by deindustrialization might win majority support in the country and even in a divided Congress, but one directed only at blacks will not. An affirmative action program in college admissions that gave a leg up to applicants from low-income households and communities might also win majority support.

There are distinct legacies of American slavery and Jim Crow that persist. Americans' perception is still guided by the "one-drop rule" that a person with African or African American ancestors (even if only a single grandparent) are "black" or "negro"—a rule, except as practiced by the Census, that doesn't apply, say, to the offspring of mixed marriages involving Hispanics or Asians with whites. The rule is no longer a legal basis for discrimination—it is not embedded in a structure or system of law—but it can subtly encourage illegal practices in housing or employment by those who hold racist views. America's goal, embodied in its laws, should be to effectively end such discrimination. In the long run, its objective should be to eliminate, as King proposed, the perception of racial difference. Cultural and ethnic differences will endure, but will not carry invidious implications that lead to discrimination. What's disturbing about the current racial radicalism is that through its language, theories, and demands for strict proportionality, it reinforces the perception of racial difference as a natural fact and appears to rule out as a possibility and as an objective its eventual disappearance.

Chapter Nine

The Immigration Imbroglio

There have always been conflicts over immigration. Prior to the Civil War, the American Party, dubbed the Know-Nothings, agitated against Irish and German immigrants. You could say the Civil War itself was fought over the forced immigration of Africans. After the Civil War, the Knights of Labor led the battle to exclude Chinese laborers who had been imported to build the railroads in the West. The American Federation of Labor and Henry Cabot Lodge's Immigration Restriction League campaigned successfully for the immigration acts of 1920 and 1924 that created quotas to choke off immigration from eastern and southern Europe. That highly discriminatory legislation quieted temporarily the uproar over immigration, but it began again after Congress in 1965 passed the Immigration and Nationality Act that removed the quotas and led to growing numbers of immigrants from Latin America and from Asia.

There is no question that over the long haul America has benefited from its history of immigration and continues to do so. The country as constituted wouldn't exist without immigrants. And its successive industrial upsurges, from the early nineteenth to the late twentieth centuries, would not have been possible without immigrant labor and inventiveness. But immigration has often had a dark side that invited conflict: not just over slavery, but also over employers' use of the newly emigrated and illegally emigrated to bring down wages and undermine unions. Divisions among immigrants and between immigrant and native workers was one reason why America failed to develop an effective labor and social democratic movement before World War I. Ironically, the restriction of immigration after 1920 was one reason why Roosevelt and the Democrats could unite the working class behind the New Deal during the 1930s.

From 1965 to 1995, over twenty million legal and illegal immigrants entered the United States, three times the number that had entered in the prior thirty years. This new wave of immigrants—many of them unskilled or low-skilled—has sown divisions. Employers used these workers, as they had used the immigrants from eastern and southern Europe before World War I, to drive down wages and undermine unions. Democrats, and in particular labor Democrats, initially understood the drawbacks of the new immigration, and promoted legislation that would ease the tensions that were being created, particularly among working-class Americans who were once the heart of the Democratic coalition.

But over the last two decades, Democrats, convinced they could win the support of immigrant constituents by championing the new legal and illegal arrivals, have abandoned that effort. Instead, they have largely ignored the issue of border security while championing a path to citizenship for illegal immigrants. As was the case with racial radicalism, this stand has met the approval and support of Democratic-leaning foundations, political groups, publications, and lobbies. Republicans, sensing an opening, stoked the grievances of workers and small businesses who felt threatened by the successive waves of legal and illegal immigrants. By the 2016 election and the victory of Donald Trump—who highlighted his opposition to illegal immigration in his campaign—it was becoming clear that the Democrats had badly miscalculated.

The Upsurge in Illegal Immigration

The 1965 legislation that opened immigration to all the peoples of the world was not supposed to lead to a dramatic increase in the numbers of immigrants. Lyndon Johnson's attorney general Nicholas Katzenbach told a Senate committee, "This bill is not designed to increase or accelerate the numbers of newcomers permitted to come to America. Indeed, this measure provides for an increase of only a small fraction in permissible immigration." But the bill included a provision allowing for family reunification, which created what came to be called "chain migration": children could bring their parents or vice versa, brothers and sisters, and then spouses and their brothers and sisters and parents and children. Family reunification encouraged large-scale legal migration.

Some of the upsurge in illegal immigration came after Congress in 1964 outlawed the Bracero program, under which growers imported several hundred thousand seasonal farmworkers from south of the border. These workers were poorly paid and subjected to harsh conditions. Cesar Chavez's newly formed United Farm Workers and the AFL-CIO had led the battle to repeal the Bracero program. But instead of stopping the inflow from the South, the program's repeal led to many thousands of Mexicans illegally crossing the border to gain employment. Illegal immigration had averaged in the low 20,000s prior to 1965, but by 1968, it was in the low six digits and by 1974 was over 400,000 annually. By 1980, legal and illegal migration to the United States was running over a million a year, about 300 percent higher than the 400,000 annual entries that were initially projected.

By the early 1980s, Americans were once again up in arms over immigration. In a June 1980 Roper poll, 91 percent of respondents agreed that the United States should make an "all out effort to stop illegal entry into the United States" and 80 percent wanted the United States to reduce the overall number of immigrants. In response, Congress had set up a Select Committee on Immigration and Refugee Policy under Notre Dame president Theodore Hesburgh, a noted liberal who had chaired the United States Commission on Civil Rights, to make recommendations to modify the 1965 law. In 1981, Hesburgh's committee proposed a two-prong approach that would "close the back door to undocumented and illegal migration [and open] the front door a little more to accommodate legal migration." To eliminate an exploitable underclass, it would grant an amnesty to those already in the United States. To discourage new entries, it would require that employers verify the status of employees. But the committee was divided on how to verify employees' status. With the business representatives objecting, it voted only 8 to 7 to require a counterfeit-proof Social Security card. That lack of consensus would prove fatal to any attempt to curb illegal immigration and would spur the next four decades of discontent.

In 1986, Congress adopted a version of the Hesburgh Commission's recommendations. The Immigration Reform and Control Act granted amnesty to illegal immigrants already in the country and established a requirement for employer verification. But to avoid any penalties, an employer need only submit a form saying that the employee had provided some evidence of legal residence. The employer was not required to authenticate the evidence, and there was no means given to do so. It was a hollow provision that inspired counterfeiters. The grant of amnesty also encouraged illegal immigration by suggesting that those who entered illegally after 1986 could look forward to being eventually granted residence and even citizenship. In 1990, Congress adopted the final plank in Hesburgh's recommendations, raising quotas of legal immigrants with a view to dampening the pressure for illegal immigration. But in the 1990s, illegal immigration rose sharply—partly as a result of a downturn in Mexico's economy after NAFTA passed. (By increasing border security personnel, the immigration acts had the unintended consequence of increasing illegal immigration, as migrants who might otherwise have gone back and forth between Mexico and the United States, stayed in the United States out of fear of being apprehended when they tried to recross the border.)

In 1994, the battle lines over illegal immigration were drawn in California. Proposition 187 was put on the ballot blocking illegal immigrants from receiving social services. Up in arms in a time of economic austerity about the rising costs of providing social services to illegal immigrants, Californians passed the proposition easily by 59 to 41 percent. In September that year, President Bill Clinton, mindful of the uproar in California, established Operation Gatekeeper, which erected a wall and increased enforcement at the state's southern border. In 1996, Democrats and Republicans joined in passing the Illegal Immigration Reform and Immigrant Responsibility Act, which increased enforcement at the southern border and penalties for illegal entry. Operation Gatekeeper did reduce illegal entry across the California southern border, but that only shifted the flow of illegal migrants to the Arizona border, where it sparked another punitive referendum in 2004, Proposition 200, which also passed easily, but failed to reduce illegal immigration.

All in all, Operation Gatekeeper and the 1996 bill failed to stem illegal immigration. Illegal entry just shifted from one place to another. And many of the illegal entries—by some estimates, about 40 percent—came from foreigners who remained in the country after their visas expired. As Hesburgh had argued, the only way to genuinely discourage illegal immigrants was by

blocking their employment through a counterfeit-proof verification program that imposed harsh penalties on employers
who flouted it. But under pressure from business and also from
Hispanic lobbies, Congress proved unwilling to pass such a program. As a result, the uproar over illegal immigration, and secondarily over the rise of unskilled immigrants, has continued. If
anything, it has grown more explosive politically.

The Jordan Commission

In the first decades of the battle over immigration, the divisions on policy were not partisan. Both the 1986 and 1996
bills enjoyed bipartisan support and passed by large margins.
(In the Senate, the final version of the 1996 bill was adopted
by voice vote.) If there were an initial division it was between
old-style liberals and labor, on one side, and business interests
and Hispanic lobbies on the other. During the 1986 debate over
verification, Hesburgh, the NAACP, and the AFL-CIO pushed
for stronger employer verification while the Chamber of Commerce and Agribusiness resisted. The high point of the liberal-
labor and bipartisan push for adjustments to the 1965 bill came
from a new commission on immigration, which was established
by the 1990 immigration bill.

The commission was headed by Texas Democrat Barbara
Jordan, who had served three terms in the House of Representatives. Jordan was a product of the civil rights movement, but
also a New Deal liberal and protégé of Lyndon Johnson who as
Texas's first African American state senator had succeeded in
getting the state to adopt a minimum wage. The commission's
other members were divided equally between Democrats and
what would now be called "moderate" Republicans.

In a series of reports, the Jordan Commission recommended
creating a computerized registry of Social Security numbers that

employers would have to check to verify an employee's eligibility to work. The commission also recommended tightening the requirements for family reunification, reducing the annual number of immigrants and emphasizing skilled over unskilled workers. The commission urged measures to assist "Americanization," which included the rapid acquisition of English. It took into account the strains created by the 1965 law and by illegal immigration. These included fiscal costs, particularly on education, and wage competition with native unskilled workers.

By the time the Jordan Commission began its hearings, there was already ample evidence that the massive increases in legal and illegal unskilled and low-skilled workers were wreaking havoc in what had been mid-scale unionized jobs in manufacturing, particularly the garment industry, construction, and meatpacking. At the time of the 1965 immigration bill, meatpacking jobs paid 25 percent higher than the average manufacturing job. Meatpacking plants were 80 percent unionized. But in the late '60s, meatpackers, led by Iowa Beef Processors (IBP), had begun moving their plants out of cities into small towns. In 1969, IBP brought in Mexican workers to break a strike and replace the workers at its Nebraska plant. Over the next thirty years, the meatpackers replaced a predominately white and African American unionized workforce with a predominately Hispanic and predominately nonunion workforce. Somewhere between a quarter and a half of the workforce were in the country illegally. The *New York Times* reported in 2001:

> Until 15 or 20 years ago, meatpacking plants in the United States were staffed by highly paid, unionized employees who earned about $18 an hour, adjusted for inflation. Today, the processing and packing plants are largely staffed by low-paid non-union workers from places like Mexico and Guatemala. Many of them start at $6 an hour.

In spite of Chavez's successes in organizing, California's farmworkers also suffered from illegal immigration. During the 1980s, agricultural economist Don Villarejo estimated, farmworker wages had fallen 8.7 percent. The average farmworker, Villarejo reported, was Mexican-born or a Mexican citizen, had six years of education, and was making $4,300 a year. Villarejo blamed declining wages on an oversupply of labor created by a "large and continuing flow of undocumented workers."

The Jordan Commission's proposals spoke to this oversupply of unskilled and low-skilled labor that was driving down wages and undermining unions, and was particularly affecting African Americans and recent legal immigrants with no more than a high school education. (In 2010, the U.S. Civil Rights Commission would issue a report on the harm that illegal immigration had done to the employment prospects of black workers.) In the history of immigration policy, the Jordan Commission proposals occupied a place similar to William Julius Wilson's books on race and class. But the commission proved to be the last gasp of liberal bipartisanship and of immigration reform that took the condition of American workers fully into account. Even as the commission was drafting its proposals, Democrats and Republicans had already begun to diverge in their approaches to immigration. While Republicans would eventually under Trump make opposition to illegal immigration their signature issue, Democrats would go in the opposite direction.

Labor Changes Course

In the early 1980s, in the debates over employer verification, Hispanic organizations and the leading Hispanic congressman Ed Roybal, from Los Angeles, had joined forces with business lobbies to try to block the requirement for employer verification. The groups, League of United Latin American Citizens (LULAC), the Mexican-American Legal Defense Fund (MALDEF), and the National Council of La Raza, argued that the requirement for employer verification would encourage discrimination against Hispanic citizens. They failed to win the argument in 1986, and they also failed when they pressed the case in hearings for the 1990 bill before Senator Edward Kennedy's Judiciary Committee. But with an assist from the American Civil Liberties Union (ACLU), they did succeed in convincing Kennedy and the committee's liberal Democrats, as well as the NAACP and Congressional Black Caucus, that the verification requirements were discriminatory. These liberals now joined them in backing a proposal to eliminate the requirement altogether.

A decade later, the AFL-CIO, the other major Democratic organization to back employer verification, also called for an end to employer verification, but its motive was different from that of the NAACP and the liberals. The federations' social service unions had found that when they tried to organize janitors or hotel workers, many of the workers turned out to be illegal immigrants. Chavez's UFW had made a similar finding. The employers were in a win-win situation. They would not be heavily penalized for hiring illegal immigrants, but they could use the threat of turning them in to the Immigration and Naturalization Service (INS) to deter them from joining unions. In 2000, the Service Employees International Union (SEIU), the Hotel Employees and Restaurant Employees Union, and the UFW persuaded the AFL-CIO Executive Council to reject employer sanctions and to press instead for amnesty for the illegal workers. The manufacturing and construction unions were unhappy, but the SEIU was the fastest-growing union in the federation, and a former SEIU official, John Sweeney, had become the federation's president. SEIU carried the day.

The AFL-CIO's abandonment of employer verification and

sanctions undermined any humane and reasonable attempt to stop illegal immigration. Democrats were left with two options: either they could respond to public pressure for stopping illegal immigration by taking measures that, although ineffective, would appear to be taking the threat seriously; or they could ignore or even reject the threat itself and opt, in effect, for the kind of "open borders" stance favored by the *Wall Street Journal* and the free market Cato Institute.

In his 2006 book *The Audacity of Hope*, Senator Barack Obama appeared to understand the problem with illegal immigration and with unskilled immigrants.

> There's no denying that many blacks share the same anxieties as many whites about the wave of illegal immigration flooding our Southern border—a sense that what's happening now is fundamentally different from what has gone on before . . . If this huge influx of mostly low-skill workers provides some benefits to the economy as a whole . . . it also threatens to depress further the wages of blue-collar Americans and put strains on an already overburdened safety net.

When he became president, Obama limited his efforts to deporting illegal immigrants who had committed crimes. Even that effort earned him the ire of the Hispanic lobbies and their liberal allies, who branded him the "deporter-in-chief." "We consider him the deportation president, or the deporter-in-chief," Janet Murguia, the president of the National Council of La Raza, declared in March 2014.

In the 2016 presidential election, Hillary Clinton gave even shorter shrift to discouraging illegal immigration. In the March debate hosted by Univision, she declared that Obama was "wrong on the issue of deportation." She said she would deport only "violent criminals" and "terrorists." (That permitted burglars, car thieves, embezzlers, sex traffickers, slavers, and major drug dealers to avoid deportation.) Her platform made only a vague and passing reference to discouraging illegal immigration. "We believe immigration enforcement must be humane and consistent with our values," the platform said. That amounted to 12 of 940 words devoted to proposals on immigration.

In 2017, Republican senators Tom Cotton and David Perdue unveiled a bill, dubbed "Reforming Immigration for Strong Employment," that very closely resembled the Jordan Commission's proposals from 1997. Their bill gave priority to skilled immigrants, narrowed the criteria for family reunification, and reduced slightly the annual number of immigrants. It was designed to take pressure off the market for low-skilled and unskilled labor. Illinois's Dick Durbin, the Democratic whip, denounced the plan, charging it with "gutting legal immigration" and of being "nothing more than a partisan ploy appealing to the racist and xenophobic instincts Trump encouraged during [the] campaign." Minority Leader Chuck Schumer dismissed it as a "non-starter." No Democratic official even considered their plan worthy of debate.

During the 2020 presidential primary, the Democratic candidates vied to see who could appear least concerned about illegal immigration. In a June 2019 debate, nine of the ten candidates called for "decriminalizing" border crossings. Two candidates, Elizabeth Warren and Kirsten Gillibrand, advocated dismantling U.S. Immigration and Customs Enforcement (ICE), an agency within the Department of Homeland Security that polices cross-border crime and illegal immigration that threatens national security. Sanders initially refused to back abolishing ICE, but after the *New Republic* ran an article critical of his stand entitled "Bernie Sanders is not the left," he shifted ground, saying he would "break up" the agency.

The Publications Lean In

The Democrats were pushed toward extremes by the liberal-leaning foundations, policy groups, lobbies, and media. The foundations and national media were moved partly by ethical concerns. They thought the United States should welcome and take care of poor people who came to the United States to work—as in the oft-quoted Emma Lazarus lines, "Give me your tired, your poor/Your huddled masses yearning to breathe free." At the extremes, elites actually advocated "open borders." Arguments for open borders were aired in the *Atlantic*, the *Nation*, *Vox* (whose editors criticized Sanders for his rejection of "open borders"), *Jacobin*, and *Dissent*.

The proponents of these views have edged toward a rejection of the very idea of a nation. In "The Case for Getting Rid of Borders—Completely," Alex Tabarrok wrote in the *Atlantic*, "No defensible moral framework regards foreigners as less deserving of rights than people born in the right place at the right time."

During the first decades of debate over illegal immigration, the *New York Times* had backed employer sanctions. In a 2000 editorial, it had criticized the AFL-CIO's decision to opt for amnesty and to reject sanctions, arguing that the federation should have honored "America's proud tradition by continuing to welcome legal immigrants and find ways to punish employers who refuse to obey the law." But during the subsequent decade, it changed its tune. Its editorial writer Lawrence Downes rejected the term "illegal" for illegal immigrants. "It pollutes the debate. It blocks solutions," he wrote. In an editorial in 2009, the *New York Times* described illegal immigrants as "Americans-in-waiting." In a 2012 editorial entitled "Migrants' Freedom Ride," it criticized Obama for "rachet[ing] up deportations." It compared illegal immigrants crossing the border to the civil rights freedom riders who had desegregated southern buses.

The foundations, policy groups, and publications also attempted to dictate the language in which the subject of immigration was discussed and to stigmatize those who depart from the terms and outlook they promoted as "racist" or "xenophobic." The ACLU followed up Downes's editorial in the *New York Times* by publishing an "issue brief" accusing those who use the term "illegal alien" of "criminalizing undocumented immigrants." "Undocumented" rather than "illegal" became the acceptable term, as though those who broke the nation's law by crossing the border or overstaying their visas were equivalent to someone who arrived at a formal event without the proper attire. *Slate* branded "assimilation"—which denotes a long-standing American ideal and the aspiration of many immigrants—as a "racist code-word." (One can imagine what *Slate* would have said about the Jordan Commission's proposals for "Americanization.")

During the 2016 campaign, Democratic groups responded to Trump's attacks against illegal immigration by committing the Fox News Fallacy. To claims by Trump and his allies that immigrants had brought down wages, the Center for American Progress, run by ardent Clinton supporters, published a paper asserting that "economists have found that immigrants complement native-born workers and increase the standard of living of all Americans." The first of these claims—that immigrants merely complement native-born workers—is wrong but arguable; the second—that immigrants increased the standard of living for *all* Americans—is ludicrous and is certainly not embraced by the findings on immigration by the National Academy of Sciences.

The Democrats' shadow party also tried to stigmatize the work of groups that take a similar position on immigration to the Jordan Commission and whose research doesn't bear out claims like those from the Center for American Progress. In 2017, the Southern Poverty Law Center (SPLC), which made its name as a foe of the Ku Klux Klan and supporter of civil rights but which like the ACLU has strayed from its original mission and become a fundraising magnet, branded the Center for Immigration Studies in Washington a "hate group." This research organization has published studies on immigration by Cornell University labor economist Vernon Briggs, University of California, Davis, agricultural economist Philip Martin, who worked on the Hesburgh Committee, and Pulitzer Prize–winning journalist Jerry Kammer. The SPLC associated it with, among others, the Proud Boys, the Knights of the Ku Klux Klan, the Daily Stormer, and the Racial Nationalist Party of America. The *New Republic* followed up by describing the Center for Immigration Studies as "far-right fringe group" and accusing it (without any evidence) of "cooking up" the numbers in its studies.

Some Democratic groups and publications have contended that by advocating amnesty and downplaying or rejecting enforcement, Democrats would maintain the allegiance of the huge and growing Hispanic voting bloc that would underpin a "new American majority." In a 2013 report from the Center of American Progress, Philip E. Woglin and Ann Garcia wrote, "Supporting real immigration reform that contains a pathway to citizenship for our nation's 11 million undocumented immigrants is the only way to maintain electoral strength in the future." In *Dissent* in 2016, University of Southern California professor Manuel Pastor maintained that "getting it right on a single key issue—immigration—can open up a conversation with Latinos on many other issues." But on its ethics, as well as its politics, the policy groups and publications got it wrong.

A Misguided Electoral Strategy

According to a March 2021 Gallup Poll, 60 percent of Americans were worried "a great deal" or a "fair amount" about illegal immigration. That represents a large part of the electorate, and those who are the most concerned tend to be more likely to vote on that issue than those who are least concerned. As expected, the results break down according to party; 91 percent of Republicans, 56 percent of independents, and 41 percent of Democrats are worried about illegal immigration. And the opinions also divide sharply by education. Only 46 percent of the college-educated are worried compared to 64 percent of those who have gone to college but do not have a four-year degree, and 69 percent of those with only a high school or less education. What these polls describe is not so much a difference in education but a difference in experience on either side of the Great Divide. They also show that by downplaying a concern about illegal immigration, Democrats have contributed to the loss of support among those working-class voters who once buoyed the party.

For an extreme example, take the Iowa congressional district that spans the small towns of western Iowa. It's one-third blue collar, and three-quarters of its voters do not have a college degree. Over the last thirty years, it has gone from Democratically-inclined to solidly Republican. It went almost two-to-one for Trump in 2016 and 2020. A key industry in the area is meatpacking, but the industry was transformed in the last three decades of the twentieth century. Asians and Hispanics migrated to Storm Lake, Marshalltown, and other small towns and went to work at much lower wages in the jobs that whites once had. Deep resentment over what happened endures.

In 2002, Storm Lake's district elected Steve King, whose signature issue was opposition to illegal immigration. King voiced the resentment and anger of his constituencies. King said of the argument that illegal immigrants were doing jobs that Americans won't do.

Every job in this country is being done by Americans, there's no job they won't do. But you need to pay them what it's worth.

And I would like to see a tighter labor supply in this country, so that a person could get out of bed, go to work, and make enough money to pay for a modest house, educate their children, and plan for retirement. It used to be that way.

When King's opposition to illegal immigration careened into white nationalism and nativism, Republicans in the House and Senate repudiated him, and in 2020 he was defeated in the primary by a well-funded opponent, who promised to be less strident, but who was also outspokenly opposed to illegal immigration. One of the first bills that Randy Feenstra sponsored was the Illegal Immigrant Payoff Prohibition Act. Democrats' acquiescence in illegal immigration had cost votes in western Iowa.

Democrats have also had to learn the hard way that their stand on illegal immigration was not the "single key" to winning over Hispanic voters. There were warning signs before the Hispanic vote turned in 2020. Arizona's Proposition 200 in 2004 contained a provision, which was later thrown out by the courts, that appeared to stigmatize the state's Latinos. It required proof of citizenship in order to register to vote. It also denied public benefits to illegal immigrants. Yet according to exit polls 47 percent of the state's Latinos supported Proposition 200.

After Cotton and Perdue issued their immigration bill, Morning Consult conducted an extensive poll in August 2017 on its different provisions. The results showed that Hispanics did not have dramatically different views of immigration from other Americans. Forty-two percent believed that the United States was allowing too many low-skilled immigrants annually, while 18 percent believed there were too few. A plurality of 49 percent believed that job skills were more important than family ties in evaluating who to admit; 33 percent favored family ties. (The rest had no opinion.) A plurality of 50 percent thought an ability to speak English should be an important factor; 37 percent thought it should not be. In other words, almost half—and a majority of those who had an opinion—thought major provisions of the Cotton-Perdue bill were acceptable. They didn't share the Democratic leaders' perception that the bill "gutted legal immigration."

The results of the 2020 election once again showed that the Democrats' acquiescence in illegal immigration had failed to give them an edge among Hispanics. Trump's views on illegal immigration—evident as early as his June 2015 presidential announcement speech when he characterized illegal immigrants from Mexico as drug dealers and rapists—were laced with bigotry. By Democratic calculations, his views on illegal immigration and his attempt to fortify border security should have turned off Hispanic voters. But Trump gained support in 2020 among Hispanic voters.

Trump gained support in big metro areas, including Chicago and New York, and in Florida, Texas, and California, three states with large Hispanic populations. In Texas's Rio Grande Valley, Trump carried an overwhelmingly Hispanic county that no Republican had won since 1920. According to postelection interviews and surveys, many Hispanics cared far more about the economy and government COVID-19 policies than they did about immigration, and they gave Trump high marks on the economy and for opposing COVID-19 lockdowns. Some Hispanics, particularly in South Texas, backed Trump's border policies. According to an extensive survey by Equis Research, 61 percent of Hispanics in South Texas wanted spending on border security boosted, and 58 percent wanted the numbers of asylum seekers limited. (Nationally, 55 percent backed boosting border security spending and 51 percent supported limiting asylum seekers.) In other words, significant numbers of Hispanics favored policies that they thought would reduce illegal immigration. The Democrats were out of step with the people they assumed were their loyal base.

In September 2022, we listened to a focus group run by progressive organizations. The focus group was composed primarily of middle-aged Hispanic women who had voted for Biden, but weren't sure about voting in the November election. They were from different parts of the country. The moderator asked them about Biden's immigration policy and about Florida governor Ron DeSantis flying migrants to the liberal upper-class island Martha's Vineyard. What he got back was not anger at DeSantis, but frustration at the administration's border policy. Here are excerpts from what the women said.

- We've allowed the undocumented to be insured fully. When does it end? . . .
- Trump's border policy was not to have an influx of migrants. President Biden reversed that. There are now more than two million expected this year.
- They are dumped on our doorstep. It stinks . . .
- We're taking in more than we can. Our homeless problem is worsening . . .
- [DeSantis and Texas governor Greg Abbott] are from border states. They are the first line of defense. They are not getting the support they need . . .
- I haven't heard much from the Democrats [on what to do about the border] . . .
- Make it harder for them to cross. It is getting out of control. Don't have them live off the government.

As was the case with Democratic views on racial justice, Democrats had a reasonable position thirty years ago that spoke to their older working- and middle-class constituents, but they abandoned it in favor of one championed by Washington lobby-ists, Democratic think tanks, and left-leaning publications. That original position, spelled out by the Hesburgh and the Jordan Commissions, had fully backed legal immigration but wanted to sharply reduce illegal immigration. It recognized that if you want to stem illegal immigration, you have to prevent employ-ers from hiring illegal immigrants. And it recognized that if you want to prevent the illegal immigrants already here from becom-ing a permanent, exploitable underclass, you need to grant them a path to citizenship. Amnesty alone would lead to increased illegal immigration, as the 1986 law had done. And verification alone without amnesty would plunge illegal immigrants that are already in the United States into the underground economy.

The Jordan Commission also recognized that if you want to improve the lot of less-educated and -skilled Americans already here, you have to limit the flow of legal and illegal unskilled immigrants into the country. There is reason to believe that the uncontrolled onrush of unskilled and low skilled migrants after 1965 was a factor in perpetuating African American ghettos in major cities, keeping down the wages of first generation migrants, and creating resentful left-behinds in small towns through the Midwest. There is also reason to believe these groups are begin-ning to understand this and that their growing rejection of the Democrats' stand on immigration is a consideration in their abandoning Democratic candidates.

Chapter Ten

Sexual Creationism

As with the politics of race and immigration, the politics of sex, gender, and women's rights was rooted in a quest for democracy and equality. The women's movement that emerged in the sixties inspired a spate of reform, much of which was backed by legislation, that transformed America's schools, workplaces, health care, and criminal justice system, and that altered men's and women's private and home lives. Like the civil rights movement, after which it was modeled, it, too, spawned new movements, including that for gay rights, which won protection against discrimination, and, finally, the legalization of gay marriage.

There was always a radical edge to these movements, as there had been to the black liberation and anti-war movements of the late '60s. It could be seen in hostility to marriage and to the family as an institution and even to heterosexuality. These radical sub-movements helped provoke a backlash, but they eventually died out, and were subordinated to the larger movements for reform. To some extent, that remains the case today—witness the organized protest against the Supreme Court's *Dobbs* decision that contributed to Democratic victories in the 2022 election. But there is also a movement that has arisen out of the old that threatens to subsume the women's and gay rights reform movements.

The movement for transgender rights, which grew out of the women's and gay rights movements, and adopted some of the language of the civil rights movement, has had a reformist side that advocates protection against discrimination in employment, housing, and school admissions suffered by people who were born as one sex but who now claim to be the other. The Supreme Court ruling in 2020 in *Bostock v. Clayton County, Georgia* sanctioned these protections in employment, which are consistent with the expansion of democratic rights, but the movement, buttressed by national organizations such as Planned Parenthood and the ACLU that are part of the shadow Democratic Party, has expanded its agenda well beyond the prevention of discrimination.

The movement now demands that individuals who were regarded as transgender (signified by their adopted gender being prefaced by the adjective "trans") be taken pure and simply for the sex they claim to be and that they be accorded all the rights and protections pertaining to that sex. That hasn't proven particularly controversial for women who claim to be men, but it has become very controversial for men who claim to be women and demand the protections that the women's movement won for women over the last sixty years. On behalf of this group of trans women, transgender groups have demanded that they be able to participate in competitive women's sports, as well as being admitted to rape centers and other "safe spaces" reserved for women who have suffered violence.

The transgender movement has also sought to transform the very language by which people refer to sex and gender, introducing such expressions as "pregnant people" and "vagina owners." The new movement and its allies have replaced the straightforward demand for women's or gay rights with an alphabet soup of sexual designations—for instance, LGBTQIA+. For most Americans, including those that Democrats should represent and attract, these terms are incomprehensible and, in some cases like "pregnant people," offensive.

The transgender activist groups have also championed what they call "gender-affirming care" for children and teenagers who declare themselves uncomfortable with the sex in which they were born—that is, their biological sex. This includes extensive hormonal therapy and surgery to change a minor's sexual appearance. Some Republican governors and state legislatures have reacted by banning these procedures outright. Democrats, including the Biden administration, have responded by denying that there are *any* drawbacks to or reasonable questions to ask about "gender-affirming care." That hard-line stance, exemplifying the Fox News Fallacy, has reinforced the cultural insularity of the Democratic Party.

Sex and Gender

There is nothing new about individuals of one sex attempting to pass as another, but what is new is the understanding of what this entails medically and what it means. The modern debate over what a sex change means probably began with German sexologist Magnus Hirschfeld who practiced during the first three decades of the last century until he was shut down by the Nazis. Hirschfeld, who was gay, contended that there was a continuum between male and female filled by "sexual intermediaries" that contained elements of both. He used castration to enable male patients to become more female.

In the United States, the general public didn't pay attention to what were then called "transvestites" or "transsexuals" until Christine (nee George) Jorgensen returned from Denmark in 1952, where he had had surgery and hormone injections to make him into a woman. Jorgensen was treated as a kind of interesting freak—"Ex-GI Becomes Blonde Bombshell," the *New York Daily News* declared. Men who wanted to become women—who until the last decade made up the vast majority of aspiring transgender individuals—could obtain hormones in the U.S., but sex-change clinics were not established until the late '60s. And even then, these clinics admitted male patients under strict requirements that they fit female stereotypes in their interests, be homosexual, and agree afterward not to socialize with other transgender individuals, but to blend into the sex they wanted to pass for.

The first attempt of transgender political organization came in the wake of the Stonewall riots in New York in June 1969, which were sparked by a police raid against a gay bar. Two transgender women who had participated in the riot founded Street Transvestite Action Revolutionaries (STAR) to defend and house the city's transgender homeless. But it dissolved in three years. Over the next two decades, trans women who wanted to make common cause with lesbians, gays, and radical feminists were spurned as males in disguise who, in the words of feminist Robin Morgan, were "leeching off women who have spent entire lives *as women* in women's bodies." In *Transgender History*, Susan Stryker called the '70s and '80s the "difficult decades."

Transgender politics really began in earnest in the 1990s. One factor was the end of the Cold War and the election of a socially liberal administration in 1992 that was not focused on the values of family, faith, and nation the way the Reagan administration had been. As Stryker notes, transgender politics also benefited from the militance of ACT UP, the gay-led group that pressed for government to address the AIDs epidemic. ACT UP saw itself as the tribune for "queers"—a designation that included any people who deviated from the heterosexual norm. When ACT UP spawned Queer Nation groups, some trans women formed Transgender Nation groups. In 1992, Leslie Feinberg, a trans man (who later went back to being a woman) and member of the Marxist-Leninist Workers World Party, put out a widely circulated pamphlet titled "Transgender Liberation" that called for a "movement" for people who "defy the 'man'-made boundaries of gender."

Transgender politics also got a boost from the universities and from the fields of women's and gender studies that had sprouted up earlier. At a conference at the University of California, Santa Cruz, in 1991, the term "queer studies" was born. The doyen of the new sexology was University of California, Berkeley, philosopher Judith Butler. Butler, who was heavily influenced by the French philosopher Michel Foucault, published *Gender Trouble* in 1990, which, for those who could penetrate its dense prose, laid down what would become the ideology of the transgender movement.

The commonsense understanding of sexuality, which conforms with biology and Darwin's theory of evolution, is that human beings are divided into two distinct sexes defined by their complementary reproductive function. These differences contribute to physical differences in body shape and size and appearance. Hirschfeld, of course, had ignored this distinction, but many transgender advocates had tried to get around it by drawing a distinction between sex and gender. While sex was rooted in reproductive biology, gender was based on appearance and behavior and could be modified with hormones and surgery, as it had been in the case of Christine Jorgensen.

Butler went beyond this distinction. She argued that both sex and gender were social constructions based on the authority of experts (on superior power, in Foucault's terms), and defined by behavioral criteria. Gender wasn't based on sex, but the concept of sex was based on criteria that described gender. "The production of sex as prediscursive [that is, as having a foundational reality] ought to be understood as the effect of the apparatus of cultural construction designated by *gender*," Butler wrote. In other words, Butler inverted the relationship between gender and sex. One couldn't easily shuck off one's gender—it was a product of the "regulation of sexuality within the obligatory frame of reproductive heterosexuality"—but one was not bound by it and could defy authority.

Butler's theory was an example of what the philosopher Ludwig Wittgenstein described as "language gone on a holiday." Differences in sex are the product of evolution not of medical whim, and the everyday perception reflects biology. But Butler's theory of sex and gender fit what an aspiring movement wanted to hear, and some version of it became gospel in the leadership of the transgender movement. The political implications of her theory were profound: trans men and women were fully justified in demanding that they be treated as members of the sex to which they had transitioned. Trans men were fully men; trans women were women.

In different variations, Butler's theory became echoed in the movement's political statements. In Emi Koyama's influential work, "The Transfeminist Manifesto," which appeared in 2001, she wrote, "Transfeminism holds that sex and gender are both socially constructed; furthermore, the distinction between sex and gender is artificially drawn as a matter of convenience." Butler's theory has even invaded medical terminology. Medical writings have become peppered with the acronyms "AFAB"—assigned female at birth—and "AMAB"—assigned male at birth—the Foucauldian implication being that these sexual designations were not products of natural history but were the result of assignments by the medical establishment.

On the other side, Butler's view of gender as the defining mode has underpinned a blizzard of new identities based on how individuals experience their gender. LGBTQIA+, for instance, stands for lesbian, gay, bisexual, transgender, queer, intersex, asexual, and any other possible (+) sexual identities. A new favorite among the young is "non-binary," meaning an individual is neither a man nor a woman. These designations, which also require customized pronouns, are expressions of a subculture within the college towns and postindustrial metro areas. They create a wall of separation between a sexual avant-garde and the rest of the country and, in so far as they are voiced approvingly by Democrats, isolate the party from many of what had been its core supporters, as well as from many more conventional college-educated voters it had acquired over the last three decades.

LGB Becomes LGBT

Since the early '90s, the transgender movement has gone through two phases. The first lasted until 2015 and saw the steady growth of the movement and of groups dedicated to advancing the rights of transgender individuals. The sheer increase in numbers was largely the product of the internet. Prior to the internet, many transgender people were isolated from each other. They weren't clustered in neighborhoods like gays, and didn't have regular social institutions where they hung out. The internet created a virtual community. "Before the rise of the internet," Rodrigo Heng-Lehtinen, the executive director of the National Center for Transgender Equality, told us, "most trans people felt like they were the only trans person on planet Earth. In terms of politics and activism, you need a kind of a critical mass of people, to coordinate with each other to make any kind of loud enough noise for someone else to notice."

In the early 2000s, national groups like Heng-Lehtinen's center, the National Transgender Advocacy Coalition, and the Transgender Law Center were founded. Much of the funding for new organizations came from sympathetic foundations, including the Gill Foundation, the Tawani Foundation, which was begun by trans woman and Hyatt heir Jennifer Pritzker, and the Arcus Foundation. During this period, transgender groups succeeded in getting anti-discrimination ordinances passed in more than a hundred cities. But the movement's greatest success during this phase was in being accepted as part of the shadow Democratic Party's cluster of liberal groups. These included, of course, feminist, women's, gay, and lesbian organizations, but also organizations like American Civil Liberties Union and Planned Parenthood. That acceptance was, however, the product of a long conflict that had begun in the early 1970s and was renewed in the 1990s.

There were two major skirmishes along the way. The first was little known outside of feminist and transgender movement circles, but created a furor within them. In 1991, the organizers of the annual Michigan Womyn's Music Festival barred a trans woman from attending. The transgender woman's case, Susan Stryker wrote, became a "litmus test for whether 'queer' was indeed transgender inclusive." In 1994, Leslie Feinberg organized a counter "Camp Trans" nearby and called for a boycott of the festival. With the backing of the ACLU and GLAAD (the Gay and Lesbian Alliance Against Defamation), the protests continued and even grew more provocative. In 1999, a pre-operative trans woman got into the festival and exposed her penis in a shower room.

The other battle directly impacted Democratic politics. In 1994, the Human Rights Campaign, which was by far the largest of the gay and lesbian groups, drafted a bill—the Employment Non-Discrimination Act (ENDA)—that barred discrimination on the basis of sexual orientation. The bill, which didn't include discrimination against transgender individuals, failed in the Senate by one vote. Transgender activists protested their exclusion. They picketed HRC fundraising events, and HRC agreed to include "gender identity" in the bill. But the new bill got nowhere in the Clinton years.

After Democrats took back control of Congress in November 2006, congressman Barney Frank reintroduced the original ENDA. He feared that the bill couldn't pass with "gender identity" included. Instead, he introduced a separate bill on gender identity. To the consternation of the transgender activists, HRC backed Frank's main bill. Seven hundred gay and lesbian groups formed a coalition called United ENDA to protest Frank's and the HRC's action. Frank's bill, which George W. Bush had promised to veto, barely passed the House, and never came to a vote in the Senate.

Frank was right about the politics. The separate bill on gender identity never even got out of a House committee. But as far as democratic rights were concerned, the transgender activists had a point. Someone shouldn't be denied employment on the basis of their gender identity any more than because of their sexual orientation. In the aftermath of the bills' failures, HRC faced a major revolt from its membership upon which, unlike the other organizations, it strongly relied for fundraising. "It made them scared about their fundraising model," Heng-Lehtinen explained.

HRC once again agreed to include gender identity in all its efforts.

The heated revolt against HRC's exclusion of gender identity and HRC's surrender marked a turning point. "No one is every going to try that again. So now it's like everything is sexual orientation and gender identity," said Heng-Lehtinen. After that, the movements and the shadow Democratic Party became defenders not just of "LGB" but of "LGBT."

With HRC in the lead, the groups now acted in unison on behalf of transgender rights. And that included the protest against the Michigan Womyn's Music Festival. In 2014, a gay and lesbian group, Equality Michigan, called for a boycott of the festival. HRC, along with GLAAD, the National Center for Lesbian Rights, and the National LGBTQ Task Force, endorsed the boycott. Rather than accede to their demand to include trans women, the festival's organizer shut it down permanently. The transgender activists had triumphed.

The Bathroom Bills

In the last two years of the Obama administration, there were two seemingly unrelated events that propelled transgender politics onto the national stage as a leading player in the culture war between Democrats and Republicans. The first of these events was the Supreme Court's decision in *Obergefell v. Hodges* in June 2015, which legalized gay marriage. Prior to that, the fight for gay marriage and secondarily for the admission of self-identified gays to the military (which the Obama administration had endorsed in 2011) were the principal preoccupations for the large groups' activism and fundraising. With *Obergefell*, the main battle had been won.

The groups' attention now shifted to transgender rights. In *Transgender History*, Susan Stryker writes that after *Obergefell* "transgender emerged as the 'cutting edge' civil rights issue for LGBT organizations. Mainstream advocacy groups like the Human Rights Campaign that had previously marginalized trans concerns suddenly developed a keen interest in the topic." That year, the foundations followed suit. The Arcus Foundation, for one, pledged $15 million to transgender rights groups and to projects within groups like the ACLU. (In 2021, Arcus would give $15 million to the ACLU alone, which responded by renaming its LGBT project after one of Arcus's founders.) The foundations also contributed to the spread of discussion about transgender rights and ideology. The Pritzker foundation gave the University of Virginia $2 million to set up a chair for transgender studies.

The second event that occurred could be called the "bathroom battle." Transgender groups, which now mostly described themselves as LGBTQ ("Q" for queer) groups, had continued to lobby cities and states to pass laws that included gender-identity in anti-discrimination ordinances. In 2014, the Houston City Council passed a sweeping anti-discrimination law, HERO, or the Houston Equal Rights Ordinance, that included gender identity. After a succession of court battles, social conservative groups and Republican officials got a referendum on HERO on the November 2015 ballot. The debate over the bill focused on whether men who identified as women could use women's bathrooms. Polls showed the ordinance in the lead, but voters repealed it by 61 to 39 percent, delivering a sharp rebuke in a Democratic Party–controlled city to the LGBTQ groups.

The battle over HERO set off conflicts around the country between LGBTQ groups, which continued to lobby for ordinances, and socially conservative organizations, most of which were identified with the Republican Party. In February 2016, LGBTQ groups successfully lobbied the Charlotte, North Carolina, City Council to pass an anti-discrimination ordinance that included gender identity. The Republican governor and state legislature struck back by passing a bill, HB2, that prevented people from using a restroom or locker room that did not correspond to their sex on their birth certificates. (Persons who underwent surgery could change their birth certificates.)

The battle over HB2 showed the power of the transgender lobby. Businesses canceled expansion plans in their state. The professional and collegiate basketball organizations canceled major events. And the Obama administration's Justice Department responded with a guidance stating that protections for transgender students came under the 1972 amendment to the

1964 civil rights act, Title IX, that banned sex discrimination
at any school that receives federal funding. The Justice Department's stance showed that transgender politics had succeeded in
the highest circles of the Democratic Party. The Obama Justice
Department was not merely defending a vulnerable group from
discrimination, but buying into the extreme gender ideology
that the LGBTQ groups had begun to promote.

There were good civil rights arguments for protecting transgender people from being denied housing, employment, health
care, and admission to schools *because* they were transgender. But
the controversy over bathrooms and locker rooms and other facilities dedicated to women raised thorny questions. Weren't these
spaces—such as publicly funded rape centers—intended to secure
the privacy and security of women as a vulnerable group? And if
a school's bathrooms fell under this order against discrimination
according to Title IX, why not its sports teams? And if gender and
not sex were the criterion for who could enter these spaces or play
on a school's teams, what did a biologically born male have to do
to qualify as a woman?

The Justice Department adhered to the new transgender ideology in answering these questions. It included discriminating
against transgender individuals under the rubric of "sex discrimination," even though the word "sex" in Title IX had been
directed at discrimination against women. It stated that "a person's gender identity may be different or same as the person's sex
assigned at birth" and defined "gender identity" as an "individual's internal sense of gender." In other words, a boy or man who
felt he was a woman could use women's locker rooms or bathrooms. And it failed to exclude the possibility that a biological
male could participate in women's sports in schools and colleges.

Twenty-one states subsequently sued the Obama administration claiming that it had unjustifiably expanded the meaning of
Title IX, but the new Trump administration would render these

suits moot by rescinding the administration's guidance. The Obama administration's statement showed, however, that the leadership of the Democratic Party had fully bought into the questionable interpretation of sex and gender that went back to Butler and that was being promoted by the LGBTQ groups and backed up by lawsuits from the ACLU. It was a green light to the LGBTQ groups and their allies.

The Women's Team

In the years since the Obama guidance, the LGBTQ groups and their allies have campaigned strenuously not just for civil rights for transgender people, but for the acceptance of transgender ideology. Their efforts have been met with strong opposition, especially from Republican-controlled states. One key area of contention has been the participation of trans women (who were born male) in women's sports. No controversy better illustrates the difference between transgender politics as civil rights reformism and transgender politics as a radical attempt to expand the rights of one group (transgender individuals) at the expense of another (women).

Title IX, which was backed by the women's movement and opposed by conservative Republicans, required equal funding for men's and women's athletics at schools that got federal money. In the wake of Title IX, women's participation in competitive sports skyrocketed. In 1972, there were 300,000 girls and women playing competitive sports in high school and college. By 2012, it was more than three million, about one in five of girls and women. Playing sports was a source not just of fun and glory and self-esteem, but also of college scholarships and job opportunities. It was important not just to participate but to excel and win.

There is no question that men have a physical advantage over women in competitive sports that require strength and stamina. Men on average have larger torsos, broader shoulders, bigger hands and feet, less fat, and greater lung and heart capacity. Serena Williams, perhaps the greatest women's tennis player ever, once boasted that she could defeat any man who was rated below the top two hundred. The 203rd rank man challenged her, and beat her 6–1. Similar comparisons can be made with the best male and female swimmers and track and field athletes. So to give women a fair chance to compete, their sports were always separate from men's sports.

But in recent years, the LGBTQ groups and their allies have backed efforts by trans women who were born men to participate in women's sports. The best known case was that of University of Pennsylvania swimmer Lia Thomas. Thomas had initially swum as a man for three years at the university and had been a mediocrity. He ranked fifty-fifth nationally, for instance, in the 500 yard freestyle event. He then changed his gender identity and, after a year had gone by, competed on the women's team and won the NCAA championship in the 500 yard freestyle. He was the best in the country. Thomas had taken hormone drugs that were supposed to reduce his power, but he clearly had an advantage over biological women. Half of the women on the Penn team protested Thomas's participation, as did parents of swimmers that competed with him, but he was unrepentant. "I'm not a man. I'm a woman, so I belong on the woman's team," he told *Sports Illustrated*.

Thomas's stance was backed by the LGBTQ organizations and their allies. The Human Rights Campaign said, "Living your truth is an incredible and powerful feeling. We're in solidarity with Lia and all athletes who compete in the sports they love and on teams consistent with their gender identity." The ACLU, which had already gone to court to back other transgender women who wanted to participate in women's sports, said, "It's not a women's sport if it doesn't include ALL women athletes. Lia Thomas belongs on the women's Penn swimming and diving team."

Bleeding People

In line with their view of sex and gender, the LGBTQ groups and their allies also challenged the way people talk about men and women. They took particular aim at the description of organs and activities that are biologically associated with women, demanding that they be referred to with neutral designations. They excised the term "women" from their descriptions of abortion or cervical cancer or motherhood. During the controversy over the Supreme Court's *Dobbs v. Jackson* decision to overturn *Roe v. Wade*, NARAL abandoned its prior support for a "woman's choice." Now it talked about "birthing people."

The groups' campaign to excise the term "women" resonated within the media. *Teen Vogue* offered its readers a "no-nonsense, 101 guide to masturbation for vagina owners." *USA Today* demoted a deputy editor after he tweeted that "people who get pregnant are also women." Private corporations incorporated the new language in their ads. Tampax celebrated "the diversity of all people who bleed."

But the groups' campaign had the most telling impact on medical institutions, including federal government bodies. The American Cancer Society has recommended screenings for "people with a cervix." The Centers for Disease Control (CDC) has described "care for breastfeeding people." Oregon's Health and Science University has put out a guide to "gender-inclusive language" that advises replacing "mother/mom" with "parent/birthing parent" and "breastfeeding" with "chestfeeding/lactation."

The controversy over language erupted on Capitol Hill in the wake of the *Dobbs* decision. At a Senate hearing on the decision in July 2022, Khiara Bridges, a University of California law professor, referred to "people with a capacity for pregnancy" in describing who was affected by the decision. Republican senator Josh Hawley asked Bridges, "You've referred to people with a capacity for pregnancy—would that be women?" Bridges responded that other people besides "ciswomen" are capable of pregnancy. ("Ciswoman" is a term that LGBTQ groups use to refer to women who were born and still describe themselves as women.) Hawley responded, "So this hearing is not about women's rights?" Bridges, exasperated by Hawley's line of questioning, said, "I want to recognize that your line of questioning is transphobic. And it opens up trans people to violence by not recognizing them."

Afterward, publications aligned with the Democratic Party applauded Bridges, in the words of *HuffPost*, for "school[ing] Hawley for his transphobic questions." Reflecting the Fox News Fallacy, they assumed that his questions were "transphobic" and that Bridges's responses were reasonable. But as *Washington Post* columnist Megan McArdle noted afterward, "few Americans would struggle with the question . . . whether women give birth." Bridges's answer, McCardle said, "won't do for a political debate in which the majority of voters disagree with you." Bridges's answer—and the attempt by the LGBTQ groups to alter language to reflect their very questionable theories of sex and gender—bore out the division between the avant-garde culture of the college towns and postindustrial metro centers and the rest of the country.

Drugs and Surgery

The most important battleground for gender politics in the Biden years has been over the use of drugs and surgery to change the sexual appearance and makeup of children and teenagers.

Like the debate over the bathroom bill, it draws extreme positions. The LGBTQ groups strongly favor what they call "gender affirmation," which creates a path from a child's initial worries about his or her true sex to drugs and eventually surgery. In response, many conservative groups have won support in some state legislatures for an outright ban on such medical procedures for minors. The Biden administration, which might have been expected to take a careful stance in the center, has thrown its weight behind those who favor gender-affirming medical intervention.

In the United States, the debate over what is called "transitioning" began with Harry Benjamin, an endocrinologist who became Christine Jorgensen's physician after she returned from Denmark. Benjamin's view anticipated that of Butler and the gender radicals. He believed that gender trumped biology. He therefore counseled people unhappy with their sex to change it through hormonal drugs and surgery. One of Benjamin's wealthy patients set up the Harry Benjamin Foundation in 1963, which later morphed into the World Professional Association for Transgender Health (WPATH). It became the arbiter of medical treatment for aspiring transgender men and women.

In the United States, few physicians accepted Benjamin's view of sex and gender. In Europe, however, there were clinics that specialized in gender transitions. In the 1990s, the Dutch developed a three-stage strategy for treating children and adolescents who suffered from confusion about their identity. Called "watchful waiting," it consisted of an initial therapeutic diagnosis with counseling, following by puberty blockers that delayed but did not necessarily prevent the hormonal changes that normally took place. Only after that, if the patient still wanted a sex change, cross-sex hormones and surgery would be permitted. In 2007, clinics began to sprout up in the US that dispensed puberty blockers and hormonal drugs and did surgery.

At present, there are more than sixty gender clinics in the United States. But the American LGBTQ groups and the psychologists and physicians that backed them favored a highly accelerated version of the Dutch protocol.

The approach favored by the groups is called "gender affirmation." Its main proponent is San Francisco psychologist Diane Ehrensaft who has been on the board of directors of Gender Spectrum and has been a consultant to WPATH. In line with Benjamin, Ehrensaft believes that there are many genders. Gender, in Ehrensaft's words, comes "in all shapes and sizes." Ehrensaft has argued that even toddlers can indicate a gender preference different from their biological sex, and she advocates encouraging children who indicate a preference other than their biological sex by providing them with the appropriate clothing, toys, activities, and first name and pronoun. Ehrensaft writes:

> When it comes to knowing a child's gender, it is not for us to tell, but for the children to say. In contrast to the watchful waiting model, once information is gathered to assess a child's gender status, action is taken to allow that child to exercise that gender. Therefore, if after careful consideration, it becomes clear that a young child is affirmed in their gender, demonstrating that the gender they know themselves is different than or opposite to the gender that would match the sex assigned to them at birth, the gender affirmative model supports a social transition to allow that child to fully live in that gender, whether that child is 3, 7, or 17 years old.

That transition includes the use of puberty blockers and cross-sex hormones that can irreversibly alter a child's sexual functioning as well as appearance. To deny a child "cross-sex hormones," Ehrensaft argues, "can create trauma in living in a body that is so alien to you and spoils any of your chances of moving gracefully in the world in your affirmed gender, increases the chances that you will always feel like a freak."

In the early 2000s, Ehrensaft's approach was countered by that of Toronto psychologist Kenneth Zucker who argued that if parents helped "children feel comfortable in their own bodies" rather than immediately encouraging them to adopt the appearance and activities of the opposite sex, many would eventually be reconciled to their biological sex. "Zucker's research showed that most young children who came to his clinic stopped identifying as another gender as they got older. Many of them would go on to come out as gay or lesbian or bisexual, suggesting previous discomfort with their sexuality, or lack of acceptance, for them or their families," the *New York Times* reported. But Canadian transgender activists succeeded in 2015 in getting the Canadian government to shut down his clinic. In WPATH, Ehrensaft's approach carried the day. Children who said or felt they were of a different sex were put on a path that led to drugs and surgery.

The Biden administration aggressively sided with the LGBTQ groups' view of transgender rights and of medical transitions. In response to the controversy over bathrooms and locker rooms, Biden's Department of Education had issued a statement threatening a cutoff of federal aid to schools that do not permit transgender students to use the facilities they choose. Biden appointed Dr. Rachel Levine, a trans woman, to be the assistant secretary for health in the Department of Health and Human Services (HHS). In response to states' banning or wanting to ban hormonal drugs and surgery for minors, HHS put out a statement that said:

> For transgender and nonbinary children and adolescents, early gender-affirming care is crucial to overall health and well-being

as it allows the child or adolescent to focus on social transitions and can increase their confidence while navigating the health-care system.

In an interview on National Public Radio and in a speech at Texas Christian University, Levine affirmed "the positive value of gender-affirming care." She told NPR, "There is no argument among medical professionals, pediatricians, pediatric endocrinologists, adolescent medicine physicians, adolescent psychiatrists, psychologists, etc., about the value and the importance of 'gender-affirming care.'" In a statement from its Office of Population Affairs, HHS has put its mark of approval on puberty blockers and "hormone therapy" during "early adolescence onward." HHS's statement lists as "resources" articles from the ACLU, Gender Spectrum, and the Human Rights Campaign.

Contrary to Levine's assertion, however, there is considerable argument about "gender-affirming care," and particularly about the use by minors of puberty blockers and cross-sex hormones. In Europe, where drugs and surgery for transitioning originated, and were more widely practiced than in the United States, Sweden, Finland, the United Kingdom, and France have all begun to back away from allowing such practices on minors. In Sweden, the National Board of Health and Welfare ruled out drugs, let alone surgery. Its 2022 report stated "that the risks of puberty suppressing treatment with GnRH-analogues and gender-affirming hormonal treatment currently outweigh the possible benefits, and that the treatments should be offered only in exceptional cases."

The Sweden reversal is particularly interesting. It came in the wake of a flood of requests from teenage girls (rather than, as before, boys) who wanted to change their gender. Many of the girls had concurrent mental illnesses and had only recently decided they wanted to be boys—suggesting that they might have been influenced through media-induced social contagion. After Swedish television and medical specialists began to air misgivings about transitioning, the girls' requests for transition plummeted.

In the United States, physicians and even federal agencies have expressed doubts about the medications used in gender-affirming care. The Food and Drug Administration warned against the side effects of puberty blockers. In 2020, before the Biden administration took charge, the Agency of Healthcare Research and Quality, which was part of the Department of Health and Human Services before Trump defunded it in 2018, stated that "there is a lack of current evidence-based guidance for care of children and adolescents who identify as transgender, particularly regarding the benefits and harms of pubertal suppression, medical affirmation with hormone therapy, and surgical affirmation." In other words, there has been plenty of argument about the benefits of gender-affirming care.

Like the LGBTQ groups' support for allowing trans women in competitive sports and their attempt to cleanse the language of the word "woman," the campaign for gender-affirming care has posed a threat to the achievements of the women's and gay movements. Part of their goal had been to reject the stereotypes of male and female behavior: to affirm that a boy who liked dolls was still a boy and a girl who cut her hair short was a girl. But according to the new transgender ideology, a boy who is accused of being a "sissy" and who begins to harbor doubts about whether he is really a boy should have his doubts reinforced; similarly, the girl who is accused of being a "tomboy" should be told that it's fine to *become* a boy.

Andrew Sullivan, the noted gay author who initiated the campaign for gay marriage, asks, "How do we know for sure if a pre-pubescent child really is trans and not just experimenting with gender the way gay kids do?" Eva Kurilova, who was chided as a child for acting "boyish," and grew up to be lesbian, makes a similar point. "The widespread belief that there is such a thing as a 'trans child' instills the notion that there is a 'wrong' way to be a little boy or a little girl. It makes kids, teens, and even adults feel like there is something wrong with not conforming to sex stereotypes."

The Impolitics of Gender Ideology

The attempt by the LGBTQ groups to protect transgender people from discrimination in housing, employment, and school admissions falls well within America's democratic tradition. But their attempts to subvert the very category of women, and the protections won by the women's movement, and to subvert the understanding of being gay and lesbian won by those movements have very little to do with democracy. It is an attempt to impose a new social conformity based on a dubious notion of gender that flies in the face of the theory of evolution. It's as if the perception that the earth is flat supersedes the findings of astronomy. The groups' efforts along these lines are also very unpopular.

As the vote in Houston in November 2015 showed, the polls may, if anything, underestimate the opposition to the extreme demands of the transgender movement. According to a May 2022 Pew Research Poll, respondents favored protecting transgender people from discrimination in employment and housing, but they didn't buy any of the radical stances of the LGBTQ groups. By 58 to 17 percent, they wanted trans athletes only to compete on teams that corresponded to their biological sex. They thought a person's gender is determined at birth by 60 to 38 percent—a spread that has been increasing since 2017. (It's also worth noting that 68 percent of blacks and 65 percent of Hispanics thought a person's gender is determined at birth.) Pluralities wanted to ban medical transitions for individuals under age eighteen and to require that trans individuals use the bathrooms of their biological sex.

Americans are also leery of the attempt to teach gender ideology to young children, which the LGBTQ groups have advocated and which some school districts, including those in Portland and Seattle, have undertaken. The Florida bill prohibiting teachers from instructing students from kindergarten to third grade about "sexual orientation or gender identity" was very popular in the state. When a polling group, Public Opinion Strategies, read the actual text of the bill to a thousand registered voters nationally, they supported it by 61 to 26 percent. When they asked specifically about discussing "gender identity" with young children, 67 percent of the respondents opposed doing so. That included a plurality of Democrats.

Local elections, particularly to school boards, could hinge on support or opposition to some form of gender ideology. It's unlikely that elections for president or Congress will. But voters' identification of Democrats with this ideology through the public declarations of the institutions of the shadow party and, in this case, through the actual positions of the Biden administration will strengthen voters' view of Democratic politics as the expression of a cultural elite that is out of touch with the sentiments and morals of most of the country.

Chapter Eleven

Apocalypse Now

Today's concern about climate change goes back to NASA scientist James Hansen's testimony before the Senate in June 1988: "Earth is warmer in 1988 than at any time in the history of instrumental measurements . . . With 99 percent confidence we can state that the warming during this time period is a real warming trend. . . . Carbon dioxide is changing our climate *now*." That same year, the United Nations created the Intergovernmental Panel on Climate Change (IPCC) to provide a mechanism for synthesizing the exploding scientific research on the issue.

The core concept that Hansen, the IPCC, and other scientists established was that the "greenhouse effect" was real, was caused by emissions of human origin, and was, in fact, changing the climate of the planet. Specifically, it was making the planet warmer over time. If the greenhouse effect was allowed to go unchecked, the climate could get warm enough to have very serious adverse effects on human societies, from rising sea levels to extreme temperatures and weather. Thus, a real problem with a real scientific basis presented itself and called for action.

That problem still exists and then some, as the level of emissions has continued to increase over the last thirty-five years.

But there remains little agreement in the United States about how to deal with it. Much of the public debate has centered on two extreme alternatives: a denial, favored by many Republicans and their supporters, that climate change exists and that anything needs to be done about it; and a radical affirmation that it does exist, poses an immediate threat to the planet, and requires draconian measures to address it, including the achievement of net zero emissions in the United States by 2030 and on the entire planet by 2050. The two extremes feed on each other. The denial of climate change induces those who favor draconian measures to raise the stakes of failure even higher, and the more dire the forecasts the more likely they will meet with denial.

The radical position is favored by prominent Democratic groups and individuals in the shadow party and by some politicians as well. It has dominated the discussion of the issue among Democrats. In our view, that's unfortunate, because the position itself is based on a selective reading of the science and a vast overestimation of what is politically and technically possible in the United States and elsewhere during the next decades. It has also, predictably, deepened the political divide between voters who live in the big postindustrial centers and those who live and work in places that depend upon steel, fertilizers, and other materials that require fossil fuels for their production—in other words, those who live in parts of America where material things are produced. There is, however, a middle ground between these extremes, and it is one that some politicians, faced with public reality, are groping toward.

The Rise of the Climate Radicals

Radical environmentalism around climate really took off from an intervention by former vice president Al Gore. His hugely influential 2006 movie *An Inconvenient Truth* did not hold back in its assessment of the direness of the climate change situation and the lateness of the hour. Gore deliberately emphasized the worst of the worst case situations in an effort to spur immediate and massive action. In fact, graphic depictions of the effects of a twenty-foot sea level rise are included in the show when that possibility is nowhere to be found in the IPCC projections for this century and for centuries and perhaps millennia to come.

In that spirit, Bill McKibben, author of the influential climate change book *The End of Nature*, and some college graduates who had been working with him, founded 350.org in 2008. Its tone was explicitly radical and apocalyptic. Its goal was to address the climate "crisis" by creating an international movement that could end the use of fossil fuels and hasten the transition to renewables (essentially, wind and solar). As the group recounts its history on its website:

> When we started organizing in 2008, we saw climate change as the most important issue facing humanity—but climate action was mired in politics and all but stalled. We didn't know how to fix things, but we knew that one missing ingredient was a climate movement that reflected the scale of the crisis.

The radicalism of the group is suggested by the name, 350 .org, which aspires to limit the CO_2 concentration in the atmosphere to 350 parts per million (ppm). But when founded, that target had already been passed so they were aspiring not just to limit global warming by moving to net zero carbon emissions but to *reverse* processes that had already taken place. In a position paper, the group was adamant that reaching their goal was necessary to "ensure that future generations are not consigned to irreversible catastrophe." Over time, they have moved from fossil fuel divestment campaigns on campuses and Days of Action demonstrations to a campaign to stop *all* new fossil fuel projects (including natural gas) and move to 100 percent renewables (no nuclear!). The group now has over 200 employees, a presence in 188 countries, and an annual budget of over $25 million. Over half of funding comes from the Tides Foundation and a host of other liberal foundations.

Naturally, expectations were high among 350.org and other climate activists when the Obama administration took office in 2009. And the administration did allocate a substantial amount of money to clean energy in the 2009 stimulus bill, the American Recovery and Reinvestment Act. The bill poured $90 billion into clean energy, more than fourteen times what Bill Clinton had proposed in 1999 and that was rejected by Congress. The administration's goal was to double renewable power generation within Obama's first term, which it did achieve.

Nevertheless, climate advocates were still quite unsatisfied with what the Obama administration initially accomplished. They viewed the failure to make fighting climate change the central focus of his administration as a sellout to fossil fuel interests. Even the administration's further actions on climate change, including the Clean Power Plan, which aimed to cut 32 percent of emissions from electrical power plants, and its agreeing to the 2015 international Paris Agreement, failed to satisfy advocates who wanted more action and faster. After all, went the thinking, the earth was burning and this was all Obama was doing?

Climate advocates had been dismayed by Obama's embrace in March 2012, in the run-up to the 2012 election, of an "all-of-the-above" approach to energy policy and the clean energy transition. He said, "We need an energy strategy for the future—an all-of-the-above strategy for the 21st century that develops every source of American-made energy." He boasted that his administration had "quadrupled the number of operating oilrigs to a record high" and "opened up millions of new acres for oil and gas exploration."

They were even more dismayed by the further development of Obama's strategy in 2014, summarized in a forty-three-page White House report, "The All-Of-The-Above Energy Strategy as a Path to Sustainable Economic Growth." The report confirmed Obama's 2012 approach noting that "The United States is producing more oil and natural gas [and] generating more electricity from renewables such as wind and solar" while prominently promoting natural gas as a "transitional fuel" to a clean energy future and advocating for more nuclear and for "clean coal"—coal where carbon emissions would be captured and stored (CCS).

The report and the strategy it outlined recognized, implicitly or explicitly, several key realities of a clean energy transition: (1) fossil fuels, especially natural gas, would continue to play a big role in the American energy mix for a long time to come; (2) energy policy has to be considered in the context of energy security; (3) energy policy has to be about economic growth and jobs not just clean energy; and (4) wind and solar, while important, are just one part of an all-of-the-above strategy.

The climate movement was appalled. 350.org denounced the strategy as "a disaster for communities and the climate." A letter was sent to Obama by eighteen other environmental organizations, including Earthjustice, Sierra Club, Environmental Defense Fund, League of Conservation Voters, and the Natural Resources Defense Council. They characterized the policy as "a compromise that future generations can't afford. It . . . locks in the extraction of fossil fuels that will inevitably lead to a catastrophic climate future."

Bill McKibben and 350.org duly upped the ante with a "A Call to Arms" for a massive climate march, which wound up getting 1,500 organizational cosponsors. On September 21, 2014, 400,000 people marched in New York for the People's Climate March, easily the biggest climate demonstration yet. By 2015, fossil fuel divestment had become the fastest-growing divestment movement in history. The climate movement, especially its radical wing around 350.org, felt it was gaining momentum.

But the election of Donald Trump threw the climate movement for a loop, as it did all movements on the left. Trump quickly repealed Obama's Clean Power Plan and withdrew the United States from the Paris Agreement. As the planet, the climate movement believed, was burning, the country was now being run by a "climate denier."

Sunrise and the Green New Deal

Rhetoric from climate activists became increasingly heated over the course of Trump's term. Organizations emerged to harness the sense of urgency around the issue, particularly among the young. In 2017, the Sunrise Movement was formed, whose tagline is "We are the climate revolution." Showing the extent to which the new climate politics was winning support, the group was initially funded by the Sierra Club, an old-line environmental organization that traditionally advocated for gradual reform and steered clear of radical organizations.

Sunrise crystallized the sense in the radical climate movement that time was running out and it was necessary to ratchet up pressure and tactics, including direct action and civil disobedience, to force a rapid transition to clean energy. Enough, said Sunrise cofounder Varshini Prakash, with "pathetic incrementalism." The group advocated for a Green New Deal—a term previously used by columnist Thomas Friedman, the U.S. Green Party, and even Bernie Sanders in 2016—that would completely transform the economy in the process of attaining carbon neutrality by 2030. The goal of their aggressive tactics, said Prakash, was to "make it politically impossible for a Democratic lawmaker to vote no on the Green New Deal."

Initially they focused their energy on allying with politicians who would support that approach and, through that, pressuring others to do so. They hit the jackpot when newly elected House representative Alexandria Ocasio-Cortes joined the organization in a sit-in at Nancy Pelosi's congressional office in November 2018, greatly elevating its profile. Riding the wave of publicity from this sit-in, Sunrise and allies pushed incoming members of Congress to support the formation of a Congressional Select Committee specifically on the Green New Deal. They got forty congressional sponsors to sign on including Senators Cory Booker, Bernie Sanders, and Jeff Merkley. The idea failed but publicity kept building.

In December, Sunrise staged another larger sit-in at Pelosi and Steny Hoyer's offices, resulting in 143 arrests. Over three hundred local elected officials from forty states issued a letter endorsing a Green New Deal. In January, over six hundred environmental and progressive organizations, including Sunrise and 350.org, did likewise. In the groups' letter, they urged a Green New Deal that would end all fossil fuel usage, including natural gas. They explicitly rejected the use of nuclear or CCS to achieve emission objectives. The transition was to be to 100 percent renewables.

In February 2019, Ocasio-Cortez and Senator Edward Markey formally introduced a congressional resolution advocating a Green New Deal. This Green New Deal proposal was everything the radicals at Sunrise could have wished for and more. The proposal affirmed that the United States must become net zero on carbon emissions by 2030 through a dramatic and far-reaching transformation of every aspect of the economy. And far from entailing sacrifice, this economic transformation would provide full employment in high-wage jobs, accompanied by universal high-quality health care and housing. It would end all oppression of indigenous people, "communities of color," migrant communities, and other "frontline and vulnerable communities." Who could ask for anything more?

The full employment aspect of the proposal was key to making it politically palatable. It countered the obvious objection that eliminating fossil fuels so quickly and disrupting the economy might result in job loss and lower wages. The proposal asserted that, on the contrary, there would be more jobs and they would all be high-wage. No trade-offs at all would be necessary.

The proposal generated enormous publicity and was injected into the mainstream of Democratic Party discourse. Six senators who would become contenders for the Democratic presidential nomination endorsed it: Cory Booker, Kirsten Gillibrand, Kamala Harris, Amy Klobuchar, Bernie Sanders, and Elizabeth Warren. Sanders would go on to release a $16.3 trillion Green New Deal plan of his own during his campaign for the Democratic nomination.

Climate Catastrophism and the Green New Deal

As Ocasio-Cortez and Markey were unveiling the Green New Deal, a young New York intellectual, David Wallace-Wells, published a highly influential *New York* magazine article that dramatized the threat that climate change posed. "The Uninhabitable Earth" was subheaded "famine, economic collapse, a sun that cooks us: What climate change could wreak—sooner than you think." In the book that came out of it, he warned that even if warming could be kept to two degrees, "The ice sheets will begin their collapse, 400 million more people will suffer from water scarcity, major cities in the equatorial band of the planet will become unlivable, and even in the northern latitudes heat waves will kill thousands each summer."

While a number of climate scientists pointed out that Wallace-Wells departed in many places from established findings and deceptively focused on only the worst possible outcomes, the general effect of his work was to raise the specter of climate catastrophe among the general public and raise receptiveness to drastic measures. As Wallace-Wells repeatedly noted, no matter how much you think you know, it's "worse than you think." It was time to contemplate "the prospect of our own annihilation."

In 2018, a fifteen-year-old Swedish activist, Greta Thunberg, came to the attention of the world's media. She stood outside the Swedish parliament every Friday with a sign, "School Strike for Climate," demanding immediate action. As she became an international media star, she warned in speeches that the world was on the verge of the apocalypse. In 2019 she told the English parliament: "Around the year 2030, 10 years 252 days and 10 hours away from now, we will be in a position where we set off an irreversible chain reaction beyond human control, that will most likely lead to the end of our civilization as we know it." At Davos, she told the great and mighty, "I don't want you to be hopeful, I want you to panic."

Thunberg's jeremiads were greeted rapturously by the world's press. But Thunberg was largely pushing on an open door. UN Secretary-General Antonio Guterres had already been talking regularly about a "climate crisis" and "climate emergency." He would later refer to the situation as a "code red for humanity." The mainstream media were under pressure by organizations like Al Gore's Climate Reality project and Extinction Rebellion to formally adopt the use of such language and align their perspective with that of the activists.

The UK *Guardian* formally updated its style guide that year to favor "climate emergency, crisis or breakdown." *Guardian* editor in chief Katharine Viner noted: "The phrase 'climate change' . . . sounds rather passive and gentle when what scientists are talking about is a catastrophe for humanity." The *Guardian* and hundreds of news organizations joined Covering Climate Now, an initiative founded in 2019 by the *Columbia Journalism Review* and the *Nation*. The initiative aimed to promote more aggressive coverage of the climate story since humanity has "just 12 years to slash heat-trapping emissions in half or else face catastrophic temperature rise and the record-breaking extreme weather it unleashes."

This was quite a significant development and helped shift the entire left of the political spectrum, including the Democratic Party, toward the catastrophist view of climate change already held by climate radicals and toward the Green New Deal as the appropriate response to the crisis. The climate radicals' theory of the case had rapidly become the Democrats'. That theory has the following components:

> Climate change is not a danger that is gradually occurring, but an imminent crisis that is already upon us in extreme weather events. It threatens the existence of the planet if immediate, drastic action is not taken. That action must include the immediate replacement of fossil fuels, including natural gas, by renewables, wind and solar, which are cheap and can be introduced right now if sufficient resources are devoted to doing so, and which, unlike nuclear power, are safe. Not only that, the immediate replacement of fossil fuels by renewables will make energy cheaper and provide high wage jobs.
>
> People resist rapidly eliminating fossil fuels only because of propaganda from the fossil fuel industry. Any of the problems with renewables that are being cited, such as their intermittency and reliability, are being solved. This means that as we use more renewables and cut out fossil fuels, political support for the transition to clean energy should go up because of the benefits to consumers and workers.

This philosophy of the Green New Deal has now taken hold in the Democrats' shadow party. It is being advanced not only by groups like 350.org, but by many groups whose traditional focus has nothing to do with climate. These include the ACLU, Planned Parenthood, and Amnesty International. President Biden, Chuck Schumer, and Nancy Pelosi and other top Democrats now unreservedly refer to climate change as an existential threat. The reformist perspective of the Obama years, which was attentive to standard Democratic concerns about jobs and prices and to the practical difficulties of a transition from fossil fuels, has been left in the rearview mirror.

The Reformist Alternative

The climate radicals' view of the issue, instantiated in the Green New Deal and now embraced by the Democrats' shadow party, is neither particularly accurate nor practical. There is an alternative, and much sounder, reformist view of climate change and energy production that is technically feasible and that would help heal the Great Divide between postindustrial metros and working-class middle America.

The basic idea of global warming is not in dispute. It is definitely happening due to human causes—about 1.1 degrees centigrade since pre-industrial times—and it is likely to go up further this century. The more it goes up, the higher the probability of large negative effects on human society. Therefore, it is important how high we expect that it will rise on our current course.

Prior to the most recent IPCC report, the most widely used scenario for future climate change was fairly extreme. Technically referred to as RCP 8.5, it projected warming of 4–5 degrees centigrade by the end of the century. This was regarded as the "business as usual" scenario—what would happen in the absence of strenuous countermeasures. It included fanciful assumptions—for instance, that the global use of coal would go up six times by 2100. Catastrophic projections of climate change effects generally used this scenario. But the latest IPCC report, based on recent changes in energy use and energy policy, now judges RCP 8.5 to have low likelihood. More moderate scenarios are judged to be much more likely, projecting warming of between 2–3 degrees C, with a best guess of around 2.6 degrees.

Climatologists Zeke Hausfather and Glen Peters noted in *Nature* that the worst-case climate scenario grows "increasingly implausible with every passing year." David Wallace-Wells of "Uninhabitable Earth" fame admitted in the *New York Times* that "we have cut expected warming almost in half in just five years."

Then there is the question of extreme weather, which is the single most important driver of the catastrophist perspective. The media and climate advocates are uniform in attributing extreme weather—all of it—to climate change. But the IPCC does not. In the IPCC report's chapter on "Weather and Climate Extreme Events in a Changing Climate" the report's authors have high confidence that heat waves, heavy precipitation, and fire weather have increased due to climate change. But they do not endorse the commonly held views that hurricanes, flooding, winter storms, tornadoes, extreme winds, and droughts with prolonged dry weather and low water supply have increased as a result of global warming.

Even where one can reasonably attribute *part* of a weather event to climate change, that does not mean that climate change precipitated the event. Take the 2021 Northwest summer heat wave. The heat wave was not caused by climate change; a lot of meteorological factors came together to produce the heat wave, which didn't have anything to do with climate change. However, the peak temperature of the wave was perhaps 1–2 degrees F higher than it would have been without global warming. But the wave's high temperatures were 30–40 degrees F over normal. Climate change was a secondary or even tertiary factor in this extreme weather event.

Finally, there is the toll that extreme weather has on human society and lives. In economic terms, increasing damages are largely accounted for by how much richer and denser human societies are; there is simply more exposure to any given disaster. In human terms, deaths from natural disasters are way down. A century ago, it was not uncommon for natural disasters to kill more than a million people annually. The average in the 2020s so far is about 13,000 per year. This is because richer societies are more resilient and far better at coping with disasters. Since societies will become richer this century, resilience will only increase.

None of this is consistent with the climate radicals' perspective. The situation is not as dire as they portray and, therefore, the necessity for drastic action is less compelling. There is space for reform and adaptation to change instead of a rapid and radical transformation of our entire economic system.

The Impracticality of Climate Radicalism

There are immense practical difficulties to attaining "net zero" in a world overwhelmingly based on fossil fuels. You simply cannot get rid of fossil fuels as fast as climate radicals want and that a Green New Deal envisions. About 84 percent of world energy consumption is from fossil fuels. It is only a point lower in the United States. This global figure is down only 2 percentage points in the last twenty years. The percent of fossil fuel usage is lower in the electricity sector—62 percent globally and 61 percent in the United States. But, and this is widely underappreciated, only 20 percent of world energy consumption is from electricity and it's only barely higher in the United States at 22 percent. The rest consists mostly of direct use of hydrocarbons to power transportation and industry, including producing what environmental scientist Vaclav Smil has called "the four pillars of modern civilization": steel, ammonia, cement, and plastics.

As Smil notes:

> [W]e are a fossil-fueled civilization whose technical and scientific advances, quality of life and prosperity rest on the combustion of huge quantities of fossil carbon, and we cannot simply walk away from this critical determinant of our fortunes in a few decades, never mind years. Complete decarbonization of the global economy by 2050 is now conceivable only at the cost of unthinkable global economic retreat.

Setting formal goals and deadlines that contravene these realties just makes it harder to achieve the progress that can be made. As Smil pointed out in an interview with the *New York Times*: "People toss out these deadlines without any reflection on the scale and the complexity of the problem . . . What's the point of setting goals which cannot be achieved? People call it aspirational. I call it delusional."

As Smil indicates, there is only one realistic way to achieve the net zero goal by 2050: economic retreat, meaning drastic cuts in our standard of living. No airplane flights. Little driving. No meat. No plastics. Energy rationing. Less consumption of all consumer goods. A lot less economic growth. That would do it but that is not a world anyone, with exception of "degrowth" advocates, wants to live in. It would be resisted vigorously in the West, particularly by the working classes, and in the developing world by the billions trying to escape from poverty into the middle class. Such a recipe for social instability would certainly not be accepted by the people and leaders of the two most populous countries in the world, China and India.

The point should be to do what works and do lots of it but not to expect a sudden and complete transformation of the fossil fuel economy. Instead, fossil fuels will be with us for quite some time while the world's economies are shifting to clean energy sources. In fact, fossil fuels have an important role to play in reducing emissions during this transition. In short, all-of-the-above was, and continues to be, the best energy policy both for the country and for a long-term clean energy transition. As Smil puts it, "We need to favor a multitude of approaches rather than relying on any single (and purportedly perfect) solution."

Consider the role of natural gas, demonized as a fossil fuel. While not widely acknowledged, the significant decline in emissions in electricity production has primarily been driven by the substitution of natural gas for coal rather than by the use of renewables. According to the U.S. Energy Information Agency (EIA), natural gas is responsible for about two-thirds of the emissions decline between 2005 to 2019 compared to 30 percent for renewables. This underscores the role natural gas will play in the future, not just in the everyday economy, but serving as a bridge fuel in a clean energy transition. The EU, reflecting this, recently recognized gas, along with nuclear, as "green" energy sources. Not only that but, as Smil notes in the interview, a concerted effort to get rid of "fugitive emissions" of methane in natural gas production would make gas even more low carbon.

Renewables will also need to be backed up for the foreseeable future by other types of energy. Renewable energy sources, due to the intermittency problem, *always* have to be backstopped by "firm" power that can be switched on when necessary. That means coal, nuclear, and, most commonly these days, natural gas. Having to keep these firm sources around and always ready to be turned on is a hidden cost of renewables; the larger the share of renewables in the energy mix, the higher these costs are and the higher the potential of unreliability, blackouts, price spikes, and other symptoms of "energy crises" when the requisite firm power has not been provided for or is cut off due to weather events or geopolitical shocks like the Russia-Ukraine war. That is one reason why increased use of renewables has *not* produced lower energy prices for consumers so far; quite the opposite, especially in heavy renewables-dependent places like Germany and California. This does not sit well with consumers, particularly working-class consumers. And those consumers vote.

What people want—and need—is abundant, cheap, reliable energy. Therefore if what you are advocating appears to call that goal into question, no amount of rhetoric about a roasting planet and no amount of effort to tie every natural disaster to climate change is likely to generate the support needed for what is sure to be a lengthy energy transition. In opinion polls, respondents generally rate climate change low on the ladder of which problems government should address. According to a 2022 Gallup Poll, only 3 percent of respondents saw climate change as the "most important problem." In a Pew survey that asked the public to rank what should be a top policy priority, climate change came in way behind strengthening the economy, reducing healthcare costs, dealing with the coronavirus, improving education, defending against terrorism, improving the political system, reducing crime, and improving the job situation. It also trailed dealing with immigration, reducing the deficit, addressing the criminal justice system, and dealing with the problems of poor people. That's twelve issues in front of climate change.

Climate change did come in sixth among college-educated respondents, but it came in fourteenth among working-class respondents. While having a very high salience in the Democratic shadow party, climate change has low salience for ordinary voters, particularly working-class voters. Working-class voters are not willing to sacrifice much to combat it—less than half of working-class voters say they would be willing to pay even an extra dollar per month on their electricity bills to combat climate change.

These voters are also right not to be taken in by the claims that the Green New Deal will create high-wage full employment.

That has certainly not been the case so far. Instead, projects on renewables have created short-term construction jobs that bear little resemblance to the middle-class jobs promised and to the high-wage jobs in the fossil fuel industry they are supposed to replace. A *New York Times* investigation of jobs in the solar and wind sectors described them as looking less like the mid-century blue collar jobs that lifted workers into the middle class and more like jobs in an "Amazon warehouse or a fleet of Uber drivers: grueling work schedules, few unions, middling wages and limited benefits." A utility workers organizer described the industry as "a lot of transient work, work that is marginal, pre-carious and very difficult to be able to organize."

What voters do want is an all-of-the-above strategy that pushes forward renewables while continuing to use a mix of energy sources including fossil fuels. They say they prefer that approach to one that relies exclusively on renewable sources by 67 to 31 percent. In this case, what voters want corresponds to the most practical course in pursuing a clean energy transition while ensuring a reliable and secure supply of cheap energy and solid growth. To go against this approach, as urged by climate radicals, is to accentuate the Great Divide between postindus-trial metros and middle America, between the Democratic shadow party and the working class.

Back to All-of-the-Above

On the very first day Biden came into office, he signed two executive orders on U.S. oil and gas production. The first said that America would rejoin the Paris climate accords. The other blocked oil and gas exploration in the Arctic National Wildlife Refuge as well as drilling in large parts of Utah. And critically, it canceled the Keystone XL pipeline between the United States and Canada. A week later, Biden stopped issuing new oil and gas leases on public lands. This was definitely not consistent with an all-of-the-above strategy but it was completely in line with what climate radicals and supporters of the Green New Deal demanded.

As a result of the war in Ukraine, the energy situation became more dire in Europe and began to bite in the United States through rising energy prices. The administration relented and began calling for more oil from domestic and international producers, as well reopening oil and gas leasing on a limited basis. However, this tentative step back toward an all-of-the-above approach was not accompanied by a plan to ensure long-term supplies of oil and gas in the country, which will continue to be necessary for the economy's smooth functioning and to backstop a renewables rollout.

The Biden administration managed to pass $1.5 trillion in new spending through the Infrastructure Investment and Jobs Act, the CHIPS and Science Act, and the Inflation Reduction Act or IRA in addition to the stimulus-oriented American Rescue Plan. Of that $1.5 trillion, half a trillion is on climate—some in the bipartisan infrastructure bill but mostly in the IRA. Commendably the bill stepped away from the Green New Deal and back toward an all-of-the-above approach. While that half a trillion is still centered on promotion of renewables and related infrastructure, there is some serious support in the bill for nuclear, geothermal, and CCS. There was even some support for opening up more federal lands to oil and gas development.

The oil and gas provisions were at the insistence of Senator Joe Manchin, without whose support the bill could not have passed. Manchin also extracted support for a side deal to reform the permitting process for infrastructure projects in order to allow these projects, both for fossil fuel and for non–fossil fuel purposes, to move forward faster. Critically for Manchin, the side deal would have allowed completion of the natural gas

Mountain Valley Pipeline in his home state. However, the climate radicals and their supporters in Congress were already extremely upset that there was any support at all for oil and gas in the IRA and they opposed Manchin's permitting reform as a "dirty deal." Sunrise, 350.org, the Sierra Club, Greenpeace, Earthjustice, the Wilderness Society, the League of Conservation Voters, and hundreds of other environmental groups came out against it, as did more than seventy House Democrats and ten Senate Democrats, including Green New Deal supporters Booker, Markey, Sanders, and Warren. In the end, the side deal for permitting reform failed miserably.

This was an amazing result. It contradicted the all-of-the-above spirit of the IRA by rejecting a bill simply because it would have allowed some fossil fuel projects to go ahead. And it even kneecapped the renewable energy commitments of the IRA. Reducing carbon emissions depends on an absolutely massive build-out of infrastructure, especially interregional high voltage transmission lines. It is very hard to build such things fast in the United States, given permitting obstacles. Even with the permitting reform bill, the pace at which this infrastructure could plausibly have been built was likely far below what would be needed to hit administration timetables. Without permitting reform, the pace will be truly glacial.

The lack of permitting reform also interferes with the IRA's commitments to nuclear energy. Partly due to the war-induced sanctions on Russian natural gas, there is now a renaissance in nuclear energy throughout the world, as country after country reverses course and embraces the necessity of a nuclear build-out: the Czech Republic, Netherlands, Poland, South Korea, the UK, Sweden, and even Japan, which had anathematized nuclear after the 2011 Fukushima incident. But the United States will be hard-pressed to participate in this renaissance without regulatory changes that would facilitate the building of new reactors.

Instead, the Nuclear Regulatory Commission released a draft of new rules in September 2022 that would make it harder, not easier, to build them.

All these problems—the clear imbalance of support between renewables and alternatives like nuclear and CCS, the tepid support for natural gas, and the failure to implement permitting reform that would jointly benefit renewables, gas, and nuclear—undercut what could have been a decisive move back toward a practical climate policy. These problems are the result of the climate radicals' fanatical hostility to fossil fuels and millenarian faith that renewables can rapidly deliver the world from a climate catastrophe. The view of the radicals reflects an apocalyptic strain in American thinking that periodically arises in response to crises, but does little to solve them.

Climate change is a serious problem, but one that can only be solved over decades with massive technological innovation across potential energy sources, serious nuclear and CCS programs, and a long-term role for natural gas, rather than through a quixotic attempt to remake the global economy around renewables in a short span of time. But the Democrats, influenced by the climate radicals and the illusory promise of a Green New Deal, still do not have a practical approach to the issue. What started as a reasonable attempt to deal with a genuine problem, in the spirit of reformist environmentalism, has been hijacked by a millenarian, quasi-religious commitment to rapidly zeroing out fossil fuels and creating a renewables-based economy. This hasn't worked and will not work. It will also widen the Great Divide and undermine the Democrats as an electoral force.

Conclusion

The War of Words

There is no common meaning of the term "liberal." In Australia, the Liberal Party espouses what by American usage would be called "conservative" politics. But in the United States, the term "liberal" has undergone changes in the last century that perfectly track the transformation of the Democratic Party. What we are proposing can be expressed in terms of the changes that have occurred. We are proposing that the Democrats embrace the economic liberalism that was handed down to Franklin Roosevelt from David Lloyd George, John Maynard Keynes, and the British Liberal Party of the early twentieth century and reject today's post-sixties version of social liberalism, which is tantamount to cultural radicalism. We're not guaranteeing that if Democrats do so they'll win every election. This is not a guidebook for political consultants. What interests us is the Democratic Party becoming the kind of party this country, which is coming apart geographically and economically, desperately needs.

The History of Liberalism

The use of "liberal" as signifying a set of political beliefs goes back to early-nineteenth-century England and to the founding of the Liberal Party. Liberals like Richard Cobden and John Bright believed, above all, in free trade, which they argued would lower the price of food imports and raise the real wages of British workers and help British manufacturers sell their products abroad. The Liberals also believed in the expansion of the franchise, and freedom of the press and religion. Like America's Jacksonians, they opposed government intervention as an instrument of monopoly. The group today that they most resemble in political platform is the right-wing Cato Institute in Washington and the Libertarian Party, but in the context of the times the early British Liberals were more on the left than the right.

In the first decade of the twentieth century, eager to incorporate the growing labor movement and labor politics, the British Liberal Party abandoned laissez-faire economics and became the champion of what would become the modern British welfare state. Liberal thinkers like Leonard Hobhouse and John Hobson drew a distinction between negative liberty—freedom from government restraint—and positive liberty—freedom to be employed and to enjoy economic security, which required government intervention. The Liberals introduced a progressive income tax and an old-age pension program and broached the idea of national health insurance.

In the United States, the *New Republic* began using the term "liberal" in the late 1910s to describe Woodrow Wilson's domestic and foreign policy. The term then lay fallow until 1932 when, during his presidential campaign, Franklin Roosevelt resurrected it. Roosevelt admired Lloyd George and the British Liberals and understood their attempt to find a middle ground between conservative laissez-faire and socialist collectivism. The liberal, Roosevelt told author Anne O'Hare McCormick, "recognizes the need for new machinery, but works to control the processes of change, to the end that the break with the old pattern might not be too violent."

Roosevelt's liberalism, like the nineteenth-century variety, included a defense of political and religious liberty, but its central tenet, and what it came to be known for, was the use of the "new machinery" of government to effect major social and economic changes for ordinary working Americans. In his 1944 State of the Union address, only a year and three months before he died, Roosevelt spelled out his Second Bill of Rights.

- The right to a useful and remunerative job in the industries or shops or farms or mines of the Nation;
- The right to earn enough to provide adequate food and clothing and recreation;
- The right of every farmer to raise and sell his products at a return which will give him and his family a decent living;
- The right of every businessman, large and small, to trade in an atmosphere of freedom from unfair competition and domination by monopolies at home or abroad;
- The right of every family to a decent home;
- The right to adequate medical care and the opportunity to achieve and enjoy good health;
- The right to adequate protection from the economic fears of old age, sickness, accident, and unemployment;
- The right to a good education.

Roosevelt's New Deal liberalism became the faith of Democratic liberals after World War II. It was clearly articulated in Arthur Schlesinger's 1949 book *The Vital Center*. It was central to the party's claim to be the party of the common man and woman. But two decades later, the term "liberal" began to change its meaning.

During the '60s, new left activists and scholars criticized "Cold War liberals" and "corporate liberals." They condemned the "liberals" of the Kennedy and Johnson administrations for supporting the Vietnam War and liberals, including Roosevelt, for tailoring their economic reforms to please big business. But after the Vietnam War ended and what was called "the movement" expired, many of the causes new left groups had begun to champion—abortion rights, the Equal Rights Amendment, civil rights and affirmative action, gay rights, and consumer and environmental protection—became associated with being liberal. The new associations with liberalism stuck and even began to overshadow the old.

It happened due to the decline of the labor movement and the disappearance of the big city machines, which had anchored the party's economic liberalism, and the growth and endurance of the post-sixties social and environmental organizations. These changes in the party's political infrastructure were matched by the transformation of the party's electorate from one that was based in the blue-collar working class to one that included and was highly influenced by college-educated professionals whose principal concerns were social and environmental.

By the early twenty-first century, the change in the meaning of liberalism was complete. Being liberal had come to refer primarily to stands on such issues as abortion, gun control, affirmative action, and climate change. If you look online for sites that tell you whether you are a liberal or conservative, you'll find that most of the questions are about your support or opposition to flag burning and kneeling when the national anthem is played, gun control, the death penalty, gay marriage, abortion, sex change operations, affirmative action, criminal justice, and illegal immigration. The American Enterprise Institute offers "32 Questions to Determine Whether a Friend or Relative Is a Liberal or Leftist?" Only one of the questions pertains directly to economics.

Liberals vs. Conservatives

Oddly enough, the term "conservative" has undergone a similar transformation. The hallmark of the Reagan conservatives who took control of the Republican Party in 1980 had been militant opposition to Soviet Communism (the rollback rather than merely the containment of Communism) and opposition to government regulation and taxation of business. Many of them had opposed the civil rights acts but, in contrast to the Wallace supporters, had not made that their defining cause. Similarly, some of them had opposed *Roe v. Wade* and the Equal Rights Amendment, but that, too, was not a defining cause. As governor of California, Reagan had signed the country's first abortion rights law.

But during the last three decades of the twentieth century, Republican ranks were swelled by three groups that overlapped: southern and also some northern Democrats who opposed racial desegregation and later busing, affirmative action, and welfare legislation; opponents of illegal immigration and of gun control; and conservative Fundamentalists and Pentecostals who opposed the Supreme Court rulings on abortion and school prayer and who saw the Democrats as having embraced the "sex, drugs, and rock n' roll" counterculture of the sixties. Many of these voters had also been ardent anti-Communists but, with the Cold War's end, they lost enthusiasm for foreign intervention except in cases where they felt their own lives and livelihoods were directly threatened. Advocates for these groups became in many states the most visible manifestation of the Republican Party.

These new groups, epitomized in the twenty-first century by the Tea Party, began to redefine what conservatism meant, and what the Republican Party stood for. If you look at online questionnaires for whether someone is a conservative, they mirror the questions asked to determine whether someone is a liberal. One site, for instance, lists eighteen questions to determine whether you are a conservative. Only one—on balanced budgets—is directly about economics. None are directly on foreign policy, once the defining cause of the conservatism of William F. Buckley Jr.'s *National Review* or the 1964 Barry Goldwater presidential campaign.

The transformed meanings of liberal and conservative became reinforced by political campaigns. Democrats would campaign against the more extreme version of Republican social conservatism, and Republicans against the most extreme version of Democrats' social liberalism. In 1984, the Mondale campaign discovered that the only issue on which he could gain traction against Reagan was Reagan's support for a constitutional amendment to overturn *Roe v. Wade*. In 1988, George H. W. Bush, trailing Democrat Michael Dukakis by 17 points on the eve of the Republican convention, began attacking Dukakis for his veto as Massachusetts governor of a bill requiring teachers to lead students in reciting the Pledge of Allegiance and for his opposition to capital punishment. The campaign's most memorable ad was of a black convict, Willie Horton, who, the ad claimed, had committed rape and armed robbery when furloughed under a program Dukakis had backed. Bush's attacks turned around his campaign and he won easily in November.

In Virginia, Democrats were able to use the Republican Party's close association to religious right leaders Pat Robertson and Jerry Falwell and their organizations to turn what had once been a conservative Democratic state and then a dependably Republican state into a state that tilted Democratic. In California, Democrats were able to use the xenophobic undertones of the Republican campaign for Proposition 187 in 1994 to win over the state's Hispanic electorate.

In almost every election since 2016, the result has rested on which party is able to best link the other party's candidate to the cultural radical strands within their party. In 2016, Trump pilloried Clinton on political correctness and immigration; in 2018 and 2020, Democrats got Trump on his casual bigotry; in 2022, Democrats won races where the Court's *Dobbs* decision on abortion and Trump's assault on democracy were the major issues; and the Republicans defeated the Democrats when crime and immigration were more salient.

Rejecting Cultural Extremes

There are, of course, people who score 100 percent on these tests of whether they are liberal or conservative. They belong, we would suspect, to the activist extremes of either party— the people who staff the shadow party organizations. But most Americans fit somewhere in between the extremes, and are leery of both. When voters are asked to rate themselves as a scale from liberal to conservative, they usually come out in the middle. As the parties themselves have become increasingly identified with their cultural extremes, more voters identify themselves as "independents." According to Gallup, Democrats and independents took up equal parts of the overall electorate in 2008, but the ranks of people who identified as independents began to swell after that. In 2022, 41 percent identified as "independent" compared to 28 percent as Republican or Democrat.

When you look at individual issues, it's clear that both parties are failing the electorate. As the 2022 election showed, most of the country opposes outright bans on abortion. But when the question is whether there should be any limits on abortion, many people are hesitant to support the Democrats' version of cultural radicalism, which is for, in the words of a Democratic bill that passed the House, "every individual to have the right to make their own decisions about having children regardless of their circumstances and without interference and discrimination." In a 2019 Gallup Poll, only 28 percent of respondents thought there should be no restrictions on abortion during the second trimester. There is a lesson here for both parties.

In May of 2022, we got a polling group, Public Policy Polling, to ask primary voters in Wisconsin whether they agreed with statements we formulated that represented a midpoint between the extremes on current controversies about race, immigration, patriotism, sex and gender, political correctness, and the police. Here is what they found.

America is not perfect, but it is good to be patriotic and proud of the country. 71 percent of Democrats and 93 percent of Republicans agreed.

Discrimination and racism are bad, but they are not the cause of all disparities in American society. 62 percent of Democrats agreed and 91 percent of Republicans.

Equality of opportunity is a fundamental American principle; equality of outcome is not. 66 percent of Wisconsin Democrats and 73 percent of Republicans agreed.

No one is completely without bias, but calling all white people racists who benefit from white privilege and American society a white supremacist society is not right or fair. 55 percent of Democrats agreed and 87 percent of Republicans agreed.

America benefits from the presence of immigrants, and no immigrant—even if illegal—should be mistreated. But border security is still important, as is an enforceable system that fairly decides who can enter the country. 74 percent of Democrats and 89 percent of Republicans agreed.

Police misconduct and brutality against people of any race is wrong, and we need to reform police conduct and recruitment. More and better policing is needed for public safety,

and that cannot be provided by "defunding the police."
69 percent of Democrats and 91 percent of Republicans
agreed.

*There are underlying differences between men and women,
but discrimination on the basis of gender is wrong.* 90 percent of Democrats and 91 percent of Republicans agreed.

*There are basically two genders, but people who want to live as
a gender different from their biological sex should have that
right and not be discriminated against. However, there are
issues around child consent to transitioning and participation in women's sports that are complicated and not settled.*
65 percent of Democrats and 76 percent of Republicans
agreed.

*Racial achievement gaps are bad and we should seek to close
them. However, they are not due just to racism, and standards of high achievement should be maintained for people
of all races,* 64 percent of Democrats and 91 percent of
Republicans agreed.

*Language policing has gone too far. By and large, people
should be able to express their views without fear of sanction by employer, school, institution, or government. Good
faith should be assumed, not bad faith.* 61 percent of Democrats and 91 percent of Republicans agreed.

The various statements were agreed to on average by 87.3
percent of Republicans and 67.7 percent of Democrats. In liberal Massachusetts, where one might imagine voters were more
supportive of cultural radicalism, a pollster, Louis DiNatale, who
asked these questions, got a very similar response. For instance,
the statement that "discrimination and racism are bad, but they
are not the cause of all disparities in American society" drew 72
to 20 percent agreement from likely voters, including 63 percent of blacks, 70 percent of Asians, and 65 percent of Hispanics.

Do you agree with the following statements?

Among 2022 Wisconsin primary voters

■ Democrats (%) ■ Republicans (%)

"America is not perfect, but it is good to be patriotic and proud of the country."

71
93

"Discrimination and racism are bad, but they are not the cause of all disparities in American society."

62
91

"Equality of opportunity is a fundamental American principle; equality of outcome is not."

66
73

"No one is completely without bias, but calling all white people racists who benefit from white privilege and American society a white supremacist society is not right or fair."

55
87

"America benefits from the presence of immigrants, and no immigrant—even if illegal—should be mistreated. But border security is still important, as is an enforceable system that fairly decides who can enter the country."

74
89

"Police misconduct and brutality against people of any race is wrong, and we need to reform police conduct and recruitment. More and better policing is needed for public safety, and that cannot be provided by 'defunding the police.'"

69
91

"There are underlying differences between men and women, but discrimination on the basis of gender is wrong."

90
91

"There are basically two genders, but people who want to live as a gender different from their biological sex should have that right and not be discriminated against. However, there are issues around child consent to transitioning and participation in women's sports that are complicated and not settled."

65
76

"Racial achievement gaps are bad and we should seek to close them. However, they are not due just to racism, and standards of high achievement should be maintained for people of all races."

64
91

"Language policing has gone too far. By and large, people should be able to express their views without fear of sanction by employer, school, institution, or government. Good faith should be assumed, not bad faith.

61
91

Source: Public Policy Polling survey of Wisconsin primary voters, May 2022.

Similarly, the statement about reforming but not defunding the police was backed by 63 to 26 percent of voters, including two to one support among blacks, Hispanics, and Asians.

What these results show is that the seemingly harsh differences in cultural outlook that have come to define liberalism and conservatism don't reflect the positions of most American voters. They are products partly of the American two-party system, which encourages each party to try to unearth what is most controversial in the other and of the shadow party groups and individuals on both sides who for decades have promoted cultural radicalism on race, immigration, sex and gender, the environment, faith, family, and flag.

The Alternative

If you look at the country's voters, and put aside the culture wars, what you find are genuine differences between the parties' voters over economic issues. In the Democratic Party, you'll find wide agreement among voters on Roosevelt's Second Bill of Rights, support for unions and labor law reform, support for campaign finance that will eliminate dark money and limit the roll of the very rich, support for progressive taxation of income and wealth, support for revising our tax laws to remove incentives for corporations to flee our shores, support for an industrial policy that will encourage our most advanced industries, and support for a sensible, incremental transition to a low-carbon economy that takes advantage of nuclear power and natural gas. You'll also find support for strong government regulation of finance, including hedge funds and cryptocurrency, and support for environmental and consumer protection. If you start talking about huge programs that will cause higher taxes, or programs that are targeted to specific groups, you get disagreement. You'll also find disagreements about unions, free trade, financial regulations, and wealth taxes from some of the party's supporters in Silicon Valley and Wall Street, but they make up a very small minority of the Democratic electorate.

In today's Republican Party, if you strip away the protestations of the religious right and the nativism and racism and xenophobia of the alt-right, you will find extensive support for lower taxes on business and individuals, including the wealthy, an end to the inheritance tax, limits on financial regulation, support for reducing spending on targeted social welfare programs, opposition to the practices of the Internal Revenue Service, and hostility to unions and environmental and consumer product regulation. You'll also find skepticism about whether or how much humans have contributed to climate change and about a conversion to clean energy sources. But, as Trump's vote revealed, you might not find support for cutting Social Security or Medicare except among some business elites and the party's ideologues.

Election results depend, of course, on circumstances that may be beyond the control of any party. Business cycle turndowns remain unavoidable, and the party in power at the time is bound to be penalized. Foreign policy ventures that alienate public opinion— which Democrats as well as Republicans have undertaken—can discredit a party and its candidates. But if you were to hold an election that simply pitted Democratic against Republican economics, shorn of hyperbolic claims about government, and of cultural differences over abortion, crime, and other social issues, Democrats would have an advantage except, perhaps, on the economics of immigration. Democrats could even win elections in what seem like Republican bastions. In 2014, a Republican year, voters in Alaska, Arkansas, South Dakota, and Nebraska approved referenda to raise their minimum wage. Over the last six years, voters in South Dakota, Idaho, Nebraska, Utah, Missouri, and Oklahoma voted to expand Medicaid eligibility within the Affordable Care Act. In Idaho in 2018, the referenda won 60.6 percent of the vote.

What these kind of results suggest is that if the Democrats could focus on liberal economics, they could win elections even in places like Idaho.

Why don't they or haven't they? There are two reasons. As we argued in the first part of this book, Democratic economic policy, when in power, has been heavily influenced by Wall Street and Silicon Valley. The decline of the labor movement has undermined the Democrats' New Deal liberal economic agenda. The second reason, which we have described in the second part of this book, is the influence of cultural radicals and their organizations within the Democrats' shadow party. As our polling in Wisconsin and Massachusetts clearly showed, most voters do not agree with the party's cultural radicals, and as long as the party is identified with them, it will not win the majorities it needs in order to enact its liberal economic agenda.

Our argument is that America needs a Democratic Party that is liberal on economics and moderate and conciliatory on cultural issues. And being "moderate" doesn't mean simply splitting the differences between positions. On the headline issues of race, immigration, gender, and climate change, the Democrats have advanced substantive reform measures that take seriously racial inequality, the plight of illegal immigrants and the need for border security, discrimination against transgender people and the rights of women, and the genuine threat posed by climate change, but under the influence of cultural radicals, it has abandoned these positions. Democrats need to go back and take a second look at William Julius Wilson's *The Truly Disadvantaged*, at the reports of the Hesburgh and the Jordan Commissions on immigration, at the traditional stands of the women's and gay movements, and at the Obama administration's approach to climate change.

If readers have arrived at this point in our argument, they may wonder why we have written an entire book about the failings of the Democratic Party to maintain a popular majority and have not dwelled on the failings of the Republican Party. Why not write a book about the January Sixth assault on the Capitol, the Republican-dominated Supreme Court's hostility to workers' and women's rights, the Republican book bans and rejection of science (whether over climate or disease), the Republican-sponsored concealed carry laws that allow gunslingers into public places, Republican support for tax breaks for the rich and the gutting of the EPA—the list goes on? There are, however, many articles and books written about the Republicans. There are already more books written about Trump's four years in office than about the last three Democratic presidents combined. Democrats, we believe, need to look in the mirror and examine the extent to which their own failures contributed to the rise of the most toxic tendencies on the political right.

We are living at one of those times when a host of assumptions that have governed our foreign and domestic policy and our civic life are being thrown into question. Trump's victory in 2016 was a clear warning sign that something was amiss: that the policies on trade, markets, immigration, Russia, and China were in need of repair. During his first two years in office, Biden gave an inkling of the kind of new economic approaches that might be needed, but the new Republican majority in the House of Representatives is likely to block any further advance. Washington will be back to debating whether to raise the debt ceiling and to ban abortion outright and whether the sins of Joe Biden's remaining son should be visited upon his father. We will not get a new New Deal, but more of the old nonsense that has driven Americans to distraction over the last decades and that has threatened America's ability to respond to challenges at home and abroad.

Our argument is that the Democrats, for all their failings, are better positioned to meet those challenges. But they can only do so if they reclaim the majority that was once theirs. That majority was based on their being the party of the common, average, ordinary man and woman. Such a party can accommodate six-figure techies and socially minded Wall Streeters and industry CEOs, but it has to be based squarely on the interests of the many rather than the few. The Democrats have to be the party of the people.

Notes

Introduction

1 **In the 2016 election:** Baltimore county government website, https://www.bal timorecountymd.gov/departments/elections/results. Thanks to Andrew Cherlin for deciphering these tables.

1 **We interviewed Robert Price:** Interview with John B. Judis.

2 **The Democratic Party:** On Jackson and Roosevelt's appeal, see Michael Kazin, *What It Took to Win: A History of the Democratic Party* (New York: Farrar, Straus and Giroux, 2022), chapter one.

4 **"Well, I think":** Correspondence from Bill Moyers.

6 **Biden won 83 percent:** Kevin Forestieri, "Mountain View Swings Left, but Rejects Statewide Changes to Rent Control," *Mountain View Voice*, Monday, November 9, 2020, https://mv-voice.com/news/2020/11/09/election-recap-mountain-view -swings-left-but-rejects-statewide-changes-to-rent-control?fbclid=IwAR17en2fsShjd cJREPbkSszEwU4Yuf1j2yU041-44Jn6ga0-_9B5vE4ylWM.

6 **His constituents, Khanna explained:** Interview with John B. Judis.

7 **Former Mountain View mayor Lenny Siegel:** Interview with John B. Judis.

12 **Prior to the 2022 election:** Justin Fox, "Are Republicans Right About America's Crime Wave?" *Bloomberg*, November 4, 2022, https://www.washingtonpost .com/business/are-republicans-right-about-americas-crime-wave-lets-look-at-the -data/2022/11/04/dccc85ba-5c34-11ed-bc40-b5a130f95ee7_story.html.

12 **Philip Bump:** Philip Bump, "Crime Is Surging (in Fox News Coverage)," *Washington Post*, October 6, 2022. On the crime wave, see Council on Criminal Justice, "Pandemic, Social Unrest, and Crime in U.S. Cites: Year-end 2022 Update," January 25, 2023, https://counciloncj.org/pandemic-social-unrest-and-crime-in -u-s-cities-year-end-2022-update/.

12 **The New Deal liberals:** On the conservative social outlook of the New Deal and the thirties, see Warren I. Susman, "The Culture of the Thirties," in *Culture as History: The Transformation of American Society in the Twentieth Century* (New York: Pantheon Books, 1984); and T. V. Smith, "The New Deal as a Cultural Phenomenon," in *Ideological Differences and World Order*, ed. F. S. C. Northrop (New Haven: Yale University Press, 1949).

Chapter One: The Rise and Fall of the Emerging Democratic Majority

19 **In the 1950s, professionals made up:** The 1950s estimate is derived from deflating the combined figure for professional, technical, and kindred workers found in Census Bureau, *Historical Statistics of the United States*, 1976, https://www2.census.gov/library/publications/1975/compendia/hist_stats_colonial-1970/hist_stats_colonial-1970p1-chD.pdf; 2021 estimate is from Bureau of Labor Statistics, detailed occupation statistics tables, https://www.bls.gov/cps/cpsaat11.pdf.

19 **Around half of adult women:** Census Bureau, "America's Families and Living Arrangements: 2021," November 29, 2021, https://www.census.gov/data/tables/2021/demo/families/cps-2021.html; Howard Fullerton Jr., "Labor Force Participation: 75 Years of Change, 1950–98 and 1998–2025," *Monthly Labor Review*, December 1999, https://www.bls.gov/mlr/1999/12/art1full.pdf; and U.S. Bureau of Labor Statistics, "Civilian Labor Force Participation Rate by Age, Sex, Race, and Ethnicity," https://www.bls.gov/emp/tables/civilian-labor-force-participation-rate.htm.

20 **In 2020, women:** Catalist, "What Happened in 2022 National Crosstabs," https://www.dropbox.com/s/re0gtn1o57fzwp5/Catalist_What_Happened_2022_Public_National_Crosstabs_2023_05_18.xlsx?dl=0.

21 **rising groups, Obama received:** Catalist, "What Happened in 2020 National Crosstabs," https://www.dropbox.com/s/ka9n5gzxwotfu1a/wh2020_public_release_crosstabs.xlsx?dl=0.

21 **We hadn't included:** Karlyn Bowman and Samantha Goldstein, "The Exit Polls: A History and Trends over Time, 1972–2020," American Enterprise Institute, January 2022, https://www.aei.org/wp-content/uploads/2022/01/The-Exit-Polls.pdf?x91208h; and Robert Griffin, William H. Frey, and Ruy Teixeira, "America's Electoral Future: The Coming Generational Transformation," Center for American Progress, October 2020, https://www.americanprogress.org/wp-content/uploads/2020/10/StatesOfChange2020-report1.pdf.

21 **And he dominated:** Bowman and Goldstein, "The Exit Polls."

22 **lost these voters:** Catalist, "What Happened in 2022 National Crosstabs."

22 **According to Catalist:** Catalist, two-party vote data found in "What Happened in Wisconsin: 2020 Crosstabs," https://www.dropbox.com/s/tao4oclcv3xqpz9/wh2020_public_release_crosstabs_WI.xlsx?dl=0.

23 **The Democratic deficit:** Yair Ghitza, "Revisiting What Happened in the 2018 Election," Catalist, May 2019, https://medium.com/@yghitza_48326/revisiting-what-happened-in-the-2018-election-c532feb51c0.

25 **The national deficit:** Catalist, "What Happened in 2022 National Crosstabs."

25 **In Wisconsin:** Catalist, two-party vote data found in "What Happened in Wisconsin: 2020 Crosstabs."

27 **working-class voters explain:** All data in this and previous paragraph from Rob Griffin, Ruy Teixeira, and William H. Frey, "America's Electoral Future: Demographic Shifts and the Future of the Trump Coalition," Center for American Progress, April 2018, https://www.americanprogress.org/wp-content/uploads/sites/2/2018/04/ElectoralFuture-report2.pdf.

27 **The Great Divide:** Robert Griffin and Ruy Teixeira, "The Story of Trump's Appeal: A Portrait of Trump Voters," Voter Study Group, Democracy Fund, June 2017, https://www.voterstudygroup.org/publication/story-of-trumps-appeal; David Autor, David Dorn, Gordon Hanson, and Kaveh Majlesi, "Importing Political Polarization? The Electoral Consequences of Rising Trade Exposure," *American Economic Review* 110, no. 10 (2020): 3139–83; and Anne Case and Angus Deaton, *Deaths of Despair and the Future of Capitalism* (Princeton, NJ: Princeton University Press, 2020).

27 **Obama had won Iowa's:** Here and elsewhere on county 2008–12–16 comparisons, Ballotopedia, "Pivot Counties by State," https://ballotpedia.org/Pivot_Counties_by_state

28 **of the population by 2045:** William H. Freyh, "The US Will Become 'Minority White' in 2045, Census Projects," Brookings, March 14, 2018, https://www.brookings.edu/blog/the-avenue/2018/03/14/the-us-will-become-minority-white-in-2045-census-projects/; and Ruy Teixeira, William H. Frey, and Robert Griffin, "The Demographic Evolution of the American Electorate, 1974–2060," Center for American Progress, February 2015, https://www.americanprogress.org/wp-content/uploads/2015/08/SOC-reportAugust15.pdf.

29 **had checked the white box:** Ruy Teixeira, "Defining 'White' and 'Hispanic' in Majority-Minority America," Center for American Progress, June 19, 2013, https://archive.thinkprogress.org/defining-white-and-hispanic-in-majority-minority-america-e5fe78dfdc4d/.

29 **Furthermore, as sociologists:** Richard Alba, Morris Levy, and Dowell Myers, "The Myth of a Majority-Minority America," *Atlantic*, June 13, 2021.

29 **Davis by 20 points:** 2014 network exit poll, Texas governor, https://www.nbcnews.com/politics/elections/2014/tx/governor/exitpoll/.

30 **got over 40 percent:** Dave Leip's Atlas of US Election Results, Texas county results, https://uselectionatlas.org/RESULTS/.

30 **Gonzales won:** Daily Kos Elections, "House and Senate 5-Year American Community Survey Racial Demographics by Congressional District," https://docs.google.com/spreadsheets/d/14gFG9uQgJ-qTq3lkTNQ9YbhB9C8s3Gy78I1eqd7EpRM/edit#gid=1893110628l.

31 **In Nevada:** Yair Ghitza and Haris Aqeel, "What Happened in 2022," Catalist, May 2023, https://catalist.us/whathappened2022/.

31 **Trump improved:** State and national data based on change in Democratic-Republican margin in two-party vote. Yair Ghitza and Jonathan Robinson, "What Happened in 2020," Catalist, https://catalist.us/wh-national/; and Ghitza and Aqeel, "What Happened in 2022."

31 **In Chicago's predominately Hispanic precincts:** Weiyi Cai and Ford Fessenden, "Immigrant Neighborhoods Shifted Red as the Country Chose Blue," *New York Times*, December 20, 2020.

31 **Cubans had the largest shift:** Hispanic subgroup data based on change in Democratic-Republican margin in two-party vote. Yair Ghitza and Jonathan Robinson, "What Happened in 2020," Catalist, https://catalist.us/wh-national/.

31 **Among Hispanics:** Catalist, "What Happened in 2022 National Crosstabs."

31 **According to a Pew analysis:** Pew Research Center, 2016–2020 Validated Voter Detailed Tables, https://docs.google.com/spreadsheets/d/1GIovkPfwUJvFZeFPdOi0fK8Rr7aOVFCYBzrlMG4Vjro/edit#gid=0.

31 **Democrats continued to enjoy:** Catalist, "What Happened in 2022 National Crosstabs."

31 **percent of black men:** Catalist, "What Happened in 2022 National Crosstabs."

31 **Democrats failed to gain back:** All data in this pargraph from authors' analysis of Catalist, "What Happned in 2022 National Crosstabs."

32 **Then in the 2022 gubernatorial election:** Ghitza and Aqeel, "What Happened in 2022."

32 **They won college-educated Hispanics:** Data in this paragraph from 2022 AP/NORC VoteCast data, https://www.foxnews.com/elections/2022/midterm-results/voter-analysis?year=2022&state=US and personal communication on 2022 VoteCast data, Aaron Zitner, *Wall Street Journal*.

32 **In Virginia's 2021 gubernatorial contest:** Catalist 2021 Virginia data, two-party vote, https://www.dropbox.com/s/6ijh3jhxa7mx3ud/wh2021_va_public_release_crosstabs.xlsx?dl=0.

32 **In that year's New York:** Matthew Thomas, "New York Democrats Keep Losing Ground with Hispanic and Asian Voters," *Vulgar Marxism*, November 4, 2021, https://vulgarmarxism.substack.com/p/new-york-democrats-keep-losing-ground.

33 **Nationwide the Democratic advantage:** Catalist, "What Happnened in 2022 National Crosstabs."

33 **In Brooklyn and Queens:** Ross Barkan, "Where Democrats Lost," Ross Barkan substack, November 10, 2022, https://rossbarkan.substack.com/p/where-democrats-lost.

33 **Republican House candidates:** All data in this paragraph from authors' analysis of Catalist, "What Happened in 2022 National Crosstabs."

Chapter Two: The Breakup of the New Deal Coalition

35 **In July 2022:** Blake Hounshell, "How Can Democrats Persuade Voters They're Not a Party of Rich Elites?," *New York Times*, July 6, 2022.

35 **Working-class whites:** See Ruy Teixeira, *America's Forgotten Majority* (New York: Basic Books, 2000); and John B. Judis and Ruy Teixeira, *The Emerging Democratic Majority* (New York: Scribner, 2002).

36 **As C. Wright Mills and G. William Domhoff:** C. Wright Mills, *The Power Elite* (New York: Oxford University Press, 1956); and G. William Domhoff, *Who Rules America?* (Englewood Cliffs, N.J.: Prentice-Hall, 1967).

39 **During the 1950s:** Drew DeSilver, "American Unions Membership Declines as Public Support Fluctuates," Pew Research Center, February 20, 2014, https://www.pewresearch.org/fact-tank/2014/02/20/for-american-unions-membership-trails-far-behind-public-support/.

43 **They were described:** Kevin Phillips, *The Emerging Republican Majority* (New York: Arlington House, 1969), 15.

44 **The wages of production workers:** Earnings data, *Statistical Abstract of the United States*, 1976, https://babel.hathitrust.org/cgi/pt?id=mdp.39015021301612&view=1up&seq=407.

45 **In a special:** *Business Week*, December 6, 1969.

45 **In 1965, when unions:** Robert Brenner, "The Economics of Global Turbulence," *New Left Review*, May–June 1998.

45 **Between 1970 and 1980:** See Thomas Byrne Edsall, *The New Politics of Inequality* (New York: W. W. Norton, 1984), 151.

45 **According to AFL-CIO:** Elizabeth R. Jager, "The Changing World of Multinationals," AFL-CIO Papers, Silver Spring, MD.

46 **By 1973, it was down:** Lawrence Mishel, Lynn Rhinehart, and Lane Windham, "Explaining the Erosion of Private-Sector Unions," Economic Policy Institute, November 18, 2020, https://www.epi.org/unequalpower/publications/private-sector-unions-corporate-legal-erosion/.

46 **Only 175 businesses:** Sar A. Levitan and Martha R. Cooper, *Business Lobbies: The Public Good & the Bottom Line* (Baltimore: Johns Hopkins University Press, 1984).

46 **In competitive House races:** Edsall, *The New Politics of Inequality*, 184.

47 **The Black Panther:** Hugh Pearson, *The Shadow of the Panther* (New York: Da Capo Press, 1995).

49 **Business lobbies outspent:** Thomas Ferguson and Joel Rogers, "Labor Law Reform and Its Enemies," *Nation*, January 6, 1979.

50 **"The federal deficit":** Carter: "'We Must Face a Time of National Austerity,' Carter Says," *Washington Post*, October 25, 1978, https://www.washingtonpost.com /archive/politics/1978/10/25/we-must-face-a-time-of-national-austerity-carter -says/fbe9d35b-ea26-48be-bdca-62a32256152a/; Meany: Helen Dewar, "Carter Meets with Meany in Effort to Patch Up His Relations with AFL-CIO," *Washington Post*, January 13, 1979, https://www.washingtonpost.com/archive/politics/1979 /01/13/carter-meets-with-meany-in-effort-to-patch-up-his-relations-with-afl-cio /49781f73-033a-4775-adb8-7486d014c8fb/.

50 **The next year:** U.S. Inflation Calculator, "Historical Inflation Rates, 1914–2023," https://www.usinflationcalculator.com/inflation/historical-inflation-rates/.

50 **Volcker, Carter's domestic policy adviser:** Joseph Treaster, *Paul Volcker: The Making of a Financial Legend* (Hoboken, NJ: John Wiley & Sons, 2004).

51 **1981–82 recession:** Bureau of Labor Statistics, monthly unemployment rate data, https://data.bls.gov/pdq/SurveyOutputServlet.

51 **In the recessions:** Federal Reserve History, "Recession of 1981–82," https:// www.federalreservehistory.org/essays/recession-of-1981-82.

53 **According to the New York Times:** "How They Voted," *New York Times*, November 9, 1980.

53 **Reagan defeated:** American National Election Studies, "The ANES Guide to Public Opinion and Electoral Behavior," https://electionstudies.org/resources/anes -guide/second-tables/?id=403.

53 **Reagan won:** Census Bureau, Historical Income Tables—Households, https:// www.census.gov/data/tables/time-series/demo/income-poverty/historical-income -households.html.

53 **those with "some college":** Karlyn Bowman and Samantha Goldstein, "The Exit Polls: A History and Trends over Time, 1972–2020," American Enterprise Institute, January 2022, https://www.aei.org/wp-content/uploads/2022/01/The-Exit-Polls .pdf?x91208h.

53 **From 1980 to 1990:** Historical Tables: Union Membership, Coverage, Density and Employment, 1973–2021, http://unionstats.com/.

53 **"There is no chance":** Thomas Byrne Edsall, *The New Politics of Inequality* (New York: W. W. Norton, 1984), 174.

55 **Sidney Blumenthal wrote:** Sidney Blumenthal, "Mondale's Days of Rage," *New Republic*, April 2, 1984.

56 **"He kept talking":** Bob Faw and Nancy Skelton, *Thunder in America: The Improbable Presidential Campaign of Jesse Jackson* (Austin: Texas Monthly Press, 1986), 217.

57 **That year, he won:** E. J. Dionne Jr., "Jackson Share of Votes by Whites Triples in '88," *New York Times*, June 13, 1988.

57 **Dukakis, like Carter:** Bowman and Goldstein, "The Exit Polls."

57 **For the first time:** John B. Judis and Ruy Teixeira, *The Emerging Democratic Majority* (New York: Scribner, 2002), 48.

Chapter Three: The Successes and Failures of the New Democrats

60 **California congressman Tony Coehlo:** Gregg Easterbrook, "The Business of Politics," *Atlantic*, October 1986.

60 **As William Domhoff:** William Domhoff, *The Power Elite and the State* (New York: A. de Gruyter, 1990), 236.

61 **party's main funding arm:** UPI, "Democratic Business Council Gets New Chairman," February 25, 1985, https://www.upi.com/Archives/1985/02/25/Dmocratic -Business-Council-gets-new-chairman/5881478155600/.

61 **"knocking the rich.":** Robert Kuttner, *The Life of the Party* (New York: Viking, 1987), 52.

63 **Thomas J. Donohue, the head:** Al From, *The New Democrats and the Return to Power* (New York: Palgrave McMillan, 2013), back cover.

63 **In its social:** Democratic Leadership Council, "The New Orleans Declaration: A Democratic Agenda for the 1990s," 1990, https://abiasedperspective.wordpress .com/2015/04/07/repost-the-manifesto-of-the-third-way-democrats-the-new -orleans-declaration/.

64 **The DLC limited:** On the history of the DLC, see Kenneth S. Baer, *Reinventing Democrats* (Lawrence: University Press of Kansas, 2000); and From, *The New Democrats and the Return to Power.*

64 **Progressive Policy Institute's most notable:** William Galston and Elaine Kamarck, *The Politics of Evasion* (Washington, DC: Progressive Policy Institute, 1989).

65 **As Derek Shearer:** Personal correspondence with Derek Shearer.

66 **Clinton's campaign manifesto:** Bill Clinton and Al Gore, *Putting People First* (New York: Times Books, 1992), 5.

66 **George Bush, Clinton said:** Bill Clinton, presidential nomination acceptance speech, 1992, https://www.presidency.ucsb.edu/documents/address-accepting-the -presidential-nomination-the-democratic-national-convention-new-york.

67 **He promised to be tough:** David Mills interview with Sister Souljah, "In Her Own Disputed Words," *Washington Post*, May 13, 1992.

67 **corporate lobbyists and lawyers:** Sara Fritz, "Lawyers, Lobbyists Top List of Clinton Contributors," *Los Angeles Times*, July 25, 1992.

68 **"Because it was the first controversial issue":** From, *The New Democrats and the Return to Power*, 194.

69 **From 1992 to 1994:** Ruy Teixeira and Joel Rogers, *America's Forgotten Majority: Why the White Working Class Still Matters* (New York: Basic Books, 2000), 81.

69 **Clinton came under intense:** Keith Bradsher, "Last Call to Arms on the Trade Pact," *New York Times*, August 23, 1993; and Joshua Mills, "Business Lobbying for Trade Pact Appears to Sway Few in Congress," *New York Times*, November 12, 1992.

70 **labor-backed think tank:** Jeff Faux "The Failed Case for NAFTA," Economic Policy Instiute, June, 1993, https://www.iatp.org/sites/default/files/Failed_Case_for _NAFTA_The.pdf

70 **171,000 jobs:** Gary Clyde Hufbauer and Jeffrey J. Schott, *NAFTA: An Assessment* (Washington, DC: Institute for International Economics, 1993).

70 **A poll taken on the eve:** *Washington Post*/ABC poll cited in Lawrence Mishel and Ruy Teixeira, "The Political Arithmetic of the NAFTA Vote," Economic Policy Institute, November 1993, https://files.epi.org/page/-/old/briefingpapers /1993_bp_political.pdf.

70 **He signed it on December 8:** Mauro Guillén, "NAFTA's Impact on the U.S. Economy: What Are the Facts?," Knowledge at Wharton, September 6, 2016, https:// knowledge.wharton.upenn.edu/article/naftas-impact-u-s-economy-facts/.

70 **from 1994 to 2004:** Robert E. Scott, Carlos Salas, and Bruce Campbell, "Revisiting NAFTA Still Not Working for North America's Workers," Economic Policy Institute, September 2006, https://files.epi.org/page/-/old/briefingpapers/173/bp173.pdf.

71 **In the 1992 campaign:** Bridget Harrison, "A Historical Survey of National Health Movements and Public Opinion in the United States," *Journal of the American Medical Association* 289, no. 9 (2003): 1163–64.

71 **"The Clinton plan is alive":** Adam Clymer, "The Clinton Health Plan Is Alive on Arrival," *New York Times*, October 3, 1993.

72 **A poll taken in February:** Theda Skocpol, "The Time Is Never Ripe: The Repeated Defeat of Universal Health Insurance in the 20th Century United States," 26th Geary Lecture, 1995, http://aei.pitt.edu/98958/1/GLS26.pdf.

72 **The plan was killed:** John B. Judis, "Abandoned Surgery," *American Prospect*, Spring 1995.

72 **Michigan Democratic congressman John Dingell:** Dana Priest and Michael Weisskopf, "Health Care Reform: The Collapse of a Quest," *Washington Post*, October 11, 1994.

74 **From 1992 to 1994:** Data in this and subsequent two paragraphs from Teixeira and Rogers, *America's Forgotten Majority*, 82–85.

76 **Republicans were aided:** Steven A. Holmes, "Did Racial Redistricting Undermine Democrats," *New York Times*, November 13, 1994.

76 **Republican conservatives deemed:** On conservatives and revolution: Jeffrey Gayner, "The Contract with America: Implementing New Ideas in the U.S.," Heritage Foundation, October 12, 1995, https://www.heritage.org/political-process/report/the-contract-america-implementing-new-ideas-the-us. On pundits and realignment: Jack W. Germond, "Long-talked-of Political 'Realignment' Seems to Have Come to Pass," *Baltimore Sun*, November 10, 1994.

77 **State of the Union:** The White House, Bill Clinton, State of the Union address, January 23, 1996, https://clintonwhitehouse4.archives.gov/WH/New/other/sotu.html.

78 **Clinton described globalization:** Bill Clinton, Remarks at Vietnam National University in Hanoi, Vietnam, November 17, 2000, https://www.presidency.ucsb.edu/documents/remarks-vietnam-national-university-hanoi-vietnam.

78 **Rubin and his successor:** John B. Judis, "Embarrassment of Riches," *American Prospect*, June 19, 2000.

79 **By 1994, the coalition:** See Bob Davis and Lingling Wei, *Superpower Showdown* (New York: Harper Business, 2020).

79 **Business Roundtable members:** Public Citizens Global Trade Watch, "Purchasing Power: The Corporate-White House Alliance to Pass the China Trade Bill over the Will of the American People," October 2, 2000, https://www.citizen.org/article/purchasing-power-the-corporate-white-house-alliance-to-pass-the-china-trade-bill-over-the-will-of-the-american-people/

80 **Robert Kapp, the president:** Nick Carey and James B. Kelleher, "Does Corporate American Kowtow to China?," Reuters, April 27, 2011, https://www.reuters.com/article/uk-kowtow-china-special-report/special-report-does-corporate-america-kowtow-to-china-idUKTRE73Q11120110427.

80 **They predicted an immediate $5.4 billion jump:** Jordan Weissmann, "Waking the Sleeping Giant," *Slate*, September 28, 2016, https://slate.com/business/2016/09/when-china-joined-the-wto-it-kick-started-the-chinese-economy-and-roused-a-giant.html.

80 **In a speech defending:** Clinton speech, China Trade Bill, March 9, 2000, https://archive.nytimes.com/www.nytimes.com/library/world/asia/030900clinton-china-text.html.

80 **Speaking at the Woodrow:** Weissmann, "Waking the Sleeping Giant."

81 **One of the first critics:** Robert E. Lighthizer, "What Did Asian Donors Want?," *New York Times*, February 25, 1997.

81 **At EPI in 2000:** Robert E. Scott, "China and the States," Economic Policy Institute, May 2000, https://www.epi.org/publication/briefingpapers_chinastates_chinastates/.

81 **Two experts from the Peterson Institute:** Weissmann, "Waking the Sleeping Giant."

82 **These totaled 2.7 million:** Robert E. Scott, "The China Toll," Economic Policy Institute, August 2012, https://files.epi.org/2012/bp345-china-growing-trade-deficit-cost.pdf.

82 **Three economists, David Autor:** David H. Autor, David Dorn, and Gordon H. Hanson, "The China Shock: Learning from Labor Market Adjustment to Large Changes in Trade" (working paper), National Bureau of Economic Research, January 2016, https://www.nber.org/system/files/working_papers/w21906/w21906.pdf.

83 **Indeed, Autor, Dorn, Hanson, and Kaveh Majlesi:** David H. Autor, David Dorn, Gordon H. Hanson, and Kaveh Majlesi, "Importing Political Polarization: The Electoral Consequences of Rising Trade Exposure" (working paper), National Bureau of Economic Research, December 2017, https://www.nber.org/system/files/working_papers/w22637/w22637.pdf.

83 **Autor and his coauthors:** Autor et al., "Importing Political Polarization."

84 **Sarah Rosen, White House:** Michael Smallberg, "How the Clinton Team Thwarted Effort to Regulate Financial Derivatives," Project on Government Oversight, April 25, 2014, https://www.pogo.org/investigation/2014/04/how-clinton-team-thwarted-effort-to-regulate-derivatives

84 **But Nebraska Democratic senator:** Stephen Labaton, "Congress Passes Wide-Ranging Bill Easing Bank Laws," *New York Times*, November 5, 1999.

85 **In 1980, manufacturing:** Michael Lind, *Land of Promise* (New York: Harper, 2013).

Chapter Four: Obama and the Lost Opportunity

87 **The battle for the Democratic:** ABC primary exit poll compilation, https://abcnews.go.com/images/PollingUnit/08DemPrimaryKeyGroups.pdf.

88 **"There is not a liberal":** Barack Obama 2004 Democratic National Convention keynote address, July 27, 2004, https://www.presidency.ucsb.edu/documents/keynote-address-the-2004-democratic-national-convention.

88 **He denounced the "dead zone":** Barack Obama, *The Audacity of Hope* (New York: Harper, 2007), 13.

89 **One Obama supporter:** See John B. Judis, "American Adam," *New Republic*, March 12, 2008.

89 **From the Republican Convention:** Real Clear Politics rolling average of 2008 polls, https://www.realclearpolitics.com/epolls/2008/president/us/general_election_mccain_vs_obama-225.html.

90 **"This is unprecedented":** Louis Uchitelle, "US Lost 2.6 Million Jobs in 2008," *New York Times*, July 9, 2009.

90 **In the last week:** "Presidential Approval Ratings—Barack Obama," https://news.gallup.com/poll/116479/barack-obama-presidential-job-approval.aspx.

90 **According to the Gallup:** Gallup data on confidence in banks, https://news.gallup.com/poll/127226/americans-confidence-banks-remains-historic-low.aspx.

91 **According to Pew:** Pew data on party ID, 2009, https://www.pewresearch.org/politics/2009/05/21/section-1-party-affiliation-and-composition/.

92 **He got very little:** John B. Judis, "Creation Myth," *New Republic*, September 10, 2008, https://newrepublic.com/article/61254/creation-myth.

92 **A Chicago consultant:** Ryan Lizza, "Making It: How Chicago Shaped Obama," *New Yorker*, July 13, 2008.

93 **Both administrations had created:** Barack Obama speech at Cooper Union in New York City, March 27, 2008, https://www.nytimes.com/2008/03/27/us/politics/27text-obama.html.

93 **"We let the special interests":** Mike Allen, "Obama Calls for Wall Street Crack-

down," *Politico*, September 16, 2008, https://www.politico.com/story/2008/09/obama-calls-for-wall-street-crackdown-013498.

94 **In Obama's closing:** Jason Leopold, "Remarks by the President in Round-table with Progressive Journalists, January 17, 2017," Bloomberg, September 30, 2022, https://www.bloomberg.com/news/articles/2022-09-30/obama-on-trump-1-presidential-term-is-okay-but-8-years-would-be-a-problem-l8t1lk89.

94 **"Our economy is badly weakened":** The White House, Barack Obama first-term inaugural address, January 21, 2009, https://obamawhitehouse.archives.gov/blog/2009/01/21/president-Barack-obamas-inaugural-address.

95 **In his authoritative study:** We rely heavily on the account of Obama's first two years from Noam Scheiber, *The Escape Artists* (New York: Simon & Schuster, 2012).

95 **From January to October:** Bureau of Labor Statistics monthly unemployment data, https://data.bls.gov/pdq/SurveyOutputServlet.

96 **The president, the budget stated:** Office of the Management and Budget, "Budget of the U.S. Government, FY 2011," February 1, 2010, 37.

96 **In addition, a total of 10.7 million homes:** Daniel Indiviglio, "Which States Had the Most Foreclosures in 2009?," *Atlantic*, January 14, 2010, https://www.theatlantic.com/business/archive/2010/01/which-states-had-the-most-foreclosures-in-2009/33538/.

97 **Marshall Ganz, a former:** John Judis, "Can the Democrats Get Organized?: An Interview with Marshall Ganz," Talking Points Memo, February 27, 2017.

98 **Obama had a cloture-proof:** Stanford Law School, "Billionaire Donors Split with Obama on Law That May Hurt Hotels," May 7, 2009, https://law.stanford.edu/press/billionaire-donors-split-with-obama-on-law-that-may-hurt-hotels/.

99 **The former approach:** Kaiser Health Tracking Poll, April 2009, https://www.kff.org/wp-content/uploads/2013/01/7891.pdf.

99 **In January 2011:** Kaiser Health Tracking Poll, "The Public's View of the ACA," March 31, 2022, https://www.kff.org/interactive/kff-health-tracking-poll-the-publics-views-on-the-aca/#?response=Favorable—Unfavorable&aRange=all.

100 **"people who have earned":** Emily Ekins, "Tea Party Fairness: How the Idea of Proportional Justice Explains the Right-Wing Populism of the Obama Era" (PhD diss., UCLA, 2014), 74–75.

101 **Democrats lost the white:** Yair Ghitza, "Revisiting What Happened in the 2018 Election," Catalist, May 1, 2019, https://medium.com/@yghitza_48326/revisiting-what-happened-in-the-2018-election-c532feb51c0.

102 **The Democratic margin:** Catalist data, two-party vote, https://www.dropbox.com/s/tao4oclcv3xqpz9/wh2020_public_release_crosstabs_WI.xlsx?dl=0.

103 **In the wake of the Democrats' rout:** See Scheiber, *The Escape Artists*; and Elizabeth Drew, "What Were They Thinking?" *New York Review of Books*, August 18, 2011.

103 **A varied group, independents' most common complaint:** "Independents Oppose Party in Power . . . Again," Pew Research Center, September 23, 2010, https://www.pewresearch.org/politics/2010/09/23/independents-oppose-party-in-power-again/.

104 **Obama agreed finally:** The Whitehouse, Barack Obama weekly address, April 9, 2011, https://obamawhitehouse.archives.gov/blog/2011/04/09/weekly-address-president-obama-budget-compromise-avoid-government-shutdown.

104 **"Now every family":** Cited by Scheiber, *The Escape Artists*, 28.

105 **In early August:** Gallup, "Presidential Approval Ratings—Barack Obama," https://news.gallup.com/poll/116479/barack-obama-presidential-job-approval.aspx.

105 *New York Times* **columnist:** Paul Krugman, "President Pushover," *New York Times*, July 24, 2011.

104 **Elizabeth Drew wrote:** Elizabeth Drew, "What Were They Thinking?"
106 **Obama's speech:** The White House, Obama speech, Osawatomie, Kansas, December 6, 2011, https://obamawhitehouse.archives.gov/the-press-office/2011/12/06/remarks-president-economy-osawatomie-kansas.
106 **The *New York Times*:** A. G. Sulzberger, "Obama Strikes Chord with Speech on GOP Turf," *New York Times*, December 7, 2011.
107 *Mother Jones* **published:** Steve Mullis, "Leaked Video Shows Romney Discussing 'Dependent' Voters," National Public Radio, September 17, 2012, https://www.npr.org/sections/itsallpolitics/2012/09/17/161313644/leaked-video-purports-to-show-romney-discuss-dependent-voters.
107 **When Romney selected:** Helene Cooper, "Health Care Leads Campaign Dialogue in Midwest," *New York Times*, August 16, 2012.
107 **In Wisconsin:** Catalist, two-party vote data found in "What Happened in Wisconsin: 2020 Crosstabs," https://www.dropbox.com/s/tao4oclcv3xqpz9/wh2020_public_release_crosstabs_WI.xlsx?dl=0.
107 **Similarly, in Iowa:** Maggie Dart-Padover, "What Happened in the Iowa Gubernatorial Election?," Catalist, January 17, 2019, https://medium.com/@CatalistAnalytics/what-happened-in-the-iowa-gubernatorial-election-b4638ae596b9.
108 *Washington Post*/**ABC poll:** Dan Balz and Scott Clement, "Poll: Major Damage to GOP After Shutdown and Broad Dissatisfaction with Government," *Washington Post*, October 21, 2013.
108 **"Most of the stories":** The White House, Obama Remarks on Affordable Care Act, Largo, Maryland, September 26, 2013, https://obamawhitehouse.archives.gov/the-press-office/2013/09/26/remarks-president-affordable-care-act#:~:text=But%20most%20of%20the%20stories,premiums%20would%20be%20sky%20high.
109 **On November 15, Obama:** Obama remarks on Affordable Care Act rollout, Washington, DC, November 14, 2013, https://timelines.latimes.com/obama-healthcare-law-fix/.
109 **And in the same poll:** Susan Page and Kendali Breitman, "Poll: Midterm Landscape Tilts to GOP," *USA Today*, May 5, 2014.
109 **Democrats won only:** Catalist, "What Happened in 2022 National Crosstabs."
109 **And they lost middle-income voters:** $50,000–$99,999 family income in 2014 network exit poll, https://www.nbcnews.com/politics/elections/2014/us/house/exitpoll/.
109 **Also in Texas, Republican Greg Abbott:** 2014 Texas network exit poll, https://www.nbcnews.com/politics/elections/2014/tx/governor/exitpoll/.
109 **Nationally, Democrats still had:** Catalist, "What Happened in 2022 National Crosstabs."
110 **problems with the plan:** CBS News, "Bill Clinton: Obamacare 'Craziest Thing in the World,'" October 4, 2016, https://www.cbsnews.com/newyork/news/bill-clinton-obamacare/.
110 **for most of 2014:** Bureau of Labor Statistics, monthly unemployment data, https://data.bls.gov/timeseries/LNS14000000.
110 **In 2013, in the wake:** St. Louis Federal Reserve, Real GDP Growth Rate Data, https://fred.stlouisfed.org/graph/?g=8eiT.
111 **Georgetown University professor:** Sharon Cohen and Deepti Hajela, "Obama Racial Legacy: Pride, Promise, Regret—and Deep Rift," Associated Press, January 4, 2017.
112 **Obama made a serious effort:** Reena Flores, "Obama Defends Black Lives Matter Movement as Protests Heat Up," CBS News, July 10, 2016, https://www

.cbsnews.com/news/obama-defends-black-lives-matter-movement-as-protests
-heat-up/.

112 **In an interview:** Michael Wessel interview with John Judis.

113 **Brookings found:** Mark Muro and Sifan Liu, "Another Clinton-Trump Divide: High-Output America vs Low-Output America," Brookings, November 29, 2016, https://www.brookings.edu/blog/the-avenue/2016/11/29/another-clinton-trump -divide-high-output-america-vs-low-output-america/.

113 **During the Obama administration:** Pre-tax market income based on Emmanuel Saez data in Drew DeSilver, "U.S. Income Inequality, on Rise for Decades, Is Now Highest Since 1928," Pew Research Center, December 5, 2013, https://www .pewresearch.org/fact-tank/2013/12/05/u-s-income-inequality-on-rise-for-decades -is-now-highest-since-1928/.

113 **And there was a net:** Glenn Kessler, "The White House Claim That 800,000 Manufacturing Jobs Were Added During Obama's Presidency," Washington Post, December 9, 2016.

113 **But in the words:** Alison Bauer, "President Obama Hits Gov. Scott Walker on 'Right-to-Work,'" Milwaukee Business Journal, March 10, 2015, https://www .bizjournals.com/milwaukee/blog/2015/03/president-obama-hits-gov-scott -walker-on-right-to.html?page=2.

113 **The American Federation:** See Dan Kaufman, The Fall of Wisconsin: The Conservative Conquest of a Progressive Bastion and the Future of American Politics (New York: W. W. Norton, 2018); and John B. Judis, "What Happened to Wisconsin?," Nation, March 24, 2019.

114 **According to Gallup:** Gallup, "Presidential Approval Ratings—Barack Obama," https://news.gallup.com/poll/116479/barack-obama-presidential-job-approval.aspx

114 **Democrats had not had:** United States House of Representatives archives, "Party Divisions of the House of Representatives, 1789 to Present," https://history .house.gov/Institution/Party-Divisions/Party-Divisions/.

114 **Republicans controlled 32 governorships:** National Council of State Legislatures, 2016 legislative control by state, https://documents.ncsl.org/wwwncsl /Elections/Legis_Control_2016.pdf.

Chapter Five: Hillary Clinton, Donald Trump, and the Deplorables

115 **In 2013, consultant:** Celinda Lake, "New Voters, New Values," American Prospect, February 11, 2013, https://prospect.org/power/new-voters-new-values/.

115 **In 2015, unchastened:** Stanley B. Greenberg, "How Progressive Policies Can Lead to a Democratic Majority," American Prospect, April 24, 2015, https://prospect .org/civil-rights/progressive-policies-can-lead-democratic-majority/.

116 **"There is one sure path":** Gara LaMarche, "New American Majority Turnout Is Vital to Win in November—and Needs Sustained Investment," Democracy Alliance, September 26, 2016, https://democracyalliance.org/from-the-president/new -american-majority-turnout-vital-win-needs-sustained-investment/.

116 **Another ad that was aimed:** Tessa Berenson, "New Hillary Clinton Ad Highlights Donald Trump's Remarks About Women," Time, November 1, 2016, https: //time.com/4553101/hillary-clinton-ad-donald-trump-women/.

116 **While she had won:** Network exit poll data, American Enterprise Institute archives.

118 **In his campaign:** Bernie Sanders interview with New York Daily News Editorial Board, April 4, 2016, https://www.nydailynews.com/opinion/transcript-bernie -sanders-meets-news-editorial-board-article-1.2588306.

119 **In these speeches:** Amy Chozick, Nicholas Confessore, and Michael Barbaro, "Leaked Speech Excerpts Show a Hillary Clinton at Ease with Wall Street," *New York Times*, October 7, 2016.

120 **Sanders's campaign proved:** Gary Langer, "Wrapping Up a Wild Ride: A 2016 Exit Poll Review," ABC News, May 10, 2016, https://abcnews.go.com/Politics /wrapping-wild-ride-2016-exit-poll-review-exit/story?id=38985830.

120 **Since 2010, the popularity:** Lydia Saad, "Socialism as Popular as Capitalism Among Young Adults in U.S.," Gallup, November 25, 2019, https://news.gallup.com /poll/268766/socialism-popular-capitalism-among-young-adults.aspx.

120 **Three-quarters of those:** Heartland Monitor data in Ronald Brownstein, "Even Baby Boomers Think It's Harder to Get Started Than It Used to Be," *Atlantic*, June 11, 2015, https://www.theatlantic.com/business/archive/2015/06/even-baby-boomers -think-its-harder-to-get-started-than-it-used-to-be/395609/.

120 **An NBER study:** NBER study findings in Chloe Berger, "Millennials Are the First Generation to Prove a College Degree May Not Be Worth It, and Gen Z May Be Next," *Fortune*, August 30, 2022, https://fortune.com/2022/08/30/millennial -versus-gen-x-college-degree-value-employment-earnings/.

120 **Sanders also did better:** Dan McLaughlin, "How Bernie Sanders Lost the White Working Class," *National Review*, March 11, 2020, https://www.nationalreview .com/2020/03/how-bernie-sanders-lost-white-working-class/.

121 **In the telling:** Langer, "Wrapping Up a Wild Ride."

121 **Some commentators and later:** Rebecca Traister, "The Sanders Campaign's Sexist New Argument: Clinton Tries Too Hard," *Cut*, April 7, 2016, https://www .thecut.com/2016/04/bernie-sanders-hillary-clinton-tries-too-hard-ambitious .html; and Rebecca Traister, "Hillary Clinton Is Furious. And Resigned. And Funny. And Worried," *New York*, March 29, 2017, https://nymag.com/intelligencer /2017/05/hillary-clinton-life-after-election.html.

122 **A postelection study:** J. Lawrence Broz, Jeffry Frieden, and Stephen Weymouth, "Populism in Place: The Economic Geography of the Globalization Backlash," Social Science Research Network, September 1, 2019, https://papers.ssrn .com/sol3/papers.cfm?abstract_id=3501263. See also Jed Kolko, "Trump Was Stronger Where the Economy Is Weaker," FiveThirtyEight, November 10, 2016, https://fivethirtyeight.com/features/trump-was-stronger-where-the-economy-is -weaker/; and Robert Griffin and Ruy Teixeira, "The Story of Trump's Appeal: A Portrait of Trump Voters," Voter Study Group, Democracy Fund, June 2017, https: //www.voterstudygroup.org/publication/story-of-trumps-appeal.

126 **Katherine J. Cramer:** Katherine J. Cramer, *The Politics of Resentment: Rural Consciousness in Wisconsin and the Rise of Scott Walker* (Chicago: University of Chicago Press, 2016); and Andrew J. Cherlin, *Labor's Love Lost: The Rise and Fall of the Working-Class Family in America* (New York: Russell Sage Foundation, 2014).

126 **In England, David Goodhart:** David Goodhart, *The Road to Somewhere: The Populist Revolt and the Future of Politics* (London: Hurst, 2017).

127 **Liberal publications aligned:** A representative sampling may be found in Samuel Goldman, "Yes, Political Correctness Really Exists," *American Conservative*, January 30, 2015, https://www.theamericanconservative.com/yes-political -correctness-really-exists/; and Greg Lukianoff and Jonathan Haidt, "The Coddling on the American Mind," *Atlantic*, September 2015.

129 **Richard Healey, a founder:** Interview with Richard Healey by John Judis and Ruy Teixeira.

132 **"will take care of everybody":** Dan Diamond, "On '60 Minutes,' Donald Trump Says Obamacare Is a Disaster—But His Own Plan Is Even Worse," *Forbes*,

September 27, 2015, https://www.forbes.com/sites/dandiamond/2015/09/27/trump-tells-60-minutes-that-obamacare-is-a-disaster-heres-what-he-didnt-say/?sh=5d3abd003d99.

132 **"It's a global power structure":** Donald Trump's argument for America ad, November 6, 2016, https://www.washingtonpost.com/video/politics/team-trump-donald-trumps-argument-for-america-campaign-2016/2016/11/06/218f32d4-a443-11e6-ba46-53db57f0e351_video.html.

132 **According to a study:** Wesleyan Media Project, "2016 Election Study," March 6, 2017, https://mediaproject.wesleyan.edu/2016-election-study-published/.

132 **The Peterson Institute:** Simon Johnson, "Win or Lose, Trump Could Cause a Recession," Peterson Institute for International Economics, May 16, 2016, https://www.piie.com/commentary/op-eds/win-or-lose-trump-could-cause-recession.

133 **challenge of Trump's campaign:** Dana Milbank, "Anti-Semitism Is No Longer an Undertone of Trump's Campaign. It's the Melody," *Washington Post*, November 7, 2016.

133 **voters in South Carolina:** Nick Gass, "Clinton Takes on Trump: 'America Never Stopped Being Great,'" *Politico*, February 27, 2016, https://www.politico.com/blogs/2016-dem-primary-live-updates-and-results/2016/02/hillary-clinton-donald-trump-slogan-219908.

133 **Clinton scoffed at:** CBS News, "Clinton Calls Trump's Slogan a 'Cruel Fantasy,'" June 28, 2016, https://www.cbsnews.com/news/hillary-clinton-donald-trump-make-america-great-again-cruel-fantasy/.

134 **"Maybe he should":** Sean Sullivan, "Trump Slams Colin Kaepernick: Maybe He Should Find a Country That Works Better for Him," *Washington Post*, August 29, 2016.

134 **According to one poll:** Marty Appel, "Americans Disapprove of Kaepernick's Actions, But Support His Right to Protest," Seton Hall Sports Poll, September 28, 2016, https://www.shu.edu/news/sports-poll-on-colin-kaepernick.cfm.

134 **Whites, she told:** NBC News, Hillary Clinton remarks to NAACP convention, July 18, 2016, https://www.nbcnews.com/video/hillary-clinton-we-white-americans-need-to-recognize-our-privilege-727176259735.

134 **She told a rally:** Hillary Clinton remarks at New York City fundraiser, September 10, 2016, https://time.com/4486502/hillary-clinton-basket-of-deplorables-transcript/.

135 **these and other attacks:** Republican debate highlights, *New York Times*, September 16, 2015, https://archive.nytimes.com/www.nytimes.com/live/republican-debate-election-2016-cleveland/trump-on-political-correctness/.

135 **According to a Quinnipiac poll:** Quinnipiac University poll, August 25, 2016, https://poll.qu.edu/images/polling/us/us08252016_U88mxwn.pdf

135 **According to one survey:** ClearerThinking.org, "Predicting Trump vs. Clinton Voting," https://programs.clearerthinking.org/trump_clinton/trump_clinton_analysis.htm.

136 **An experimental study:** Lucian Gideon Conway, Meredith Repke, and Shannon C. Houck, "Donald Trump as a Cultural Revolt Against Perceived Communication Restriction: Priming Political Correctness Norms Causes More Trump Support," *Journal of Social and Political Psychology* 5, no. 1 (May 2017): 244–59, https://jspp.psychopen.eu/index.php/jspp/article/view/4987.

136 **Matt Grossman concluded:** Matthew Grossmann tweet, May 12, 2018, https://twitter.com/mattgrossmann/status/995311112030695424.

138 **"So I won the places":** Eli Watkins, "Hillary Clinton: US Does 'Not Deserve' Trump," CNN, March 12, 2018, https://www.cnn.com/2018/03/12/politics/hillary-clinton-india-donald-trump/index.html.

138 **Political scientists:** Thomas Edsall, "The Unsettling Truth About Trump's First Great Victory," *New York Times*, March 22, 2023.

Chapter Six: Trump, the Shadow Democrats, and the 2020 Election

139 **In his 2016 campaign:** John Sides, "Did Enough Bernie Sanders Supporters Vote for Trump to Cost Clinton the Election?," *Washington Post*, August 24, 2017.

141 **His approval rating:** FiveThirtyEight rolling average of Trump approval ratings, https://projects.fivethirtyeight.com/trump-approval-ratings/.

144 **The senators included four:** Bernie Sanders Senate Office, "Sanders, 14 Senators Introduce Medicare for All," April 10, 2019, https://www.sanders.senate .gov/press-releases/sanders-14-senators-introduce-medicare-for-all-2/#:~:text =Sanders%20introduced%20the%20bill%20along,)%2C%20Martin%20Heinrich%20(D%2DN.

145 **By replacing fossil:** Ed Markey Senate Office, "Senator Markey and Rep. Ocasio-Cortez Introduce Green New Deal Resolution," February 7, 2019, https://www .markey.senate.gov/news/press-releases/senator-markey-and-rep-ocasio-cortez -introduce-green-new-deal-resolution.

146 **In its introduction:** Nikole Hannah-Jones et al., "The 1619 Project," *New York Times Magazine*, August 2019.

147 **After a confused initial response:** The story of the Northam incident is told by veteran Virginia journalist Margaret Edds in *What the Eyes Can't See: Ralph Northam, Black Resolve, and a Racial Reckoning in Virginia* (Columbia: University of South Carolina Press, 2022). Edds tried, but failed, to identify the figures in the controversial photo, as did a law firm hired by the governor.

148 **The furor began to:** Peter Jamison and Scott Clement, "Virginians Split on Governor's Fate amid Blackface Scandal, Poll Shows," *Washington Post*, February 9, 2019.

148 **In a June 2019 debate:** Paulina Firozi, "Democrats Have Lurched Leftward on Health Benefits for Undocumented Immigrants," *Washington Post*, July 1, 2019.

148 **Nine of ten:** Associated Press, "Most Democrats Promise to Decriminalize Border Crossings During 2020 Debate," June 27, 2019, https://www.pbs.org /newshour/politics/most-democrats-promise-to-decriminalize-border-crossings -during-2020-debate.

149 **In their statement:** *New York Times* Editorial Board, "The Democrats' Best Choices for President," *New York Times*, January 19, 2020.

151 **It was as if:** John B. Judis, "Mayhem and Mania: The Political Psychology of the Pandemic," *American Affairs* 6, no. 2 (Summer 2022): 169–82.

152 **Their greatest gains:** Authors' analysis of Catalist, "What Happened in 2022 National Crosstabs."

152 **Their improved margins:** Analysis of States of Change data in Ruy Teixeira, "Demographic Change Giveth and Demographic Change Taketh Away," *Liberal Patriot*, June 11, 2021, https://theliberalpatriot.substack.com/p/demographic -change-giveth-and-demographic.

153 **In the exit polls:** Data in this paragraph from 2020 network exit polls, filtering on white college graduates, https://www.cnn.com/election/2020/exit-polls /president/national-results/45.

153 **As a result of his campaign's:** Authors' analysis of Catalist, "What Happened in 2022 National Crosstabs," two-party vote.

153 **Overall, too, Biden:** Authors' analysis of Catalist, "What Happened in 2022 National Crosstabs," two-party vote.

153 **His margin among these voters:** Data in this paragraph from authors' analysis of Catalist, "What Happened in 2022 National Crosstabs," two-party vote.

154 **In some cities like Chicago:** Ruy Teixeira, "The Democrats' Hispanic Voter Problem," *Liberal Patriot*, December 9, 2021, https://theliberalpatriot.substack.com/p/the-democrats-hispanic-voter-problem-dfc.

154 **Over half of Hispanic voters:** Ruy Teixeira, "The Democrats' Hispanic Voter Problem: More Evidence from the 2020 Pew Validated Voter Survey," October 7, 2021, *Liberal Patriot*, October 7, 2021, https://theliberalpatriot.substack.com/p/the-democrats-hispanic-voter-problem.

154 **Asian neighborhoods in New York:** Matthew Thomas, "Queens Is More Diverse Than Ever and More Republican Than 20 Years Ago," *Vulgar Marxism*, August 16, 2021, https://vulgarmarxism.substack.com/p/queens-is-more-diverse-than-ever.

155 **Jaime Harrison started:** Richard Luscombe, "James Clyburn: 'Defund the Police' Slogan May Have Hurt Democrats at the Polls," *Guardian*, November 8, 2020, https://www.theguardian.com/us-news/2020/nov/08/james-clyburn-defund-police-slogan-democrats-polls.

155 **Spanberger said angrily:** Quote in Manu Raju tweet, November 5, 2020, https://twitter.com/mkraju/status/1324445099430940673?lang=en.

Chapter Seven: Joe Biden's New New Deal

157 **In June 2019, at a private:** Jennifer Epstein, "Biden Tells Elite Donors He Doesn't Want to 'Demonize' the Rich," Bloomberg, June 18, 2019, https://www.bloomberg.com/news/articles/2019-06-19/biden-tells-elite-donors-he-doesn-t-want-to-demonize-the-rich#xj4y7vzkg.

157 **But a year later, in May:** Cited in Jonathan Martin and Alexander Burns, *This Will Not Pass* (New York: Simon & Schuster, 2022).

157 **Biden invoked Roosevelt:** Joe Biden presidential nomination acceptance speech, August 21, 2020, https://www.cnn.com/2020/08/20/politics/biden-dnc-speech-transcript/index.html.

158 **"Why should a firefighter":** Joe Biden Pittsburgh speech, November 2, 2020, https://www.rev.com/blog/transcripts/joe-biden-campaign-event-speech-transcript-pittsburgh-pa-november-2.

159 **In 1982, liberal:** Robert B. Reich, "Why the US Needs an Industrial Policy," *Harvard Business Review*, January 1982.

159 **It would also "defuse":** Reich, "Why the US Needs an Industrial Policy."

160 **At a talk in Washington:** Brian Deese, "Remarks on a 21st-Century Industrial Policy," Atlantic Council, June 23, 2021, https://www.atlanticcouncil.org/commentary/transcript/brian-deese-on-bidens-vision-for-a-twenty-first-century-american-industrial-strategy/.

160 **The program put $80 billion:** Justin Badlam, Stephen Clark, Suhrid Gajendragadkar, Adi Kumar, Sara O'Rourke, and Dale Swartz, "The CHIPS and Science Act: Here's What's in It," McKinsey, October 4, 2022, https://www.mckinsey.com/industries/public-and-social-sector/our-insights/the-chips-and-science-act-heres-whats-in-it.

160 **As the program neared:** Don Clark and Ana Swanson, "U.S. Pours Money into Chips, But Even Soaring Spending Has Its Limits," *New York Times*, January 1, 2023.

161 **It was centered:** Patrick Brown, "What Skeptics of the Inflation Reduction Act Get Wrong," Breakthrough Institute, August 29, 2022, https://thebreakthrough.org/blog/what-skeptics-of-the-inflation-reduction-act-get-wrong; see also Justin Badlam, Jared Cox, Adi Kumar, Nehal Mehta, Sara O'Rourke, and Julia Silvis, "The Inflation

Reduction Act: Here's What's in It," McKinsey, October 24, 2022, https://www.mckinsey
.com/industries/public-and-social-sector/our-insights/the-inflation-reduction-act
-heres-whats-in-it.

161 **The bill flouted:** Adam Stein, "The Inflation Reduction Act: How Does It Impact
Nuclear Energy?," Breakthrough Institute, July 29, 2022, https://thebreakthrough.org
/blog/the-inflation-reduction-act-how-does-it-impact-the-nuclear-energy-industry
?gclid=Cj0KCQiAtICdBhCLARIsALUBFcEkwEs6vLGH2Pz9ZZXqG0fwL5v8dvs1H
l4rxsWZ7TWjocWpFSTlSV4aAvOZEALw_wcB.

161 **S&P Global reported:** Camellia Moors and Taylor Kuykendall, "EV Announce-
ments Snowballing Post Inflation Reduction Act," S&P Global Market Intelligence,
September 12, 2022, https://www.spglobal.com/marketintelligence/en/news-insights
/latest-news-headlines/ev-announcements-snowballing-post-inflation-reduction
-act-72023626.

161 **his first two years:** Office of Acquisition Management, U.S. Department of
Commerce, "Build America Buy America," https://www.commerce.gov/oam/build
-america-buy-america.

162 **The administration responded:** Yuka Hayashi, "WTO Rules Against U.S.
Tariffs on Imported Steel, Aluminum," *Wall Street Journal*, December 9, 2022.

163 **As the Brookings Institution's:** Mark Muro, "Can the CHIPS Act Heal the
Nation's Economic Divide?," Brookings, August 2, 2022, https://www.brookings
.edu/blog/the-avenue/2022/08/02/can-the-chips-act-heal-the-nations-economic
-divides/.

163 **In the original bills:** On the limits of Biden's industrial strategy, see Robert
Kuttner, "Reclaiming U.S. Industry," *American Prospect*, February 2023; and Julius
Krein, "Where the Chips Fell," *American Affairs*, August 30, 2022, https://american
affairsjournal.org/2022/08/where-the-chips-fell/.

164 **Arizona senator Kyrsten Sinema:** Brian Schwartz, "How Wall Street Wooed
Sen. Kyrsten Sinema," *CNBC*, August 9, 2022.

165 **Biden said he intended:** The White House, Remarks by President Biden
in honor of labor unions, Washington, DC, September 8, 2021, https://www
.whitehouse.gov/briefing-room/speeches-remarks/2021/09/08/remarks-by
-president-biden-in-honor-of-labor-unions/.

166 **As Amazon workers:** Glenn Thrush, "Biden Expresses Solidarity with Alabama Workers Attempting to Unionize an Amazon Warehouse," *New York Times*,
updated March 16, 2021.

166 **While union leaders:** Amelia Lucas, "Starbucks Criticizes Biden's Visit with
Union Leaders, Requests White House Meeting," CNBC, May 6, 2022, https://www
.cnbc.com/2022/05/06/starbucks-criticizes-biden-visit-with-union-leaders-requests
-white-house-meeting.html.

167 **A provision that would have:** Lee Harris, "Industrial Policy Without Industrial Unions," *American Prospect*, October 2022; and Lee Harris, "An Industrial Policy
Without Worker Protections," *American Prospect*, July 28, 2022, https://prospect.org
/economy/industrial-policy-without-worker-protections/.

167 **His Health and Human Services:** Eric Topol, "America Is Flying Blind
When It Comes to the Delta Variant," *Guardian*, August 9, 2021, https://www
.theguardian.com/commentisfree/2021/aug/09/america-is-flying-blind-when-it
-comes-to-the-delta-variant.

168 **1.7 million migrants:** Elliot Spagat, "Illegal Border Crossings to US from
Mexico Hit Annual High," AP, October 22, 2022, https://apnews.com/article/biden
-mexico-us-customs-and-border-protection-cuba-immigration-8fbba5bde9afca3f
404eaa96bcfd136a.

168 **In January 2023:** Myah Ward, "Biden Announces New Program to Curb Illegal Migration as He Prepares for Visit to Border," *Politico*, January 5, 2023, https://www.politico.com/news/2023/01/05/biden-border-plan-illegal-crossings-00076519.

168 **Predictably, he was:** Tweet from the Young Center, https://twitter.com/theYoungCenter.

169 **The administration also gave:** Ellen Bufkin, "Biden Faces Backlash over Vow to Prioritize Minority-Owned Businesses," Sinclair Broadcast Group, January 12, 2021; and John B. Judis and Ruy Teixeira, "New York's Race-Based Preferential Covid Treatments," *Wall Street Journal*, January 7, 2022.

170 **As *New York Times* analyst:** Nate Cohn, "Why Some States Went in Different Directions in Midterms," *New York Times*, updated November 29, 2022.

171 **But the swing:** Data this paragraph, authors' analysis of Catalist, "What Happened in 2022 National Crosstabs."

171 **Democratic losses among nonwhites:** Data this paragraph, Catalist, "What Happened in 2022 National Crosstabs."

172 **that mostly comprises Asians:** Authors' analysis of AP/NORC VoteCast data.

172 **In Iowa, which Obama:** Annie Gowen, "Iowa's Sharp Right Turn," *Washington Post*, March 22, 2023.

173 **Democrats won the working-class:** Personal communication with Ruy Teixeira from Aaron Zitner, *Wall Street Journal*.

173 **He did even better:** Authors' analysis of AP/NORC VoteCast data.

173 **In fact, Florida Hispanics:** Marc Caputo and Noah Pransky, "Florida's Hispanic Voters Back DeSantis over Crist, Support Martha's Vineyard Migrant Flights," NBC News, October 24, 2022, https://www.nbcnews.com/politics/2022-election/floridas-hispanic-voters-back-desantis-crist-support-marthas-vineyard-rcna53493; and A. G. Gancarski, "Poll: Majorities Oppose Ron DeSantis-backed 'Stop WOKE' and Parental Rights Laws," Florida Politics, October 3, 2022, https://floridapolitics.com/archives/561035-poll-majorities-oppose-ron-desantis-backed-stop-woke-and-parental-rights-laws/.

173 **That's one reason:** Authors' analysis of AP/NORC VoteCast data.

173 **And he did 38 points:** Data this paragraph, authors' analysis of AP/NORC VoteCast data.

Chapter Eight: Race and Radicalism

179 **"By many measures," Shelby:** Shelby Steele, *The Content of Our Character* (New York: St. Martin's Press, 1990), 15.

179 **Charles Murray's *Losing Ground*:** Charles Murray, *Losing Ground* (New York: Basic Books, 1984) and, with coauthor Richard Herrnstein, *The Bell Curve* (New York: Free Press, 1994).

180 **They included Robert Allen:** William Julius Wilson, *The Declining Significance of Race* (Chicago: University of Chicago Press, 1978); and William Julius Wilson, *The Truly Disadvantaged* (Chicago: University of Chicago Press, 1987).

180 **In the past, the black working and middle classes:** Wilson, *The Truly Disadvantaged*, 7.

181 **"One does not have":** Wilson, *The Truly Disadvantaged*, 12.

181 **In line with this class:** Wilson, *The Truly Disadvantaged*, 110.

181 **Criticized for offering "conservative":** Wilson, *The Truly Disadvantaged*, viii.

182 **It was an "ideology":** Derrick A. Bell Jr., "White Superiority in America: Its Legal Legacy, Its Economic Costs," *Villanova Law Review* 33 (1988): 767. And on *Brown v. Board of Education*, Derrick A. Bell Jr., "Brown v. Board of Education and the Interest-Convergence Dilemma," *Harvard Law Review* 93, no. 3 (January 1980):

518–33, https://harvardlawreview.org/1980/01/brown-v-board-of-education-and-the-interest-convergence-dilemma/.

183 **Referring back to the sit-ins:** Kimberlé Williams Crenshaw, "Race Liberalism and the Deradicalization of Racial Reform," *Harvard Law Review* 130 (2017): 2298–2319, https://scholarship.law.columbia.edu/cgi/viewcontent.cgi?article=3867&context=faculty_scholarship.

183 **"We work to prevent people":** Critical Resistance, "Mission and Vision," https://criticalresistance.org/mission-vision/#:~:text=Critical%20Resistance%20seeks%20to%20build,really%20make%20our%20communities%20secure.

183 **"Racism surreptitiously defines social":** Angela Y. Davis book, *Are Prisons Obsolete?* (New York: Seven Stories Press, 2003), https://collectiveliberation.org/wp-content/uploads/2013/01/Are_Prisons_Obsolete_Angela_Davis.pdf.

184 **In 2000, TransAfrica founder:** Randall Robinson, *The Debt: What America Owes to Blacks* (New York: Dutton, 2000).

184 **Clinton and George W. Bush's:** Donald Trump presidential inauguration speech, https://www.bbc.com/news/world-us-canada-38697653.

184 **In what would become a standard:** Richard Delgado and Jean Stefancic, *Critical Race Theory: An Introduction.* (New York: New York University Press, 2001), 7.

185 **Every policy in every institution:** Ibram X. Kendi, *How to Be an Antiracist*, (New York: One World, 2019), 18.

186 **In his book *Woke Racism*:** John McWhorter, *Woke Racism: How a New Religion Has Betrayed Black America* (New York: Portfolio, 2021).

187 **These kind of sentiments:** See Judis, "Mayhem and Mania."

188 **the Movement for Black Lives:** Movement for Black Lives (M4BL), "Vision for Black Lives," https://m4bl.org/policy-platforms/.

188 **"We are intentional about amplifying":** Movement for Black Lives (M4BL), "The Preamble," https://m4bl.org/policy-platforms/the-preamble/.

188 **The platform demanded:** See various parts of M4BL "Vision for Black Lives" platform, https://m4bl.org/policy-platforms/.

189 **"We'll provide long-term support":** Brook Kelly-Green, "Why Black Lives Matter to Philanthropy," Ford Foundation, July 19, 2016, https://www.fordfoundation.org/news-and-stories/stories/posts/why-black-lives-matter-to-philanthropy/.

189 **Interviewed during the August riots:** Rob Wildeboer and Chip Mitchell, interview with Ariel Atkins, WBEZ, April 12, 2020, https://www.wbez.org/stories/winning-has-come-through-revolts-a-black-lives-matter-activist-on-why-she-supports-looting/398d0f3f-73d0–4f2e-ae32–04cceba0d322.

189 **But donations continued to pour:** Aaron Morrison, "Black Lives Matter Opens Up about Its Finances," AP, February 23, 2021, https://apnews.com/article/black-lives-matter-90-million-finances-8a80cad199f54c0c4b9e74283d27366f.

190 **Investigative reports from *New York* magazine:** Sean Campbell, "Black Lives Matter Secretly Bought a $6 Million House," *New York*, April 4, 2022, https://nymag.com/intelligencer/2022/04/black-lives-matter-6-million-dollar-house.html; and Andrew Kerr, "Black Lives Matter Art Fellowship Program, Cited as Reason for $6 Million Purchase, Nowhere to Be Found," *Washington Examiner*, July 8, 2022, https://www.washingtonexaminer.com/news/business/black-lives-matter-art-fellowship-program-mansion-purchase-nowhere-to-be-found.

190 **for services to Cullors's brother:** Andrew Kerr, "BLM Doled Out Millions to Patrisse Cullors's Family and Friends, IRS Filing Shows," *Washington Examiner*, May 17, 2022 ../customXml/item1.xml.

190 **In 2014, Coates:** Ta-Nehisi Coates, "The Case for Reparations," *Atlantic*, June 2014.

191 **"It is as though we":** Coates, "The Case for Reparations."

191 **Columbia University linguist John McWhorter:** John McWhorter, "Talking Ta-Nehisi Coates," *The Glenn Show*, October 18, 2017, https://www.youtube.com /watch?v=-jeiPKh7jEA.

191 **"The only remedy to racist":** Kendi, *How to Be an Antiracist*, 19.

192 **"A racist policy":** Kendi, *How to Be an Antiracist*, 18.

192 **Robin DiAngelo, an obscure:** Robin DiAngelo, *White Fragility* (Boston: Beacon, 2018).

192 **DiAngelo argued that white people:** DiAngelo, *White Fragility*, 7, 21, 150.

192 **In August 2019, the *New York Times Magazine*:** Nikole Hannah-Jones et. al., "The 1619 Project," *New York Times Magazine*, August, 2019, https://www .nytimes.com/interactive/2019/08/14/magazine/1619-america-slavery.html.

193 **Two sets of prominent scholars:** History News Network, "Twelve Scholars Critique the 1619 Project and the New York Times Magazine Editor Responds," January 26, 2020, https://historynewsnetwork.org/article/174140; see also Sean Wilentz, "A Matter of Facts," *Atlantic*, January 22, 2020, https://www.theatlantic .com/ideas/archive/2020/01/1619-project-new-york-times-wilentz/605152/   and David North and Thomas Mackannon, eds., *The New York Times' 1619 Project and the Racialist Falsification of History: Essays and Interviews* (New York: Mehring Books, 2021).

193 **Another scholar revealed:** Leslie M. Harris, "I Helped Fact Check the 1619 Project. The Times Ignored Me," *Politico*, March 6, 2020, https://www.politico.com /news/magazine/2020/03/06/1619-project-new-york-times-mistake-122248.

193 **It put out "The 1619 Project":** Nikole Hannah-Jones et al., *The 1619 Project: A New Origin Story* (New York: One World, 2021).

194 **In Virginia's Loudon County:** Equity Collaborative, "Loudoun County Equity Final Report," December 2, 2019, https://go.boarddocs.com/vsba/loudoun /Board.nsf/files/BCVGK644213C/$file/LCPS%20Equity%20Assessment_Ad%20 Hoc%20on%20Equity_060619.pdfhttps://www.lcps.org/cms/lib/VA01000195 /Centricity/domain/60/equity_initiative_documents/LCPS_Equity_Report _FINALReport12_2_19.pdf.

194 **Nor could "grandfather":** Stanford University IT Community, "Elimina-tion of Harmful Language Initiative," December 19, 2022, https://s.wsj.net/public /resources/documents/stanfordlanguage.pdf.

195 **In his op-ed, Cotton:** Rashika Dugyala, "NYT Opinion Editor Resigns after Outrage on Tom Cotton Op-Ed," *Politico*, June 7, 2020, https://www.politico.com /news/2020/06/07/nyt-opinion-bennet-resigns-cotton-op-ed-306317.

195 **Even though McNeil had used:** Donald McNeil Jr., "NYTimes Peru N-Word: Parts One-Four," Medium, March 1, 2021, https://donaldgmcneiljr1954 .medium.com/nytimes-peru-n-word-part-one-introduction-57eb6a3e0d95.

196 **At the Poetry Foundation:** Kaveh Akbar et al., "Letter to the Poetry Foun-dation from Fellows + Programmatic Partners," June 6, 2020, https://docs.google .com/forms/d/e/1FAIpQLSf4u5Ns8Blz0gutuanOHF6I026Xi0dE9lT36HQtg5pDK eT5uQ/viewform.

196 **The paper issued an apology:** *Philadelphia Inquirer* editors, "An Apology to Our Readers and Inquirer Employees," *Philadelphia Inquirer*, June 3, 2020, https:// www.inquirer.com/news/philadelphia-inquirer-black-lives-matter-headline-apology -20200603.html.

196 **After a shooting:** Nicole Asbury, "Montgomery County Finalizes Deal to Bring Polie Back into the Schools," *Washington Post*, April 26, 2022.

196 **In the District of Columbia:** Omari Daniels and Michael Brice-Saddler,

"DC Council Overrides Mayor's Veto of Controversial New Crime Code," *Washington Post*, January 17, 2023.

196 **The district's revision, cheered:** Troy Burner, "Bowser Should Sign the Revised Criminal Code Act," *Washington Post*, December 6, 2022.

197 **Upon coming into office:** The White House, Executive Order on Advancing Racial Equity and Support for Underserved Communities Through the Federal Government, January 20, 2021, https://www.whitehouse.gov/briefing-room/presidential-actions/2021/01/20/executive-order-advancing-racial-equity-and-support-for-underserved-communities-through-the-federal-government/.

197 **The FDA's guidance was echoed:** Judis and Teixeira, "New York's Race-Based Preferential Covid Treatments."

198 **It's a method of examination:** Caitlin O'Kane, "Head of Teachers Union Says Critical Race Theory Isn't Taught in Schools, Vows to Defend 'Honest History'," CBS News, July 8, 2021, https://www.cbsnews.com/news/critical-race-theory-teachers-union-honest-history/.

198 **A study from the Crowd Counting:** Erica Chenoweth and Jeremy Pressman, "This Summer's Black Lives Matter Protests Were Overwhelmingly Peaceful Our Research Finds," *Washington Post*, October 16, 2020.

198 **In New York City, former policeman:** Jaek Lahut, "NYC Mayoral Candidate Eric Adams Says 'Young White Affluent People' Lead the 'Defund the Police' Movement," *Business Insider*, April 7, 2021, https://www.businessinsider.com/eric-adams-defund-the-police-young-white-affluent-people-2021-4.

199 **In the Democratic primary:** Ross Barkan, "The Decline of the Working Class Voter," Ross Barkan substack, September 20, 2021, https://rossbarkan.substack.com/p/the-decline-of-the-working-class.

199 **Voters turned down the referendum:** Jane Shortal, "Breaking Down Voting Data on Minneapolis Ballot Question 2," KARE 11, November 3, 2021 https://www.kare11.com/article/news/local/breaking-the-news/breaking-down-voting-data-on-minneapolis-ballot-question-2/89-8eb28e0a-c275-4bea-b350-e9b722dedd0f.

199 **In overwhelmingly black Detroit:** Susan Page, Dana Afana, Jasmin Barmore, Sam Fogel, and Janelle James, "Exclusive Poll Finds Detroit Residents Far More Worried about Public Safety than Police Reform," *USA Today*, July 25, 2021.

199 **In spite of its prominent endorsements:** Mark DeCamillo, "Release #2020-24: Close Elections Forecast for Proposition 15 (Split Roll Property Taxes) and Proposition 22," Berkeley Institute for Governmental Studies, October 26, 2020, https://escholarship.org/uc/item/2pr670k8?.

200 **An October 2021 Pew survey:** Carrie Blazina and Kiana Cox, "Black and White Americans Are Far Apart in Their Views of Reparations for Slavery," Pew Rsearch Center, November 28, 2022, https://www.pewresearch.org/fact-tank/2022/11/28/black-and-white-americans-are-far-apart-in-their-views-of-reparations-for-slavery/.

200 **Democratic analyst David Shor:** David Shor tweet, https://twitter.com/davidshor/status/1583450872284991488.

200 **According to the current Census tabulation:** William H. Frey, "Eight Takeaways from the Census 2000," *Milken Institute Review*, April 25, 2022, https://www.milkenreview.org/articles/eight-takeaways-from-the-census-2020; note that white is technically white non-Hispanic alone in this definition.

201 **It also includes in the standard:** See Richard Alba, *The Great Demographic Illusion* (Princeton, NJ: Princeton University Press, 2020).

201 **In 2019, according to a Pew Research:** Mohamad Mosliman et al., "Facts About the U.S. Black Population," Pew Research Center, Fact Sheet, March 2, 2023,

https://www.pewresearch.org/social-trends/fact-sheet/facts-about-the-us-black
-population/.

202 **According to a Pew report:** Christine Tamir, Pew Research Center, "Key Findings about Black Immigrants in the U.S.," January 27, 2022, https://www.pewresearch
.org/fact-tank/2022/01/27/key-findings-about-black-immigrants-in-the-u-s/.

202 **Coates based his case:** Matt Bruenig, "The Racial Gap Is About the Upper
Classes," People's Policy Project, June 29, 2020, https://www.peoplespolicyproject
.org/2020/06/29/the-racial-wealth-gap-is-about-the-upper-classes/.

202 **About half of Americans:** Gabriel Zucman quoted in Noel King, "About
Half of America Has Zero Net Wealth," *Marketplace*, April 21, 2014, https://www
.marketplace.org/2014/04/21/about-half-america-has-zero-net-wealth/.

202 **Between low-income whites:** Kriston McIntosh, Emily Moss, Ryan Nunn,
and Jay Shambaugh, "Examining the Black-White Wealth Gap," Brookings, February 27, 2020, https://www.brookings.edu/blog/up-front/2020/02/27/examining
-the-black-white-wealth-gap/.

202 **In fact, according to a St. Louis:** William R. Emmons, Ana Hernandez
Kent, and Lowell R. Ricketts, "The Bigger They Are, The Harder They Fall: The
Decline of the White Working Class," St. Louis Federal Reserve, 2018, https://www
.stlouisfed.org/household-financial-stability/the-demographics-of-wealth/decline
-of-white-working-class.

203 **An affirmative action program:** Richard Kahlenberg, "A New Affirmative
Action Should Be Based on Class," *Boston Globe*, October 27, 2022.

203 **Americans' perception is still guided:** F. James Davis, "Who Is Black?
One Nation's Definition," PBS *Frontline*, n.d., https://www.pbs.org/wgbh/pages
/frontline/shows/jefferson/mixed/onedrop.html.

Chapter Nine: The Immigration Imbroglio

206 **By 1980, legal and illegal migration:** Douglas S. Massey and Karen A. Pren,
"Unintended Consequences of US Immigration Policy: Explaining the Post-1965
Surge from Latin America," *Population Development Review* 38, no. 1 (2012): 1–29,
https://www.ncbi.nlm.nih.gov/pmc/articles/PMC3407978/.

207 **In a June 1980 Roper poll:** John S. Lapinski, Pia Peltola, Greg Shaw, and
Alan Yang, "Trends: Immigrants and Immigration," *Public Opinion Quarterly* 61,
no. 2 (Summer 1997): 356–83, https://www.jstor.org/stable/2749556.

207 **That lack of consensus:** Philip L. Martin, "Select Committee Suggest Changes
in Immigration Policy—A Review Essay," *Monthly Labor Review*, February 1982.

210 **It took into account:** US Commission on Immigration Reform, "Becoming
an American: Immigration and Immigrant Policy," September 1997, https://files
.eric.ed.gov/fulltext/ED424310.pdf.

210 **"Until 15 or 20 years ago":** David Barboza, "US Meatpacker Profits Hinge
on Pool of Immigrant Labor," *New York Times*, December 21, 2001.

211 **Villarejo blamed declining wages:** Central Valley Project Improvement Act,
Hearings Before the Subcommittee on Water and Power of the Committee on Energy
and Natural Resources, United States Senate, One Hundred Second Congress,
March 18, 1991, https://www.google.com/books/edition/Central_Valley_Project
_Improvement_Act/zF4DVMORPM8C?hl=en&gbpv=1&dq=Don+Villarejo
.+%E2%80%9CEnvironmental+Effects+of+Living+and+Working+in+Agricultural
+Areas+of+California:+Social+and+Economic+Factors,%E2%80%9D&pg=PA491
&printsec=frontcover.

213 **"There's no denying that many blacks":** Barack Obama, *The Audacity of
Hope* (New York: Crown, 2006), 263.

213 **"We consider him the deportation":** Reid J. Epstein, "NCLR Head: Obama 'Deporter-in-Chief,'" *Politico*, March 4, 2014, https://www.politico.com/story/2014 /03/national-council-of-la-raza-janet-murguia-barack-obama-deporter-in-chief -immigration-104217.

213 **She said she would deport only:** David Nakamura, "Clinton's Stance on Immigration Is a Major Break from Obama," *Washington Post*, March 10, 2016.

214 **Illinois's Dick Durbin:** Dick Durban tweet, August 2, 2017, https://twitter.com /SenatorDurbin/status/892804883107196931?s=20&t=_hqH_oeAaX58e9aBmMp7-g.

214 **Sanders initially refused to back:** Sarah Jones, "Bernie Sanders Is Not the Left," *New Republic*, June 26, 2019, https://newrepublic.com/article/149378/bernie -sanders-not-left.

215 **In "The Case for Getting Rid of Borders—Completely":** Alex Tabarrok, "The Case for Getting Rid of Borders—Completely," *Atlantic*, October 10, 2015, https://www .theatlantic.com/business/archive/2015/10/get-rid-borders-completely/409501/.

215 **Its editorial writer Lawrence Downes:** Lawrence Downes, "What Part of 'Illegal' Don't You Understand?," *New York Times*, October 28, 2007.

215 **In a 2012 editorial entitled:** *New York Times* editorial board, "Migrants' Freedom Ride," *New York Times*, July 28, 2012.

215 **It compared illegal immigrants:** For the history, we benefited from Jerry Kammer, *Losing Control* (Washington, DC: Center for Immigration Studies, 2020).

216 **The ACLU followed up:** ACLU, "Criminalizing Undocumented Immigrants," February 2010, https://www.aclu.org/other/issue-brief-criminalizing-undocumented -immigrants.

216 *Slate* **branded "assimilation":** Silpa Kovvali, "The History of Trump's Favorite Racist Code Word," *Slate*, February 27, 2018, https://slate.com/news-and-politics /2018/02/the-history-of-assimilation-as-a-racist-code-word.html.

216 **To claims by Trump and his allies:** Cesar Maximiliano Estrada, "How Immigrants Positively Affect the Business Community and US Economy," Center for American Progress, June 22, 2016, https://www.americanprogress.org/article/how -immigrants-positively-affect-the-business-community-and-the-u-s-economy/.

216 **The first of these claims:** National Academies of Sciences, Engineering, and Medicine, *The Economic and Fiscal Consequences of Immigration* (Washington, DC: National Academies Press, 2017).

216 **In 2017, the Southern Poverty Law Center:** Southern Poverty Law Center, "Hate Map," https://www.splcenter.org/hate-map.

217 **The *New Republic* followed up:** Laura Reston, "Where Trump Gets His Fuzzy Border Math," *New Republic*, March 11, 2017, https://newrepublic.com /article/140951/trump-gets-fuzzy-border-math.

217 **In a 2013 report:** Philip E. Woglin and Ann Garcia, "Immigration Is Changing the Political Landscape in Key States," Center for American Progress, April 8, 2013, https://www.americanprogress.org/article/immigration-is-changing-the-political -landscape-in-key-states/.

217 **In *Dissent* in 2016:** Manuel Pastor, "Latinos and the New American Majority," *Dissent*, Summer 2016, https://www.dissentmagazine.org/article/latinos-new -american-majority-immigration-progressive-politics-union-labor.

218 **Only 46 percent of the college-educated:** Lydia Saad, "Four in Ten Americans Still Highly Concerned about Illegal Immigration," Gallup, April 19, 2022, https://news.gallup.com/poll/391820/four-americans-highly-concerned-illegal -immigration.aspx.

218 **"Every job in this country":** Jason Margolis and Marco Werman, "Storm Lake, Iowa: Meatpacking Town Fueled by Immigrant Labot," *The World*, December 29, 2011,

https://theworld.org/stories/2011-12-29/storm-lake-iowa-meatpacking-town-fueled-immigrant-labor.

219 **Yet according to exit polls:** Network Arizona exit poll, November 2004, https://www.cnn.com/ELECTION/2004/pages/results/states/AZ/I/01/epolls.0.html.

219 **The results showed that Hispanics:** Eli Yokley, "Poll Finds Voters Back Bill for Curbing Legal Immigration," Morning Consult, August 9, 2017, https://morningconsult.com/2017/08/09/cotton-perdue-immigration-bill-poll/.

220 **According to an extensive survey:** Equis Research, "2020 Post Mortem, Part Two: The American Dream Voter," December 14, 2021, https://assets.ctfassets.net/ms6ec8hcu35u/4E5a5nNoWi9JNFqeAylkmS/bf542d82f900dbfb62cc6e6d7253a24a/Post-Mortem_Part_Two_FINAL_Dec_14.pdf.

Chapter Ten: Sexual Creationism

226 **And even then, theses clinics:** This history of transgender medicine and politics is drawn from Susan Stryker, *Transgender History* (New York: Seal Press, 2017); and Genny Beemyn, "Transgender History in the United States," Oxford e-book, available at https://www.umass.edu/stonewall/sites/default/files/Infoforandabout/transpeople/genny_beemyn_transgender_history_in_the_united_states.pdf.

226 **Over the next two decades:** Beemyn, "Transgender History."

227 **"The production of sex":** Judith Butler, *Gender Troubles* (New York: Routledge, 1990), 7, 140.

228 **In Emi Koyama's influential work:** Emi Koyama, "The Transfeminist Manifesto" in Carole McCann, Seung-kyung Kim, and Emek Ergun, eds., *Feminist Theory Reader* (New York: Routledge, 2020).

228 **Medical writings have become:** Cleveland Clinic, "AFAB and AMAB: What the Sex You're Assigned at Birth Means for Your Health," November 28, 2022, https://health.clevelandclinic.org/afab-and-amab-meaning/.

229 **"Before the rise of the internet":** Interview of Rodrigo Heng-Lehtinen by John Judis.

230 **With the backing of the ACLU:** Laurie J. Kendall, "From the Liminal to the Land: Building Amazon Culture at the Michigan Womyn's Music Festival," PhD thesis, University of Maryland, 2006.

235 **In 1972, there were 300,000:** Sarah Pruitt, "How Title IX Transformed Women's Sports," *History*, June 11, 2021, https://www.history.com/news/title-nine-womens-sports.

236 **The ACLU, which had already:** On the controversy, see Michael Powell, "What Lia Thomas Could Mean for Women's Elite Sports," *New York Times*, May 29, 2022, https://www.nytimes.com/2022/05/29/us/lia-thomas-women-sports.html.

237 *Teen Vogue* **offered its readers:** Gigi Engle, "How to Masturbate If You Have a Vagina," *Teen Vogue*, October 19, 2022, https://www.teenvogue.com/story/how-to-masturbate-if-you-have-a-vagina.

237 *USA Today* **demoted a deputy:** Isaac Schorr, "Former *USA Today* Editor Recounts Witch Hunt Triggered by 'Anti-Trans' Tweet," *National Review*, July 1, 2022, https://www.nationalreview.com/news/former-usa-today-editor-describes-witch-hunt-triggered-by-anti-trans-tweet/.

237 **Tampax celebrated "the diversity":** Amanda Woods, "Tampax Sparks Firestorm for Tweet That 'Not All People with Periods Are Women,'" *New York Post*, October 26, 2020, https://nypost.com/2020/10/26/tampax-under-fire-after-tweeting-not-all-people-with-periods-are-women/.

237 **The Centers for Disease Control (CDC):** Michael Powell, "A Vanishing Word in the Abortion Debate: 'Women,'" *New York Times*, June 8, 2022.

237 **Oregon's Health and Science University:** Mirenna Scott, Gayle Stamos, and Anna Young, "Creating a Gender-Inclusive Clinical Space," Oregon Health and Science University, chrome-extension://efaidnbmnnnibpcajpcglclefindmkaj/https://www.ohsu.edu/sites/default/files/2021–04/Creating%20a%20Gender-Inclusive%20Clinical%20Space_4.20.21.pdf.

237 **At a Senate hearing:** Jo Yurcaba, "Law Professor Khiara Bridges Calls Sen. Josh Hawley's Questions about Pregnancy 'Transphobic,'" NBC News, July 13, 2022, https://www.nbcnews.com/nbc-out/out-politics-and-policy/law-professor-khiara-bridges-calls-sen-josh-hawleys-questions-pregnanc-rcna38015

238 **Afterward, publications aligned with:** Alanna Vagianos, "Professor Schools Sen. Josh Hawley For His Transphobic Questions in Abortion Hearing," *HuffPost*, June 12, 2022, https://www.huffpost.com/entry/professor-schools-sen-josh-hawley-for-his-transphobic-questions-in-abortion-hearing_n_62cda22de4b02e0ac91a484f.

238 **But as *Washington Post* columnist:** Megan McArdle, "A Berkeley Professor's Senate Testimony Didn't Go How the Left Thinks It Did," *Washington Post*, July 14, 2022.

240 **In line with Benjamin:** Diane Ehrensaft, "The Gender Spectrum" YouTube, https://www.youtube.com/watch?v=HpE3d69SiDU.

240 **"When it comes to knowing a child's":** Gender Dysphoria Affirmative Working Group, "The Gender Affirmative Model," February 17, 2020, https://www.gdaworkinggroup.com/the-gender-affirmative-model.

240 **To deny a child "cross-sex hormones":** Diane Ehrensaft, "Puberty Blockers and Hormones for Transgender Youth," Kids in the House, https://www.kidsinthehouse.com/teenager/health-and-development/puberty/puberty-blockers-and-hormones-for-transgender-youth.

241 **Many of them would go on:** The story of the battle over transitioning is told in Emily Bazelon, "The Battle Over Gender Therapy," *New York Times Magazine*, June 15 2022; see also Jesse Singal, "How the Fight Over Transgender Kids Got a Leading Sex Researcher Fired," *The Cut*, February 7, 2016, https://www.thecut.com/2016/02/fight-over-trans-kids-got-a-researcher-fired.html.

242 **In an interview on National:** Remarks by Assistant Secretary Rachel Levine, Texas Christian University, Fort Worth, Texas, April 30, 2022, https://www.hhs.gov/about/news/2022/04/30/remarks-by-hhs-assistant-secretary-for-health-adm-rachel-levine-for-the-2022-out-for-health-conference.html.

242 **She told NPR "There is no argument":** Selena Simmons Duffin, "Rachel Levine Calls State Anti-LGBTQ Bills Disturbing and Dangerous to Trans Youth," NPR, April 29, 2022, https://www.npr.org/sections/health-shots/2022/04/29/1095227346/rachel-levine-calls-state-anti-lgbtq-bills-disturbing-and-dangerous-to-trans-youth.

242 **In a statement from its Office:** Office of the Assistant Secretary for Health, "Gender-Affirming Care and Young People," Office of Population Affairs, n.d., https://opa.hhs.gov/sites/default/files/2022–03/gender-affirming-care-young-people-march-2022.pdf.

242 **Its 2022 report stated:** National Board of Health and Welfare, Sweden, "Care of Children and Adolescents with Gender Dysphoria," 2022, https://www.socialstyrelsen.se/globalassets/sharepoint-dokument/artikelkatalog/kunskapsstod/2023-1-8330.pdf.

242 **The Sweden reversal is particularly:** National Board of Health and Welfare, Sweden, "The Development of the Diagnosis of Gender Dysphoria," 2020, https:

//www.socialstyrelsen.se/globalassets/sharepoint-dokument/artikelkatalog/ovrigt/2020–2–6600.pdf.

243 **After Swedish television:** Canadian Gender Report, "The Swedish U-Turn on Gender Transitioning for Children," November 12, 2020, https://genderreport.ca/the-swedish-u-turn-on-gender-transitioning/.

243 **In 2020, before the Biden:** Agency for Health Care Research and Quality, "Treatments for Gender Dysphoria in Transgender Youth," Department of Health and Human Services, July 17, 2020, https://effectivehealthcare.ahrq.gov/get-involved/nominated-topics/treatments-gender-dysphoria-transgender-youth.

243 **Andrew Sullivan, the noted gay author:** Andrew Sullivan, "Can the Biden Presidency Be Saved?," *The Weekly Dish*, July 29, 2022, https://andrewsullivan.substack.com/p/can-the-biden-presidency-be-saved-17d.

243 **Eva Kurilova who was chided:** Eva Kurilova, "I Would Have Been a Trans Kid—Stop Medicalizing Gender Nonconformity," Reality's Last Stand, July 25, 2022, https://www.realityslaststand.com/p/i-would-have-been-a-trans-kidstop.

244 **According to a May 2022 Pew:** Kim Parker, Juiliana Menasce Horowitz, and Anna Brown, "Americans' Complex Views on Gender Identity and Transgender Issues," Pew Research Center, June 28, 2022, https://www.pewresearch.org/social-trends/2022/06/28/americans-complex-views-on-gender-identity-and-transgender-issues/.

245 **When a polling group, Public:** Robert Blizzard, "National Poll Results, Florida Law," Public Opinion Strategies, March 28, 2022, https://pos.org/wp-content/uploads/2022/03/POS-National-Poll-Release-Memo.pdf.

Chapter Eleven: Apocalypse Now

246 **Today's concern about climate:** James Hansen testimony, Senate Energy and Natural Resources Committee, June 23, 1988, https://www.sealevel.info/Hansen.0623–1988_oral.pdf.

248 **Gore deliberately emphasized the worst:** Intergovernmental Panel on Climate Change (IPCC), "Sea Level Rise," chapter 13 in *Climate Change 2013: The Physical Science Basis*, https://www.ipcc.ch/site/assets/uploads/2018/02/WG1AR5_Chapter13_FINAL.pdf.

248 **"When we started organizing in 2008":** "350 Celebrates a Decade of Action," 350.org, 2019, https://350.org/10-years/.

248 **In a position paper, the group:** 350.org and Center for Biological Diversity, "Not Just a Number: Achieving a CO_2 Concentration of 350 ppm or Less to Avoid Catastrophic Climate Impacts," Center for Biological Diversity, 2010, https://www.biologicaldiversity.org/programs/climate_law_institute/350_or_bust/pdfs/Not_Just_a_Number-v3.pdf.

249 **Over half of funding:** 350.org "2020 Financial Report," https://350.org/2020-annual-report-financial-data/.

249 **He said, "We need an energy strategy":** The White House, President Barack Obama remarks, Mount Holly, North Carolina, March 7, 2012, https://obamawhitehouse.archives.gov/the-press-office/2012/03/07/remarks-president-energy-mount-holly-nc

250 **They were even more dismayed:** The White House, Barack Obama, "The All-of-the-Above Energy Path as a Strategy for Sustainable Economic Growth," July 2014, https://obamawhitehouse.archives.gov/sites/default/files/docs/aota_report_updated_july_2014.pdf.

250 **The climate movement was appalled:** White House, "The All-of-the-Above Energy Path."

250 **350.org denounced the strategy:** Laura Barron-Lopez, "Natural Gas Big Winner in Obama SOTU Speech," *The Hill*, January 29, 2014, https://thehill.com/policy/energy-environment/196790-natural-gas-big-winner-in-speech-to-green-groups-dismay/.

250 **They characterized the policy:** American Rivers and seventeen other environmental organizations, "Open Letter to Barack Obama," January 16, 2014, https://www.washingtonpost.com/r/2010–2019/WashingtonPost/2014/01/16/National-Politics/Graphics/All%20of%20the%20Above%20letter%20Jan%2016%20FINAL%20corrected.pdf?tid=a_inl_manual.

250 **By 2015, fossil fuel divestment:** Damian Carrington, "Campaign Against Fossil Fuels Growing, Says Study," *Guardian*, October 7, 2013, https://www.theguardian.com/environment/2013/oct/08/campaign-against-fossil-fuel-growing.

251 **Organizations emerged to harness:** Sunrise Movement, https://www.sunrisemovement.org/.

251 **The goal of their aggressive:** Meteor Blades, "Five Questions for Sunrise Co-Founder Varshini Prakash about Climate Activism and a Green New Deal," *Daily Kos*, December 9, 2018, https://www.dailykos.com/stories/2018/12/9/1818010/-Five-Questions-for-Sunrise-co-founder-Varshini-Prakash-about-climate-activism-and-a-Green-New-Deal.

252 **In January, over six hundred environmental:** A Community Voice-Lousiana and 645 other environmental and progressive organizations, "Open Letter to Congress on Legislation to Address the Urgent Threat of Climate Change," January 10, 2019, https://foe.org/wp-content/uploads/2019/01/Progressive-Climate-Leg-Sign-On-Letter-2.pdf.

252 **It would end all oppression:** Alexandria Ocasio-Cortez et. al., "Recognizing the Duty of the Federal Government to Create a Green New Deal," February 7, 2019, https://www.congress.gov/116/bills/hres109/BILLS-116hres109ih.pdf.

253 **As Ocasio-Cortez and Markey:** David Wallace-Wells, "The Uninhabitable Earth," *New York*, July 2017.

253 **In the book that came:** David Wallace-Wells, *The Uninhabitable Earth* (New York: Tim Duggan Books, 2019), 16.

253 **While a number of climate:** Chris Mooney, "Scientists Challenge Magazine Story about Uninhabitable Earth," *Washington Post*, June 12, 2017.

254 **In 2019 she told the English:** Greta Thunberg speech, UK Houses of Parliament, London, UK, April 23, 2019, https://www.theguardian.com/environment/2019/apr/23/greta-thunberg-full-speech-to-mps-you-did-not-act-in-time.

254 **At Davos, she told the great:** Greta Thunberg, "'I Want You to Panic', 16 Year Old Issues Climate Warning at Davos," *Guardian*, January 25, 2019, https://www.theguardian.com/science/video/2019/jan/25/i-want-you-to-panic-16-year-old-greta-thunberg-issues-climate-warning-at-davos-video.

254 **UN Secretary-General Antonio Guterres:** Antonio Guterres remarks, 2019 Climate Action Summit, United Nations, New York, New York, September 23, 2019, https://www.un.org/sg/en/content/sg/speeches/2019–09–23/remarks-2019-climate-action-summit.

254 *Guardian* **editor in chief Katharine:** Damian Carrington, "Why the Guardian Is Changing the Language It Uses about the Environment," *Guardian*, May 17, 2019, https://www.theguardian.com/environment/2019/may/17/why-the-guardian-is-changing-the-language-it-uses-about-the-environment.

254 **The *Guardian* and hundreds:** Mark Hertsgaard and Kyle Pope, "A New Commitment to Covering the Climate Story," *Columbia Journalism Review*, July 26, 2019, https://www.cjr.org/covering_climate_now/covering-climate-partnerships .php.

255 **This philosophy of the Green:** *At Liberty* podcast, "Climate Change Is a Racial Justice Issue," ACLU, September 30, 2021, https://www.aclu.org/podcast /climate-change-is-a-racial-justice-issue; Planned Parenthood California Central Coast, "Climate Justice," https://www.plannedparenthood.org/planned-parenthood -california-central-coast/about20us/climate-justice; and Amnesty International, "Climate Change," https://www.amnesty.org/en/what-we-do/climate-change/.

257 **More moderate scenarios are judged:** Carbon Brief Staff, "In Depth Q&A: The IPCC Sixth Assessment Report on Climate Science," Carbon Brief, August 9, 2021, https://www.carbonbrief.org/in-depth-qa-the-ipccs-sixth-assessment -report-on-climate-science/; and Zeke Hausfather and Frances C. Moore, "Commitments Could Limit Warming Below 2 Degrees C," *Nature,* April 14, 2022, https://media.nature.com/original/magazine-assets/d41586-022-00874-1 /d41586-022-00874-1.pdf.

257 **Climatologists Zeke Hausfather and Glen:** Zeke Hausfather and Glen Peters, "Emissions—The Business as Usual Story Is Misleading," *Nature*, January 29, 2020, https://www.nature.com/articles/d41586-020-00177-3.

257 **David Wallace-Wells of "Uninhabitable Earth" fame:** David Wallace-Wells, "Beyond Catastrophe: A New Climate Reality Is Coming Into View," *New York Times Magazine*, October 26, 2022.

257 **The heat wave was not caused:** Patrick Brown, "What It Means for Clilmate Change to Make Heat Waves Worse," Breakthrough Institute, June 20, 2022, https://thebreakthrough.org/blog/what-it-means-for-climate-change-to-make -heatwaves-worse; Ted Nordhaus, Vijaya Ramachandran, and Patrick Brown, "The Obvious Climate Strategy No One Will Talk About," *Foreign Policy*, November 6, 2022, https://foreignpolicy.com/2022/11/06/climate-cop27-emissions-adaptation -development-energy-africa-developing-countries-global-south/#; and Cliff Mass, "Was Global Warming the Cause of the Great Northwest Heat Wave? Science Says No," Cliff Mass Weather Blog, July 5, 2021, https://cliffmass.blogspot.com/2021/07 /was-global-warming-cause-of-great.html.

258 **In economic terms, increasing damages:** Our World in Data, "Weather Disaster Losses," https://ourworldindata.org/grapher/weather-losses-share-gdp; and Roger Pielke Jr., "Weather and Climate Disaster Losses So Far in 2022: Still Not Getting Worse," The Honest Broker, July 20, 2022, https://rogerpielkejr.substack .com/p/weather-and-climate-disaster-losses.

258 **The average in the 2020s:** Our World in Data, "Natural Disaster Deaths," https://ourworldindata.org/natural-disasters

258 **About 84 percent of world energy:** Our World in Data, "Energy Mix Charts, by Country," https://ourworldindata.org/energy-key-charts.

258 **This global figure is only down:** Our World in Data, "Energy Mix Charts, Global Energy Consumption by Source," https://ourworldindata.org/energy-mix.

258 **The percent of fossil fuel:** Our World in Data, "Electricity Mix Charts," https://ourworldindata.org/energy-key-charts.

258 **But, and this is widely underappreciated:** World Energy and Climate Statistics Yearbook, "Share of Electricity in Total Final Energy Consumption," 2022, https:// yearbook.enerdata.net/electricity/share-electricity-final-consumption.html.

258 **The rest consists mostly of direct:** Vaclav Smil, *How the World Really Works* (New York: Viking, 2022), 41.

259 **"[W]e are a fossil-fueled civilization":** Smil, *How the World Really Works*, 5.

259 **As Smil pointed out:** David Marchese interview with Vaclav Smil, "This Eminent Scientist Says Climate Activists Need to Get Real," *New York Times Magazine*, April 22, 2022.

260 **As Smil puts, "We need to favor":** Nathan Gardels interview with Vaclav Smil, "Want Not, Waste Not," *Noema*, 2021, February 25, 2021, https://www.noemamag.com/want-not-waste-not/.

260 **According to the U.S. Energy:** U.S. Energy Information Agency, "Electric Power Sector CO_2 Emissions Drop as Generation Mix Shifts from Coal to Natural Gas," June 9, 2021, https://www.eia.gov/todayinenergy/detail.php?id=48296.

260 **The EU, reflecting this:** Matina Stevis-Gridneff and Somini Sengupta, "Europe Calls Gas and Nuclear Energy 'Green,'" *New York Times*, July 6, 2022.

260 **Not only that but, as Smil:** David Marchese, "This Eminent Scientist."

260 **That is one reason why increased:** Ted Nordhaus, "In Global Energy Crisis, Anti-Nuclear Chickens Come Home to Roost," *Foreign Policy*, October 8, 2021, https://foreignpolicy.com/2021/10/08/energy-crisis-nuclear-natural-gas-renewable-climate/.

261 **According to a 2022 Gallup:** Gallup data, "Most Important Problem," https://news.gallup.com/poll/1675/most-important-problem.aspx.

261 **In a Pew survey that asked:** Pew Research Center, "Public's Top Priority for 2022: Strengthening the Nation's Economy," February 2022, https://www.pewresearch.org/politics/2022/02/16/publics-top-priority-for-2022-strengthening-the-nations-economy/.

261 **Working-class voters are not willing:** Authors' analysis of AP-NORC data, "Is the Public Willing to Pay to Help Fix Climate Change?," November 2018, https://apnorc.org/projects/is-the-public-willing-to-pay-to-help-fix-climate-change/.

262 **A *New York Times* investigation of jobs:** Noam Scheiber, "Building Solar Farms May Not Build the Middle Class," *New York Times*, July 16, 2021.

262 **They said they prefer that approach:** Pew Research Center, "Americans Largely Favor U.S. Taking Steps to Become Carbon Neutral by 2050," March 1, 2022, https://www.pewresearch.org/science/2022/03/01/americans-largely-favor-u-s-taking-steps-to-become-carbon-neutral-by-2050/?utm_content=buffer6c627&utm_medium=social&utm_source=twitter.com&utm_campaign=buffer&fbclid=IwAR3f3BZq4inOZGrw3s9xAOAe3qP2WdCNqZVAbBhLAUf_imU2G1yDJ_p9uSU.

263 **The Biden administration managed to pass:** Aatish Bhatia, Francesca Paris, and Margot Sanger-Katz, "See Everything the White House Wanted, and Everything It Got," *New York Times*, October 20, 2022.

264 **Reducing carbon emissions depends on:** Jesse D. Jenkins, Jamil Farbes, Ryan Jones, Neha Patankar, and Greg Schivley, "Electricity Transmission Is Key to Unlock the Full Potential of the Inflation Reduction Act," Princeton REPEAT project, September, 2022, https://repeatproject.org/docs/REPEAT_IRA_Transmission_2022–09–22.pdf.

264 **There is now a renaissance:** Eri Sugiura and Kana Inagaki, "Japan Approves Nuclear Energy U-turn to Avert Crisis," *Financial Times*, December 22, 2022; and Michael Moran, "Nuclear Dreams, Nuclear Realities," Breakthrough Journal, November 16, 2022, https://thebreakthrough.org/journal/no-18-fall-2022/nuclear-dreams-nuclear-realities.

265 **Instead, the Nuclear Regulatory:** Matt Yglesias, "More Nuclear Power Is What Both Parties Want," *Washington Post*, December 18, 2022.

Conclusion

267 **In the United States:** The best account of this history is Richard D. Rotunda, *The Politics of Language: Liberalism as Word and Symbol* (Iowa City: Iowa University Press, 1986).

267 **The liberal, Roosevelt told author:** Anne O'Hare McCormick, "Roosevelt's View of the Big Job," *New York Times*, September 11, 1932.

269 **If you look online for sites:** See ProProfs Quizzes, "Liberal or Conservative Test: Am I Liberal or Conservative Quiz," June 24, 2022, https://www.proprofs.com /quiz-school/personality/quizreport.php?title=are-you-liberal-conservative&sid =MTkzNjM4MTE5 or https://www.politicalpersonality.org/test/.

269 **The American Enterprise Institute:** Dennis Prager, "32 Questions to Determine Whether a Friend or Relative Is a Liberal or a Leftist," American Enterprise Institute, April 2, 2021, https://www.aei.org/carpe-diem/32-questions-to -determine-whether-a-friend-or-relative-is-a-liberal-or-a-leftist/.

270 **One site, for instance, lists eighteen:** IDR Labs, "Conservatism Test," https://www .idrlabs.com/conservatism/test.php conservatism test.

272 **When voters are asked to rate:** Aliza Astrow and Lanae Erickson, "Overcoming the Democratic Brand," Third Way, November 7, 2022, https://www .thirdway.org/memo/overcoming-the-democratic-party-brand.

272 **As the parties themselves:** Lydia Saad, "Democrats' Identification as Liberal Now 54%, a New High," Gallup, January 12, 2023, https://news.gallup.com/poll /467888/democrats-identification-liberal-new-high.aspx.

272 **According to Gallup, Democrats:** Jeffrey M. Jones, "U.S. Party Preferences Evenly Split in 2022 After Shift to GOP," Gallup, January 12, 2022, https://news .gallup.com/poll/467897/party-preferences-evenly-split-2022-shift-gop.aspx.

272 **But when the question is whether:** Women's Health Protection Act of 2021, https: //www.congress.gov/bill/117th-congress/house-bill/3755/text.

273 **In a 2019 Gallup Poll, only 28:** Jean Yi and Amelia Thomson-DeVeaux, "Where Americans Stand on Abortion, in 5 Charts," FiveThirtyEight, May 6, 2022, https://fivethirtyeight.com/features/where-americans-stand-on-abortion-in-5 -charts/.

273 **In May of 2022 we got:** Ruy Teixeira and Dan Adams, "Step Away from the Noise of Social Media and Cable News and There's a Lot of Common Ground in Wisconsin," *Milwaukee Journal Sentinel*, October 10, 2022, https://www.jsonline .com/story/opinion/2022/10/10/despite-noise-social-media-theres-common -ground-wisconsin/8191449001/.

274 **In liberal Massachusetts, where one:** Ruy Teixeira, "The Democrats' Common Sense Problem," *Liberal Patriot*, March 24, 2022, https://theliberalpatriot.substack .com/p/the-democrats-common-sense-problem.

Acknowledgments

We had been mulling an updated version of *The Emerging Democratic Majority* for almost a decade. Tim Duggan of Holt, alerted by our agent Rafe Sagalyn, thought *Where Have All the Democrats Gone?* was a good idea. We are grateful to Tim for his astute editorial suggestions, to Anita Sheih for seeing the book through from draft to publication, to production editor Chris O'Connell, and to Muriel Jorgensen for copyediting.

Larry Lynn, Thomas Edsall, Richard Healey, and Jo Freeman read and commented on chapters of the book. We received advice and assistance from Andrew Cherlin, Michael Lind, Miriam Pawel, William Barry, Richard Healey, Fred Block, Rob Stein (who died, sadly, two weeks after we talked to him about our book), James Mann, William Domhoff, Jonathan Cohn, Michael Podhorzer, Margaret Edds, Jerry Kammer, Steve Rosenthal, Joel Parker, Hal Salzman, Bill Moyers, Marty Lobel, Jeff Fiedler, Karlyn Bowman, William Frey, Robert Griffin, Patrick Moore, Ted Nordhaus, Roger Pielke Jr., and Michael Shellenberger and from John Halpin, Peter Juul, and Brian Katulis of the *Liberal Patriot*. We received help on data from Dan Adams, Louis DiNatale, the States of Change project, and Catalist Analytics and research assistance from Nate Moore.

Index

Page numbers in *italics* refer to tables.

About the Authors

John B. Judis serves as editor-at-large at Talking Points Memo. Previously, Judis worked as a senior writer at the *National Journal* and a senior editor at the *New Republic*. His previous books include *The Emerging Democratic Majority*, which he cowrote with Ruy Teixeira, as well as *The Populist Explosion*, *The Folly of Empire*, and more. Judis received his BA and MA degrees in philosophy from the University of California, Berkeley.

Ruy Teixeira is a nonresident senior fellow at the American Enterprise Institute, politics editor of the *Liberal Patriot* newsletter, and a contributing columnist at the *Washington Post*. He is the coauthor of *The Emerging Democratic Majority* and *America's Forgotten Majority*, as well as the author of *The Optimistic Left*, among other titles. Teixeira holds a PhD in sociology from the University of Wisconsin–Madison.